Theory of
Knowledge

Dimensions of Philosophy Series
Norman Daniels and Keith Lehrer, Editors

Theory of Knowledge, Keith Lehrer

Philosophy of Law: An Introduction to Jurisprudence,
revised edition, Jeffrie G. Murphy and Jules L. Coleman

Philosophy of Social Science, Alexander Rosenberg

Introduction to Marx and Engels: A Critical Reconstruction,
Richard Schmitt

FORTHCOMING

Philosophy of Science, Clark Glymour

Contemporary Continental Philosophy, Bernd Magnus

Philosophy of Physics, Lawrence Sklar

Philosophy of Religion, Thomas V. Morris

Metaphysics, Peter van Inwagen

Philosophy of Mind, Jaegwon Kim

Philosophy of Biology, Elliott Sober

Political Philosophy, Jean Hampton

Normative Ethics, Shelly Kagan

Also by Keith Lehrer

Philosophical Problems and Arguments: An Introduction
(coauthored with James W. Cornman and George S. Pappas)

Knowledge

Rational Consensus in Science and Society
(coauthored with Carl Wagner)

Knowledge and Skepticism (coedited with Marjorie Clay)

Thomas Reid

Metamind

Theory of Knowledge

Keith Lehrer

UNIVERSITY OF ARIZONA

Westview Press

BOULDER AND SAN FRANCISCO

To my wife,
ADRIENNE

Dimensions of Philosophy Series

Copyright © 1990 by Westview Press, Inc.

Published in 1990 in the United States of America by Westview Press, Inc., 5500 Central Avenue, Boulder, Colorado 80301

Library of Congress Cataloging-in-Publication Data
Lehrer, Keith.
    Theory of knowledge / Keith Lehrer.
        p. cm. — (Dimensions of philosophy series)
    Includes bibliographical references.
    ISBN 0-8133-0570-5 — ISBN 0-8133-0571-3 (pbk.)
1. Knowledge, Theory of. I. Title. II. Series.
BD161.L368 1990
121—dc20
                                                                        89-37511
                                                                            CIP

Printed and bound in the United States of America

The paper used in this publication meets the requirements of the American National Standard for Permanence of Paper for Printed Library Materials Z39.48-1984.

10   9   8   7   6   5   4   3   2   1

Contents

Preface   xi

1 THE ANALYSIS OF KNOWLEDGE   1

   What Is Knowledge? 2
   Analysis, 5
   The Form and Objectives of an Analysis of Knowledge, 6
   The Analysis of Knowledge, 9
   Theories of Justification, 13
   A Counterexample, 16
   Justification Without Falsity: A Fourth Condition, 17
   A Final Analysis of Knowledge, 18
   Introduction to the Literature, 18

2 TRUTH AND ACCEPTANCE   20

   Truth, 21
   Acceptance and Knowledge, 26
   The Consistency of Knowledge and Belief, 27
   Borderline Cases of Knowledge, 32
   Memory Without Knowledge, 36
   Introduction to the Literature, 38

3 THE FOUNDATION THEORY: INFALLIBLE FOUNDATIONALISM   39

   Infallible Versus Fallible Foundationalism, 40
   The Foundation Theory in General, 41
   The Foundation as a Guarantee of Truth, 42
   Fallible Foundations, 43
   Incorrigible Foundations, 44
   Fallibility and Inference: Summary of the Argument, 54

Nomological Infallibility, 54
Meaning and Belief, 55
Justification as a Logical Guarantee of Truth for
  Nonbasic Beliefs, 57
Phenomenalism, 58
Objections to Phenomenalism, 59
Summary, 62
Introduction to the Literature, 62

4   FALLIBLE FOUNDATIONS   63

Perceptual Belief and Independent Information, 64
Justification and Innocent Belief, 65
Semantics and Justification, 68
Self-justification and Necessary Truth, 70
Contingent Self-justification, 73
Probability and Justification: Fallibilistic
  Foundationalism, 75
Three Concepts of Probability, 76
Probability, Truth, and Basic Belief, 83
Summary: Competence, Success, and Coherence, 84
Introduction to the Literature, 85

5   THE EXPLANATORY COHERENCE THEORY   87

The Regress or the Circle, 87
The Traditional Answer: Coherence as Implication, 90
Coherence as Explanation, 91
On the Justification of What Is Explained, 92
Explanatory Coherence and Justification:
  An Analysis, 93
Objections and Replies to Coherence
  as Explanation, 98
Self-explanatory Beliefs, 102
Simplicity and Conservation, 108
Summary, 110
Introduction to the Literature, 111

6   INTERNAL COHERENCE AND PERSONAL JUSTIFICATION   112

Acceptance and Belief Reconsidered, 113
Justification and Reasonable Acceptance, 114
Justification, Reasonableness, and Coherence, 115
Competition Defined, 117

The Justification Game: Replying to a Skeptic, 119
A Foundationalist Objection, 121
The Principle of Trustworthiness, 121
The Justification Game and the Definition of
    Personal Justification, 126
The Lottery Paradox, 129
The Advantages of Truth, 130
Introduction to the Literature, 131

7   COHERENCE, TRUTH, AND UNDEFEATED JUSTIFICATION   132

The Uncharitable Possibility of Error, 132
Verific Justification, 134
A Solution: Defeat and the Ultra
    Justification Game, 141
Truth Connection and the Isolation Objection, 143
Perception, Memory, and Introspection, 145
A Definition of Undefeated Justification, 146
Knowledge Reduced to Undefeated Justification, 147
Determining Justification, 151
Introduction to the Literature, 152

8   EXTERNALISM AND EPISTEMOLOGY NATURALIZED   153

Naturalism, 154
The Advantages of Externalism, 155
Knowing That One Knows: Rejection of Deductive
    Closure, 158
The Naturalistic Relation, 159
Objections to Externalism: Information Without
    Knowledge, 162
Externalism and Justification, 165
Complete Justification and Reliabilism, 167
Causation and Justification: The Basing Relation, 168
Reliability and the Justification Game, 172
Externalism, Foundationalism, and Coherence:
    An Ecumenical Reconsideration, 173
Introduction to the Literature, 175

9   SKEPTICISM   176

Skepticism and Agnoiology, 176
Conception and the Chance of Error, 177

*A Refutation of Skepticism: Fallibility, Not
    Ignorance, 178*
The Merits of Skepticism, 179
Skepticism and Closure: An Externalist Caveat, 181
Introduction to the Literature, 185

Notes   187
Bibliography   197
Index   ·   207

Preface

THIS BOOK arose out of my earlier book, *Knowledge*, in more than one way. *Knowledge* had been widely used as a textbook in theory of knowledge courses but then went out of print. Professor Marjorie Clay of Bloomsburg University and Angela Blackburn of Clarendon Press both suggested to me that a textbook based on the previous book would be useful, and Spencer Carr of Westview Press encouraged me with a contract. I am very indebted to these people for their encouragement. The result is what you read.

How similar is this book to *Knowledge*? It is a different book: Chapters 6, 7, and 8 are entirely new; the other chapters contain new material as well but incorporate material from *Knowledge*. In addition, I have included Introduction to the Literature sections that are intended to guide students to further reading on subjects covered in each chapter. Though it has a similar structure to the original, this book was written as a textbook concerning the present state of the art. I have written for students, not for my colleagues, though I hope the latter may find some edification and pleasure in it. I have explained things that I thought students would need explained. I have retained a good deal of the critical argumentation from the earlier book because the same criticisms of various views that seemed cogent to me then seem cogent to me still. I have, however, considered new theories and presented a new form of the coherence theory, leaving the most complicated refinements for my articles. I would encourage those interested in such refinements to read "Knowledge Reconsidered" in *Knowledge and Skepticism* (Westview), edited by Marjorie Clay and myself, as well as my contribution to *The Current State of the Coherence Theory*, edited by John W. Bender.

This book is an attempt to explain foundationalism, the coherence theory, and externalism to students. Of course, I was not bashful about saying where the truth lies. So a form of the coherence theory winds up in the winner's circle, but it is a form that incorporates elements from foundationalism and externalism. I thought it important to advocate a theory rather than to pretend to a balanced presentation of views. Total impartiality is unattainable and the attempt at it soporific. Students, quite understandably, like to feel that what they read is a quest for the truth. The current book is, and it reads that way. I am an analytic philosopher who thinks a philosopher, like others, should attempt to define his or her key terms. Definitions chain together as a result, and it requires some intellectual effort to proceed from beginning to end. However, I have explained each definition with an example, which should make it possible for a student who has difficulty with definitions to grasp the main arguments nonetheless.

I recommend the book to those who like argument and definition turned by examples. Those who are seeking effortless mastery of philosophical profundities will not find that here, nor, I think, anywhere else. The students who like to match wits with argumentation and definition should find a feast here. I wish them a hearty meal with good appetite and encourage them to reject what they find unsavory. They should determine the reason for the offensiveness and prepare a dish of their own—one more to their own liking. To understand philosophy, one must do philosophy. One must seek the truth to know it. That is my advice and, as it turns out, my theory of knowledge as well.

In closing I wish to thank Marian David, Scott Sturgeon, Vann McGee, Gary Gleb, and Jonathan Kvanvig for their critical reflections; my research assistant Barbara Hannan and my editor Spencer Carr for reflections and editorial work; and Lois Day for assisting me in preparing the manuscript. I owe special thanks to my research assistant Leopold Stubenberg for proofreading and compiling the index. I should also like to express my indebtedness to the John Simon Guggenheim Foundation and the National Science Foundation for supporting my research on Thomas Reid, which greatly influenced the current work, and the National Endowment for the Humanities for sponsoring the Summer Institute in Theory of Knowledge that I directed with Alvin Goldman. It was this institute that, more than any other single factor, was responsible for my writing this book.

Keith Lehrer

1

The Analysis of Knowledge

ALL AGREE THAT KNOWLEDGE is valuable, but agreement about knowledge tends to end there. Philosophers disagree about what knowledge is, about how you get it, and even about whether there is any to be gotten. The question "What is knowledge?" will be the primary subject of this chapter and of this book. Why approach the theory of knowledge by asking this question? *Epistemology*, the theory of knowledge, and *metaphysics*, the theory of reality, have traditionally competed for the primary role in philosophical inquiry. Sometimes epistemology has won, and sometimes metapysics, depending on the methodological and substantiative presuppositions of the philosopher.

The epistemologist asks what we know, the metaphysician what is real. Some philosophers have begun with an account of the nature of reality and then appended a theory of knowledge to account for how we know that reality. Plato, for example, reached the metaphysical conclusion that abstract entities, or forms, such as triangularity or justice, are real and all else is mere appearance. He also held that the real is knowable, and he inquired into how we might know this reality.[1] Aristotle, on the contrary, held that individual substances, such as individual statues or animals, are real, and inquired as to how we might have knowledge, especially general knowledge, concerning these substances.[2] It is hardly surprising that Plato and Aristotle produced vastly different theories of knowledge when they conceived of the objects of knowledge in such different ways. Their common approach, starting with metaphysics, we might refer to as *metaphysical epistemology*. The problem with this approach is that the metaphysical epistemologist uncritically assumes we know the reality posited and only concerns himself with what such knowledge is like.

Other philosophers, most notably René Descartes, turned tables on the metaphysical approach by insisting that we must first decide what we can *know* about what is real and must remain skeptical about what *is* real until we have discovered what we can know. We might refer to this as *skeptical epistemology*. However, there is also a problem with this approach. When one once enters the den of skepticism, an exit may be difficult to find. Seeking to discover what he knew by following the method of doubting all that he could, Descartes imagined a powerful demon bent on deceiving us and thus found demonic doubt.[3] It remains controversial whether such doubt admits of relief by reason. It seems natural to begin with skepticism with the hope of discovering what we know and what we do not, but if we first pretend to *total* ignorance, we shall find no way to remove it. Moreover, we shall lack even the meager compensation of knowing that we are ignorant, for that too is knowledge.

Are we then trapped between a method that uncritically assumes our knowledge of reality while assigning priority to metaphysics and one that rejects the assumption that we have knowledge and leads to skepticism? Our approach here will be neither skeptical nor metaphysical. We assign priority to neither metaphysics nor epistemology but attempt to provide a systematic and critical account of prior metaphysical and epistemological assumptions. We refer to this as *critical epistemology*. We begin with commonsense and scientific assumptions about what is real and what is known. These convictions constitute our data, perhaps even conflicting data if commonsense and science conflict. The object of philosophical inquiry, of which critical epistemology is a fundamental component, is to account for the data. The account, though, is critical. Sometimes we explain the data and sometimes we explain the data away. For the most part, it behooves a critical epistemologist to construct a theory of knowledge explaining how we know the things we think we do, but, in a few instances, a theory may explain why we think we know when we do not. In order to explain what we do know or why we do not, however, we do well to first ask what knowledge is. Indeed, we must do so in order to evaluate the claims of either the metaphysical dogmatist or the epistemological skeptic. It is to this inquiry that we now turn.

What Is Knowledge?

Some have denied that we know what is true or what is false, and they have remained skeptics. Skepticism will have a hearing, but we shall pursue our study as critical epistemologists: We assume people have knowledge. But what sort of knowledge do they have, and what is knowledge anyway? There are many sorts of knowledge, but only one, the knowledge that something is true, will be our concern. Consider the following sentences:

I know the way to Lugano.
I know the expansion of pi to six decimal places.
I know how to play the guitar.
I know the city.
I know John.
I know about Alphonso and Elicia.
I know that the neutrino has a rest mass of 0.
I know that what you say is true.
I know the sentence 'Some mushrooms are poisonous' is true.

These are but a few samples of different uses of the word 'know' describing different sorts of knowledge.[4] If we are interested in finding out what people have when they have knowledge, we must first sort out the different senses of the word 'know'. Then we may ask our question again, once it has been disambiguated.

In one sense, 'to know' means to have some special form of competence. Thus, to know the guitar or to know the multiplication tables up to ten is to be competent to play the guitar or to recall the products of any two numbers not exceeding ten. If a person is said to know how to do something, it is this competence sense of 'know' that is usually involved. If I say I know the way to Lugano I mean that I have attained the special kind of competence needed either to get to Lugano or to direct someone there. If I say that I know the expansion of pi expanded to six decimal places, I mean that I have the special competence required to recall or to recite the number pi expanded to six decimal places.[5]

Another sense of 'know' is that in which the word means to be acquainted with something or someone. When I say that I know John, I mean that I am acquainted with John. The sentence 'I know the city' is more difficult to disambiguate. It might mean simply that I am acquainted with the city and hence have the acquaintance sense of 'know', or it might mean that I have the special form of competence needed to find my way around the city, geographically and/or socially. I also might mean that I know it in both the competence and acquaintance sense of 'know'. This example illustrates the important fact that the senses of 'know' that we are distinguishing are not exclusive; thus, the term 'know' may be used in more than one of these senses in a single utterance.[6]

The third sense of 'know' is that in which 'to know' means to recognize something as information. If I know that the neutrino has a rest mass of 0, then I recognize something as information, namely, that the neutrino has a rest mass of 0. The last three sentences on the list all involve this information sense of the word 'know'. It is often affirmed that to know something in the other senses of 'know' entails knowledge in the information sense of 'know'. I must have some information about Lugano if I know the way to Lugano; about the expansion of pi if I know the expansion of pi to six decimal places; about the city if I know the city; about the guitar if I know how to play the guitar, and so forth. Thus, the information sense of the word 'know' is often implicated in the other senses of the word.

In our study, we shall be concerned with knowledge in the information sense. It is precisely this sense that is fundamental to human cognition and required both for theoretical speculation and practical sagacity. To do science, to engage in experimental inquiry and scientific ratiocination, one must be able to tell whether one has received correct information or not to obtain scientific knowledge of the world. Engaging in law or commerce requires the same sort of knowledge. This sort of knowledge goes beyond the mere possession of information. If you tell me something and I believe you, even though I have no idea whether you are a source of truth and correct information about the subject or a propagator of falsehood and deception, I may, if I am fortunate, acquire information when you happen to be informed and honest. This is not, however, knowledge in the sense that concerns us; it is merely the possession of information. Similarly, if I read some gauge or meter and believe the information I receive, though I have no idea whether the instrument is functioning properly, I may thus acquire information, but this is not knowledge. If you doubt this, consider a clock that is not running because it stopped at noon some months ago. As luck would have it, you happen to look at it just at noon and believe that it is noon as a result. You might, as a result, come to believe it is noon when indeed it is, but that is not knowledge. If the clock is in fact running properly, but, again, you have no idea that this is so, you will have received the information from a reliable source; but your ignorance of the reliability of the source prevents you from recognizing that the information is correct, from knowing that it is correct, even though you may believe it to be so. It is information that we recognize to be genuine that yields the characteristically human sort of knowledge that distinguishes us as adult cognizers from machines, other animals, and even our childhood selves.

Some philosophers, choosing to place emphasis on the similarity between ourselves and these other beings, may insist that they have knowledge when they receive information.[7] This is a verbal dispute in which we shall not engage, for it is profitless to do so. We shall remain content with the observation that our most cherished scientific achievements, the discovery of the double helix, for example, and our most worthy practical attainments, the development of a system of justice, for example, depend on a more significant kind of knowledge. This kind of knowledge rests on our capacity to distinguish truth from error.

Analysis

To indicate the information sense of the word 'know' as being the one in question is quite different from analysing the kind of knowledge we have picked out. What is an analysis of knowledge? An analysis is always relative to some objective. It does not make any sense simply to demand the analysis of goodness, knowledge, beauty, or truth, without some indication of what purpose such an analysis is supposed to achieve. To demand the analysis of knowledge without specifying further what you hope to accomplish with it is like demanding blueprints without saying what you hope to build. Before asking for such an analysis, we should explain what goals we hope to achieve with it.

First, let us consider the distinction between analysing the meaning of the term 'know' and analysing the kind of knowledge denoted. Many philosophers have been interested in the task of analysing the meaning of the word 'know'.[8] Indeed, many would argue that there is no need for philosophical analysis once we have a satisfactory analysis of the meaning of the term 'know'. This restrictive conception of philosophical analysis is sustained by a dilemma: either a theory of knowledge is a theory about the meaning of the word 'know' and semantically related epistemic terms, or it is a theory about how people come to know what they do. The latter is not part of philosophy at all, but rather that part of psychology called learning theory. It follows that if a theory of knowledge is part of philosophy, then it is a theory of knowledge about the meaning of the word 'know'. That is the argument, and it is one that would reduce the theory of knowledge to a theory of semantics.

It is not difficult to slip between the horns of the dilemma. A theory of knowledge need not be a theory about the meaning of epistemic words any more than it need be a theory about how people come to know what they do. Instead, it may be one explaining what conditions must be satisfied and how they may be satisfied in order for a person to know something. When we specify those conditions and explain how they are satisfied, then we shall have a theory of knowledge. An analogy should be helpful at this point. Suppose a person says that there are only two kinds of theories about physical mass. Either a theory of matter is a theory about the meaning of 'mass' and semantically related physical terms, or it is a theory about how something comes to have mass. This dichotomy would be rejected on the grounds that it leaves out the critical question of what mass is, or, to put it another way, it leaves out the question of what condition must be satisfied for something to have a given mass. A theoretician in physics might be concerned with precisely the question of what conditions are necessary and sufficient for an object to have mass, or more precisely, to have a mass of n. Similarly, a philosopher might be concerned with precisely the question of what conditions are necessary and sufficient for a person to have knowledge, or more precisely, to know that p.

Some philosophers have questioned whether it is possible to give necessary and sufficient conditions for knowledge, but the finest monuments of scientific achievement mark the refutation of claims of impossibility. Obviously, a necessary and sufficient condition for the application of the expression 'S knows that p' is precisely the condition of S knowing that p. This could be made less trivial with little difficulty. The objection to the idea that a philosopher can discover necessary and sufficient conditions for knowledge may rest on the confused idea that a set of conditions necessary and sufficient for the application of a term constitutes a kind of recipe for applying terms which would enable us to decide quite mechanically whether the term applies in each instance. However, we may, without taking any position on the question of whether such a recipe can be found for applying the term 'know', state flatly that this is not the purpose of our theory of knowledge or the analysis of knowledge incorporated therein. Our interests lie elsewhere.

The Form and Objectives of an Analysis of Knowledge

We shall then approach the question "What is knowledge?" with the objectives of formulating necessary and sufficient conditions for a person having knowledge (in the information sense of the term 'know') and of explaining how those conditions may be satisfied. Our project is contiguous with scientific investigations having analogous objectives. Our conception of analysis is indebted to both Carnap and Quine.[9] Carnap proposed that philosophy should aim at *explication*. This is a kind of analysis aiming at the generation of philosophically and scientifically useful concepts. More specifically, explication aims at producing concepts useful for articulating laws and theories. For example, the explication of 'fish' so as to exclude whales from the class of fish generates a scientifically useful concept for the purpose of formulating laws. One such law is that fish are cold-blooded, to which whales would constitute a counterinstance if whales were included in the class of fish. When, however, we take this purpose of explication seriously and adopt the strategy of providing analyses of this sort in philosophy, then, as

Quine argued, there can be no clear boundary between philosophy and science. Our reasoning is that it is surely the purpose of science as well as philosophy to provide concepts to facilitate the formulation of laws and theories.

Thus, we contend that the distinction between philosophy and theoretical science is a bogus distinction, whether viewed historically or systemically.[10] Historically, it is clear that the special sciences break off from philosophy when some theory emerges that deals with a circumscribed subject in a precise and satisfactory manner. Philosophy remains the residual pot of unsolved intellectual problems. To date, theories of knowledge have remained in the pot. We do not claim that the current study or other recent research has brought us to the point where the theory of knowledge should be poured out into a special science, but we hope that we are approaching closer to that goal than some suspect and others fear.

A formulation of an analysis of knowledge may be expressed by an equivalence. Again, the analogy with mass is helpful. An analysis of mass may be given in an equivalence of the following form:

O has a mass of n if and only if . . .

where the blank to the right of the equivalence is filled with a sentence describing a set of necessary and sufficient conditions. Similarly, an analysis of knowledge may be given in an equivalence of the following form:

S knows that p if and only if . . .

where the blank to the right of the equivalence is filled with a sentence describing a set of necessary and sufficient conditions.

When considering candidates for such sets of conditions, we shall ask whether there is any counterexample to the proposed analysis. What is a counterexample? First of all, any experiment of fact or thought which would falsify the resulting equivalence is a counterexample. To say that there is no experiment of thought to falsify the equivalence means that we can think of no logical possibility that is consistent with other postulates of the theory under consideration which would yield the result that one side of the equivalence is satisfied and the other is not. We shall begin by considering any logically possible case as a potential counterexample to a theory of knowledge. We may decide eventually, however, that some examples, though logically possible, are so remote in terms of real possibility that they do not constitute realistic objections to an analysis of actual human knowledge.

In addition to being immune from counterexamples, such an equivalence will be a suitable analysis only if it facilitates reaching our epistemic objectives. Thus, though some analyses are definitely mistaken because we can find acceptable counterexamples, there are other equivalences which fail to constitute satisfactory analyses simply because they are unenlightening. To say that a person knows that *p* if and only if it is known to the person that *p*, though this is immune from counterexamples, would completely fail to explain or inform. The explanatory role of an analysis is of fundamental importance and must be appealed to in support of an analysis.

It is important, therefore, to consider at the outset what sort of enlightenment one is seeking, what one is attempting to explain by means of an analysis. We shall be concerned with an analysis that will be useful for explaining how people know that the input (the reports and representations) they receive from other people and their own senses is correct information rather than error and misinformation. A person may receive a representation that *p* as input without knowing that the representation is correct and, therefore, without knowing that *p*. Suppose, for example, that some person unknown to me tells me all the perch in the Genesee River will be killed by a pollutant that has raised the temperature of the water two degrees. I might believe what I am told, being gullible, but I do not know whether my informant knows whereof she speaks. Consequently, I do not know the perch will die. My informant may be knowledgeable. I may possess accurate information as a result of believing what I was told, but I do not know that the report is correct. Similarly, if I possess some information in memory but no longer know whether it is correct formation, whether it is something I accurately remember or just something I imagine, I am again ignorant of the matter. If, on the other hand, I know that the information I possess is correct, then I have knowledge in the requisite sense.

One test of whether I know that the information I possess is correct is whether I can answer the question of how I know that the information is correct or how I would justify claiming to know. Such questions and the answers provided are the basis for critical discussion and rational confrontation in scientific inquiry and everyday life. The replies to such queries show us whether or not the conditions for knowledge have been satisfied. If a person claims to know something, how well she answers the question "How do you know?" will determine whether we accept her claim. Consequently, our analysis of knowledge should explain how a person knows that her information is correct and how her knowledge claims are justified.

The foregoing remarks indicate why we shall not be concerned with the sort of knowledge attributed to animals, small children, and simple machines that store information, such as telephones that store telephone numbers. Such animals, children, or machines may possess information and even communicate it to others, but they do not know that the information they possess is correct. They lack any conception of the distinction between veracity and correct information, on the one hand, and deception and misinformation, on the other. Any child, animal, or machine that not only possesses information but knows whether the information is correct is, of course, a candidate for being a knowing subject. In those cases in which such knowledge is lacking, however, we shall assume ignorance in the information sense of knowledge under investigation here.

The Analysis of Knowledge

With these preliminary remarks to guide us, we shall now offer an analysis of knowledge. Each condition proposed will be the subject of subsequent chapters. Moreover, in the case of some controversial conditions, we shall not undertake a detailed defense in the present chapter. Our intention here is only to provide the analysis with some intuitive justification which will subsequently be developed and defended.

A Truth Condition

The first condition of knowledge is that of *truth*. If I know that the next person to be elected President of the United States will have assets of at least one million dollars, then it must be true that the next President will have assets of at least one million dollars. Moreover, if the next person to be elected President will, in fact, not have assets of at least a million dollars, then I do not know the next President will have assets of at least a million dollars. If I claim to know, my knowledge claim is incorrect. I did not know what I said I did. Thus, we shall accept the following conditionals:

(iT) if S knows that p, then it is true that p

and

(iT') If S knows that p, then p.

The two conditionals are equivalent for all those cases in which instances of the following principle, which articulates the absolute theory of truth to be discussed in the next chapter, are necessarily true:

(AT) It is true that p if and only if p.

It is true that the U.S. has a president if and only if the U.S. has a president, and this is necessarily true. The equivalence of the conditionals

> If Lehrer knows that the U.S. has a president, then the U.S. has a president

and

> If Lehrer knows that the U.S. has a president, then it is true that the U.S. has a president

is a result of the necessary truth of

> It is true that the U.S. has a president if and only if the U.S. has a president.

We shall find in the next chapter, however, that in spite of the innocent and even trivial appearance of (AT), the absolute theory of truth, it leads to paradox in some instances.

An Acceptance Condition

The second condition of knowledge is *acceptance.* If I deceitfully claim to know that Jan and Jay married on 31 December 1969, when I do not accept it, then I do not know Jan and Jay married on that date even if they were married then. If I do not accept that p, then I do not know that p. Thus, the following conditional expresses a condition of knowledge:

> (iA) If S knows that p, then S accepts that p.

A more familiar and quite similar condition would require belief as a condition of knowledge as follows:

> (iB) If S knows that p, then S believes that p.

These two conditions would be equivalent if the following equivalence were necessarily true:

> (AB) S accepts that p if and only if S believes that p.

Principle (AB) is not true, however. There is a special kind of acceptance requisite to knowledge. It is accepting something for the purpose of attaining truth and avoiding error with respect to the very thing one accepts. More precisely, the purpose is to accept that p if and only if p. Sometimes we believe things that we do not accept for this epistemic purpose. We may believe something for the sake of felicity rather than from a regard for truth. We may believe that a loved one is safe because of the pleasure of so believing, though there is no evidence to justify accepting this out of regard for truth, indeed, even when there is evidence against it. So, there are cases in which we do not accept in the appropriate way what we believe. It is the acceptance of something in the quest for truth that is the required condition of knowledge.

Some philosophers have insisted that a person may know something is true even though she lacks conviction of its truth. Others, in diametric opposition, have contended that a person only knows that something is true when she is sure, or certain, of the truth of what she believes. Thus, some philosphers have denied condition (iB) on the grounds that a person may know something to be true that she does not believe at all,[11] and others have maintained that for a person to know something to be true she must believe it to be true with considerable certainty.[12] Our proposal is that acceptance rather than belief, condition (iA) rather than (iB), is what is needed. A person need not have a strong feeling that something is true in order to know that it is. What is required is acceptance of the appropriate kind, acceptance in the interest of obtaining a truth and avoiding an error in what one accepts.

We may, however, consider the appropriate kind of acceptance to be a kind of belief, provided we do not assume that all kinds of belief are the requisite sort of acceptance. Hence, we might adopt

(A) If S accepts that p, then S believes that p,

provided that we reject

(B) If S believes that p, then S accepts that p.

We gain some continuity with tradition as well as some expository simplification by considering acceptance to be a special kind of belief. We may, consequently, speak of belief as a condition of knowledge for the sake of tradition, but we shall recall that it is a special kind of belief—acceptance aimed at truth—that is required and introduce the terms "accept" and "acceptance" when precision is needed.

A Justification Condition

Accepting something that is true does not suffice for knowledge. If I accept something without evidence or justification, that my wife has exactly fourteen dollars in her purse, for example, and, as luck would have it, this turns out to be right, I fall short of *knowing* that what I have accepted is true. Thus, we require a third condition affirming the need for *justification*. While we allowed that a person need not be completely certain of p in order to know that p, we shall insist that he be justified, indeed, completely justified in his acceptance of p in order to be said to know that p.

The reason for requiring that a person be *completely* justified rather than simply justified is to indicate that slight justification is not enough. I may be justified in accepting that my secretary is in her office now because she is ordinarily there at this time. Not being there myself, however, I do not know that she is there, for, though justified, I am not completely justified in accepting that she is there. I am unable to exclude the possibility that she is out of the office on an errand, for example, and, in that way, my justification is incomplete. Our condition may be formulated as follows:

(iJ) If S knows that p, then S is completely justified in accepting that p.[13]

The locution 'S is completely justified in accepting that p' will be used in a somewhat technical way. We offer some clarification of what is meant here, but the analysis of this notion must be left to later chapters. In colloquial usage, a speaker may say that another is completely justified in accepting that p because the *speaker* rather than the other person has strong evidence that p. There may be no implication that the other has such evidence. For example, if someone says, 'Alexander believes his wife is unfaithful' and I reply, 'He is completely justified', I may be implying only that I have adequate evidence of her infidelity, never mind how I acquired it, without any implication that Alexander has such evidence. Thus, I could expand the previous utterance and say instead, 'He is completely justified as it happens, but he really has no evidence of her infidelity—she is too clever'.

This use of the expression 'completely justified' is not the one intended in (iJ). When we say that S is completely justified, we shall mean that if his acceptance is based on adequate evidence, then he is completely justified by the evidence he has in accepting that p. Thus, that I am completely justified in accepting that p by the evidence I have does not by itself warrant my saying that another is completely justified in her acceptance of p. She too must have evidence which completely justifies her acceptance before she is, in the required sense, completely justified in accepting that p. The moral of the preceding remarks is that we shall not be enslaved to ordinary thought and speech when we speak of "complete justification" but, for the sake of theoretical advantage, we shall delete unwanted implications and allow expedient expansion within the theory of justification articulated below.

Theories of Justification

There are three kinds of theories of justification that we shall discuss in detail in subsequent chapters. These theories constitute the heart of a theory of knowledge. The first kind of theory is a *foundation* theory of justification. According to foundationalists, knowledge and justification are based on some sort of foundation, the first premises of justification. These premises provide us with basic beliefs that are justified in themselves, or self-justified beliefs, upon which the justification for all other beliefs rests.[14]

The motives for such a theory are easy to appreciate. If one thinks of justification in terms of an argument for a conclusion, it appears that justification must either continue infinitely from premise to premise, which would be an infinite regress, or argumentation must cycle with some premise being used to justify itself. This would be a circular argument, or some premises must be first premises, for example, basic beliefs justified without appeal to other premises. The latter alternative is the one chosen by the foundation theory.

Basic beliefs constitute the evidence in terms of which all other beliefs are justified according to the foundation theorist. Some empiricist philosophers affirm the existence of basic beliefs concerning perception (*I see something red*, for example), or more cautious beliefs about mere appearance (*I am appeared to in a reddish way*, for example) and maintain that all justification would be impossible without them. They aver that unless there are some basic beliefs to which we may appeal in justification, we shall lack a necessary starting point and fall victim to skepticism. In the absence of basic beliefs the whole edifice of justification would collapse for want of a foundation.

Not all epistemologists agree with this contention. A second kind of theory of justification, a *coherence* theory, denies the need for basic beliefs. Coherentists argue that justification must be distinguished from argumentation and reasoning. For them, there need not be any basic beliefs because all beliefs may be justified by their relation to others by mutual support.[15] The edifice of justification stands because of the way in which the parts fit together and delicately support each other rather than because they rest on a concrete foundation of basic beliefs.

How can a theory of justification avoid an unceasing regress proceeding from premise to premise without appeal to basic beliefs? First, justification need not proceed until all claims to knowledge employed in the justification are themselves justified. If we consider justification in a social context, the justification of knowledge claims need proceed only as long as some claim to knowledge is disputed. Thus, if we suppose that justification is a response to a query or demand, then there is no reason to suppose that the argument need proceed beyond the point at which agreement is reached. Hence, even if all completely justified beliefs are justified by evidence, not all claims to knowledge employed to defend other such claims need themselves be justified. They need to be justified only when they engender disputation. Just as we avoid endless disputation by finding premises on which we agree, we may avoid a regress of justification without appeal to basic beliefs, says the coherence theorist, because beliefs are completely justified by the way they agree or cohere with a system of beliefs. My perceptual belief that I see something red, for example, is justified because of the way it coheres with a system of beliefs that tells me under what conditions I can tell something red when I see it. It is coherence rather than reasoning or argumentation which yields justification.

This dispute between the foundation theorist and the coherence theorist is joined by a third party, the defender of an *externalist* theory, who disagrees with both parties to the dispute. We need neither basic beliefs nor coherence to obtain knowledge, the externalist contends, but rather the right sort of external connection between belief and reality to obtain knowledge.[16] Causality is one contender for the role of the needed external connection. What makes my belief that I see something red a case of knowledge on such an account is that my belief is *caused* by my seeing some external red object. Such philosophers may even go so far as to deny that justification is necessary for knowledge, contending that only the desired external connection is necessary. We may, however, do the externalist no injury by looking upon the external connection as providing us with a kind of external justification.

The foundation theorist and the coherence theorist may together protest, however, that a person totally ignorant of the external relationship of her belief, the causal history of her belief, for example, will not know that her belief is true unless it is justified by basic beliefs or coheres with a system of beliefs. The externalist will reply that the appropriate external connection requires neither basic beliefs nor coherence to yield knowledge. We leave the dispute unresolved here to become the centerpiece of our inquiry.

We shall eventually argue, however, that complete justification is a matter of coherence within a system of things a person accepts, which is a *subjective* fact about the knower but with some features adapted from the foundation theorist and the externalist. From the former, we shall take the insight that some beliefs are justified without being conclusions of argumentation and, from the latter, we shall incorporate the idea that a system yielding coherence may contain correct representations of how our beliefs are connected to reality. Nevertheless, we shall find that the engine of justification, which pulls the epistemic lever, is something subjective, something a person accepts in the quest for truth.

Most philosophers have thought that knowledge must be based on some objective method for assessing claims of truth or falsity. Some thought the test was that of experience, others of reason, and there have been mixed methodologies as well. All have assumed that acceptance must be checked in some objective manner. They have repudiated with epistemic horror the idea that acceptance of any sort could by itself produce any sort of justification. That a person accepts something for whatever purpose is far too subjective a datum to serve as a solid basis for justification. Even those philosophers who argue that some beliefs are self-justified have sought some principle by means of which we can determine which beliefs are self-justified and which not. They have held, too, that we must somehow transcend the subjectivity of acceptance in order to demarcate the area of justification. This conception has become so ingrained philosophically as to impose itself on commonsense. However, the assumption that there is some objective method for distinguishing the honest coin of justified acceptance from the counterfeit of the unwarranted shall not go unexamined. We shall study in some detail those theories that rest on this assumption, but, to warn the reader fairly in advance, no such theory shall prevail once we have exhibited our mint for epistemic approval.

The theory of justification we shall ultimately defend may strike some as closely aligned with skepticism. We shall examine this charge, but even here it should be noted that our sympathies with the writings of the philosophical skeptics of the past are strong. Too often contemporary writers seek the most effective method for liquidating the skeptic without asking whether his teaching may not be of more importance than his mode of burial. Since the most brilliant philosophers of past and present have been skeptics of one form or another, it would behoove those who study skepticism to consider whether these skeptics have some truth in their grasp. We claim they do. At the heart of the skeptic's position is the insight that there is no exit from the circle of what one accepts from which one can sally forth to find some exquisite tool to measure the merits of what lies within the circle of subjectivity. Nor is there such a tool, as we shall show, but subjectivity when directed toward truth and away from error can provide the basis of complete justification.

A Counterexample

Some philosophers have suggested that the conditions which we have considered necessary for knowledge are jointly sufficient for knowledge as well.[17] This would amount to affirming the following equivalence as an analysis of knowledge:

S knows that *p* if and only if it is true that *p*, *S* accepts that *p*, and *S* is completely justified in accepting that *p*.

In short, knowledge is completely justified true acceptance. Nevertheless, this analysis has been forcefully disputed and requires amendment.[18]

Edmund Gettier has presented us with a counterexample to the claim that knowledge is completely justified true acceptance which runs as follows. Suppose a teacher wonders whether any member of her class owns a Ferrari and, moreover, suppose that she has very strong evidence that one student, a Mr. Nogot, owns a Ferrari. Mr. Nogot says he does, drives one, has papers stating he does, and so forth. The teacher has no other evidence that anyone else in her class owns a Ferrari. From the premise that Mr. Nogot owns a Ferrari, she draws the conclusion that at least one person in her class owns a Ferrari. The woman might thus be completely justified in accepting that Mr. Nogot owns a Ferrari.

Now imagine that, in fact, Mr. Nogot, evidence to the contrary notwithstanding, simply does not own the Ferrari. He was out to deceive his teacher and friends to improve his social status. However, another student in the class, a Mr. Havit, does own a Ferrari, though the teacher has no evidence or inkling of this. In that case, the teacher would be quite correct in her belief that at least one person in her class owns a Ferrari, only it would not be Mr. Nogot who she thinks owns one, but Mr. Havit instead. In this case, the teacher would have a completely justified true belief when she accepts that at least one person in her class owns a Ferrari, but she could not be said to know that this is true because it is more due to good fortune than good justification that she is correct.[19]

To put the argument schematically, Gettier argues that a person might be completely justified in accepting that *F* by her evidence, where *F* is some false statement, and deduce *T* from *F*, where *T* is some true statement. Having deduced *T* from *F*, which she was completely justified in accepting, the person would then be completely justified in accepting that *T.* Assuming that she accepts that *T,* it would follow from the analysis that she knows that *T.* In such a case, the belief that *T* will be true, but the only reason the person has for accepting *T* to be true is the inference of *T* from *F.* Since *F* is false, it is a matter of luck that she is correct in her belief that *T.*[20]

One might be inclined to reply that inference from a false statement can never yield complete justification, but similar examples may be found that do not seem to involve any inference. An example taken from R. M. Chisholm illustrates this. Suppose a man looks into a field and spots what he takes to be a sheep.[21] The object is not too distant and the man knows a sheep when he sees one. In such a case, it would be natural to regard the man as being completely justified in accepting that he sees a sheep in the field without any reasoning at all. Now imagine that the object he takes to be a sheep is not a sheep but a dog. Thus, he does not know that he sees a sheep. Imagine, further, that an object in the deeper distance which he also sees but does not think is a sheep, happens in fact to be a sheep. So it is true that the man sees a sheep and, moreover, accepts and is completely justified in accepting that he sees a sheep. Of course, he still does not know that he sees a sheep because what he takes to be a sheep is not, and the sheep that he sees he does not take to be a sheep.

Justification Without Falsity: A Fourth Condition

In the two cases we have described, a person has justified true acceptance but lacks knowledge and in one case does not infer what he thus accepts from any false statement. There is some merit, however, in the idea that the falsity of some statement accounts for the lack of knowledge. Somehow, it is the falsity of the two statements (that Mr. Nogot owns a Ferrari and that what the man takes to be a sheep really is one) which accounts for the problem. It is false that Mr. Nogot owns a Ferrari, and it is also false that what the man takes to be a sheep is really a sheep (because it is a dog). We may say that in the first case the teacher's justification for her belief that at least one person in her class owns a Ferrari depends on the false statement that Mr. Nogot owns a Ferrari, and in the second case that the man's justification for his belief that there is a sheep in the field depends on the false statement that what he takes to be a sheep is really a sheep.

We shall explore the kind of dependence involved subsequently, but here we may notice that the teacher would be unable to justify completely her acceptance that there is a Ferrari owner among her students were she to concede the falsity of the statement that Mr. Nogot owns a Ferrari. Similarly, the man would be unable to justify completely his acceptance that there is a sheep in the field were he to concede the falsity of the statement that what he takes to be a sheep really is a sheep.

To render our analysis impervious to such counterexamples, we must add the condition that the complete justification that a person has for what she accepts must not depend on any false statement—whether or not it is a premise in inference. We may thus add the following condition to our analysis:

(iD) If S knows that p, then S is completely justified in accepting that p in some way that does not depend on any false statement.[22]

A Final Analysis of Knowledge

The preceding condition enables us to complete our preliminary analysis of knowledge as follows:

(AK) S knows that p if and only if (i) it is true that p, (ii) S accepts that p, (iii) S is completely justified in accepting that p, and (iv) S is completely justified in accepting p in some way that does not depend on any false statement.

Our next task is to examine each of these conditions of knowledge in order to formulate a theory of knowledge explaining how and why claims to knowledge are justified. We begin in the next chapter with an account of truth and acceptance and then proceed to consider theories of justification. The discussion of such theories will lead us to an account that brings central features of the various theories under the umbrella of a coherence theory. The correct theory of knowledge must provide the correct blend of subjective acceptance and truth in what is accepted, the right match between mind and reality. A match between mind and world sufficient to yield knowledge rests on coherence with a system of things we accept, our acceptance system, which must include an account, undefeated by error, about how we may succeed in our quest for truth. When we have such a theory before us, we shall return, at the end, to the speculations of skeptical and metaphysical epistemologists supplied with the scale of knowledge to weigh their claims.

Introduction to the Literature

There are a number of good introductions to the theory of knowledge. Perhaps the best general collection of essays pertaining to both the classical and contemporary literature is *Human Knowledge*, edited by Paul K. Moser and Arnold Vander Nat. The best collection of contemporary articles is *Essays on Knowledge and Justification*, edited by George S. Pappas and Marshall Swain. Two splendid and readable traditional introductions are *The Problems of Philosophy* by Bertrand Russell and *The Problem of Knowledge* by Alfred J. Ayer. There are some excellent recent textbooks written by single authors. The best are *Contemporary Theories of Knowledge* by John L. Pollock, *Belief, Justification, and Knowledge* by Robert Audi, and *Theory of Knowledge*, 3rd ed., by Roderick Chisholm.

2

Truth and Acceptance

WE HAVE SAID that knowledge implies acceptance and truth, which commits us to the following two implications:

(iA) If S knows that p, then S accepts that p

and

(iT) If S knows that p, then it is true that p.

These two implictions of knowledge are closely connected, and we shall discuss them together in this chapter. Concerning acceptance, it is important to notice that a person may accept something for one purpose they would not accept for another. For example, if I were a *fideist*, someone whose faith is not based on reason, I might accept that God exists for the sake of piety without any concern for evidence of the existence of God or for argument intended to show that the claim is true. Sometimes a person accepts something for the sake of piety or felicity without any concern for the truth of what she thus accepts. That, however, is not the sort of acceptance that is a condition of knowledge. On the contrary, the sort of acceptance requisite to knowledge is precisely acceptance concerned with obtaining truth and avoiding error with respect to the very thing accepted.

I know that the structure of the human genome is a double helix. This is something that I accept in the interests of obtaining truth and avoiding error. The sort of acceptance that is a condition of knowledge is acceptance aimed at truth, and it is in this way that acceptance and truth are connected. Can we give a more precise account of what is meant by saying that a person accepts something in the interests of obtaining truth and avoiding error with respect to the thing accepted? It is important to notice, first of all, that these two interests, obtaining truth and avoiding error, are not in harmony with each other. If I were interested simply in avoiding errors, the rational strategy would be to accept nothing; for, if I were to accept nothing, then I would accept nothing false. On the other hand, if I were interested simply in accepting truths, the rational strategy would be to accept everything; for, if I were to accept everything, then no truth would escape my acceptance. The trouble is, neither of these simple objectives of acceptance is the stuff of which knowledge is made.

What is needed is acceptance that aims at accepting something exactly in those cases in which it is true and not otherwise. To put the matter in a formula, the relevant aim of acceptance is to accept that p if and only if it is true that p.

Truth

In order to understand this condition, we need to have some account of truth. We have already noted the following condition of knowledge:

(iT) If S knows that p, then it is true that p.

Thus, it is appropriate to inquire into the nature of truth to understand knowledge. Unfortunately, the notion of truth is shrouded in controversy and paradox. For example, philosophers disagree about what sort of objects are true or false. One natural suggestion is that it is sentences, declarative sentences—'The structure of the human genome is a double helix', for example—that are true or false.

Let us consider the attempt to provide a theory of when sentences are true or false. A complete theory or definition of truth for sentences would fill in the right hand side of the schema,

X is true if and only if . . .

and thus tell us the conditions under which each sentence is true. This would give us an answer to the question, What is truth? In fact, no such general theory of truth is possible. Why?

Suppose we attempt to give a general theory, call it T, of the conditions under which sentences are true. Accordingly, T informs us, at least minimally, of the conditions under which sentences are true. But now a nasty question arises. Under what conditions is T itself true? Either

T tells us the conditions under which *T* is itself true or it does not. If it does not, then *T* is not a *general* theory of truth, not even a minimal theory, because it does not tell us the conditions under which one sentence, *T* itself, is true. So, to be complete, *T* must tell us about the conditions under which *T* itself is true. But then it must refer to itself. Unfortunately, self-reference, whether direct or indirect, leads to a very famous paradox.

The paradox may be formulated in terms of a sentence that says of itself that it is false as follows:

S. Sentence *S* is false.

If sentence *S* is false, then since it says sentence *S* is false, what *S* says is true, and sentence *S* is true. Of course, if *S* is true, then since it says *S* is false, *S* must be false. *S* is, therefore, true if and only if it is false.

The paradox might seem to arise simply because *S* refers to itself, but the paradox runs deeper. Consider the following two sentences:

A. Sentence *B* is true

and

B. Sentence *A* is false.

Sentence *A* refers to *B*, not to itself, while *B* refers to *A*, not to itself, and yet sentence *A* is true if and only if it is false, as the reader can easily determine. The crux is that the paradox arises because sentences of a language can be used to speak about sentences of the same language and say things about their truth or falsity.

These paradoxes should not be thought of as simple logical puzzles. Every solution has problematic consequences. It is possible to lay down some rule that excludes all such sentences from the domain of legitimate discourse. One might, for example, formulate rules for legitimate or well-formed sentences of a language, as Tarski did,[1] which would exclude the paradoxical sentences as not well formed. So long as we speak according to the rules, no paradox will arise, but the remark that sentences like *S*, *A*, and *B* are not well formed itself leads to paradox. Consider the sentence

C. Sentence *C* is either false or not well formed.

Brief reflection is required to note that sentence *C* is true if and only if it is either false or not well formed. A follower of Tarski who insists that C is not well formed is then in the peculiar position of saying something about C which, if true, would appear to imply that C itself is true. For the follower says

Sentence C is not well formed

which seems to imply that

Sentence C is either false or not well formed

which, of course, is C itself.

Moreover, the new paradox arises for any way of characterizing the paradoxical sentences, for example, as meaningless or as indeterminate, that is, neither true nor false. We need only substitute for the expression "not well formed" in C our preferred characterization of the paradoxical sentence to obtain a new paradox. In fact, we can formulate a generic paradox eliciter by replacing "not well formed" with a variable "Q" to obtain

CV. Sentence CV is either false or Q

which will yield a paradox by substituting one's favored characterization of the paradoxical sentences for the variable Q.

One way to escape this paradox is to refuse to utter the paradoxical sentences or say anything about them. One may put one's hand over one's mouth in silence. Silence may be the better part of dialectical valor, but it provides meager enlightenment. Moreover, the paradoxes have an important consequence. They show that we cannot accept a very simple and minimal theory about the truth of sentences. We might call it the *disquotational* theory of truth because it gives an account of truth by dropping quotation marks around a sentence, by disquoting a sentence. One instance of the theory is

"Chisholm is a philosopher" is true if and only if Chisholm is a philosopher

and the general form consists of sentences resulting from substituting the same declarative sentence for "X" when it occurs between quotation marks and at the end of the formula in

"X" is true if and only if X.

The minimal theory, once put forth as a condition of adequacy for a definition of truth by Tarski,[2] must be given up in an unqualified form, as Tarski noted, though it may be satisfied in artificial languages which, unlike English, do not allow the formation of paradoxical sentences. Since our pretheoretical understanding of truth is probably based on the acceptance of something like the unrestricted general disquotational theory, it is important to notice that it leads to paradox and cannot be sustained.

Thus, a complete theory of truth is impossible. Tarski noted that the attempt to formulate a complete theory of truth for a language within the language itself would lead to paradox.[3] This is a technical result of major importance which contains a metaphysical insight of equal importance. It is that the attempt to give a complete account of the relationship between language and the world within language is doomed to failure. The paradoxes exhibit the failure in cases in which language is both the subject and vehicle of discourse. What should we conclude about truth? It is a primitive notion. We cannot give any perfectly general definition of truth. Does that mean that truth is mysterious? Perhaps it is for some who think that anything that cannot be defined is mysterious. Notice, however, that for any sentence that does not refer to itself either directly or indirectly, the minimal theory of truth applies. For most of the sentences of a language, though not all, the minimal theory of truth specifies a condition of the truth of the sentence.[4]

The paradoxes transfer from words to ideas, from sentences to acceptings and thus become directly relevant to our inquiry. We can obtain paradoxes from an analogy to the disquotational theory applied to acceptance. It is natural to assume that

> S's accepting that Chisholm is a philosopher is true if and only if S accepts that Chisholm is a philosopher and Chisholm is a philosopher

and in general

> (G) S's accepting that p is true if and only if S accepts that p and p,

but this leads to paradox. Consider the following:

> (F) What the only person in 226 is now accepting is false.

Suppose that, without being aware of the fact, I am that person. Given (G) and my being the person in 226, my accepting that (F) is true if and only if I accept that (F) and what I am accepting is false. So, my accepting what I do is true if and only if it is false.

What is the upshot of this discussion for our inquiry? First of all, we must proceed without assuming that we can give any general theory or definition of truth pertaining to either sentences or acceptances we have considered. We may, nevertheless, retain the proposal that the sort of acceptance germane to knowledge is acceptance that aims at truth. The paradoxes concerning truth do not imply that it is paradoxical to aim at accepting *p* if and only if it is true that *p*. We may even formulate the objective without using the word "true" at all by saying that the aim of acceptance is to accept that *p* if and only if *p*. This objective, however formulated, is not rendered paradoxical by the truth paradoxes. The paradoxes simply are cases in which the objective cannot be attained.

Consider the claim (F) above. Given the objective of accepting that *p* if and only if *p*, I have the objective of accepting that what the only person in room 226 is now accepting is false if and only if what the only person in room 226 is now accepting is false. When I am the only person in room 226 and accept that what the only person in 226 is now accepting is false, I shall be frustrated in my attempt to obtain my objective because what the only person in 226 is now accepting is true if and only if it is false. In general, paradoxical acceptances will yield cases in which there is no way in principle of fulfilling the objective in question and, therefore, in those cases the objective has no application.

Moreover, paradoxical acceptances will, as we have noted, arise from the attempt to accept a complete theory of when what we accept is true, of the relationship between acceptance and reality. This should not be seen as a counsel of despair, however. Most instances of (G) do not lead to paradox, indeed, almost none do, and the general assumption (G) is nonproblematic with respect to such instances. It supplies us with at least a minimal account of truth for those instances. Similar remarks apply to the absolute theory of truth

(AT) It is true that *p* if and only if *p*

considered above. The claim (F) above will generate paradox when substituted for the variable '*p*' in (AT) as well as in (G). But most substitutions in (G) and (AT) will lead to nonparadoxical equivalences, indeed, to equivalences that are necessarily true.

Moreover, the account of truth offered for nonparadoxical instances allows for further theoretical articulation. For example, one might claim for such instances that *S*'s acceptance that *p* is true if and only if *S*'s acceptance that *p* corresponds to the fact that *p*. Given the correctness of the assumption (G), however, it must be the case that *S*'s accepting that p corresponds to the fact that p if and only if S accepts that p and p. In that case, S's acceptance that p corresponds to the fact that p just in case S accepts that p and p. Thus, it appears that an account of what it is to accept that p, what it is for a mental state of acceptance to be an acceptance that p, to have that content rather than another, yields an account of correspondence.

To return to our example, if we can obtain an account of what makes a state of accepting something a state of accepting that Chisholm is a philosopher, of what gives it that specific content, we shall thereby have obtained an account of what it is for my accepting that Chisholm is a philosopher to correspond to the fact that Chisholm is a philosopher. It is whatever is required for my state of accepting to have the content that Chisholm is a philosopher, exactly when Chisholm is a philosopher. Thus, we may conclude that a theory of the content of acceptance and thought generally subsumes or, indeed, constitutes a theory of correspondence. To understand how our states of acceptance have the content they do is to understand the relationship between acceptance and reality. The rest is only disquotation.

Acceptance and Knowledge

Let us now turn to a reconsideration of the acceptance condition of knowledge contained in the following conditional:

(iA) if S knows that p, then S accepts that p.

As we noted in the first chapter, the more common proposal is the following conditional:

(iB) If S knows that p, then S believes that p.

Conditional (iB) has been a battleground of controversy, and, though we have replaced (iB) with (iA), it is reasonable to assume that some of the objections raised against the former would be called into battle against the latter as well, for we have said that acceptance of the required sort may be considered to be a kind of belief so that

(A) If S accepts that p, then S believes that p

which together with (iA) yields (iB). It will, therefore, be useful to explore the objections to conditional (iB) at the outset to defend our proposal.

Two kinds of arguments have been employed in the effort to refute (iB). The first depends on certain facts of linguistic usage. For example, it makes sense and is sometimes quite correct to say 'I do not believe that; I know it', or 'She does not believe that; she knows it'. This kind of argument represents an attempt to show that it is inconsistent to say both that a person knows that p and that he believes that p and, consequently, that the former does not imply the latter.[5] The second form of argument is less ambitious and consists of offering a counter-example to (iB), the favored kind being one in which a person gives correct answers to questions he is asked without believing that his answers are correct.

The Consistency of Knowledge and Belief

Let us consider the first form of argument. From the fact that it makes sense and is even correct to say 'I do not believe that; I know it', or 'He does not believe that; he knows it', it hardly follows that the thesis (iB) is false. The reason it makes sense to say these things is to be found in the study of rhetoric rather than logic. It makes sense to say, 'I do not believe that; I know it', not because it is logically inconsistent to say that a woman believes what she knows but rather because this is an emphatic way of saying, 'I do not only believe that: I know it'. To say the latter, however, is quite consistent with conceding that the person referred to does believe, though not only believe, what she is said to know. Similar remarks apply to the locution, 'She does not believe that; she knows it'. An exact analogy to these cases is one in which it makes sense to say, 'That is not a house, it is a mansion', and the reason it makes sense is not that it is logically inconsistent to say that a house is a mansion but rather that this is an emphatic way of saying, 'That is not only a house, it is a mansion'. Indeed, that something is a mansion entails that it is a house. Once the rhetoric of emphatic utterance is understood, the logic is left untouched.

It is worth noting how the replacement of acceptance for belief makes the objection less plausible. It is odd to say 'I do not accept that; I know it' or, 'She does not accept that; she knows it', though one would probably be understood. Such expressions are less natural, however, which suggests that the contrast between knowledge and acceptance is less salient than the contrast between knowledge and belief. Acceptance makes a more natural ingredient of knowledge than belief.

'I Know' as a Performative Utterance

A more sophisticated attack on (iB) resting upon considerations of linguistic usage is derived from the writings of J. L. Austin. In a famous passage Austin compares the locution, 'I promise', to the locution, 'I know'.[6] His basic contention is that uttering such words is the performance of a certain ritual which alters one's relations to others. As he puts it, "When I say, 'I promise', I have not merely told you what I intend to do, but by using this formula (performing this ritual), I have bound myself to others, and staked my reputation in a new way."[7] Similarly, Austin says, "When I say 'I know!', I give others my word: I give others my authority for saying that 'S is P'."[8] Austin goes on to remark, "To suppose that 'I know' is a descriptive phrase is only one example of the descriptive fallacy, so common in philosophy. Even if some language is now purely descriptive, language was not in origin so, and much of it is still not so. Utterance of obvious ritual phrases, in the appropriate circumstances, is not describing the action we are doing, but doing it."[9]

Even if Austin is correct in declaring that when I say, 'I know that S is P', I give others my authority for saying that S is P, the performance of this act is perfectly consistent with describing oneself as accepting with complete justification that S is P. Indeed, the assumption that I am making such a descriptive claim about myself when I say, 'I know that S is P', helps to explain the way in which I give my authority for saying that S is P by saying, 'I know that S is P'. If I were not claiming to be completely justified in accepting that S is P when I say, 'I know that S is P', then why in the world should my saying, 'I know that S is P' be taken as giving my authority for saying that S is P? It might be more reasonably be taken as an expression of opinionless agnosticism.

Knowing Implies Believing: An Alleged Counterexample

Let us now consider the second form of argument directed against (iB), the attempt to produce a counterexample. The best instance of such an argument that I have found is in an article by Colin Radford.[10] Radford's alleged counterexample to (iB) would, if correct, succeed as well against (iA). The distinction between belief and acceptance is not germane to the example. It concerns a man, John, who protests quite sincerely that he does not know any English history, but when quizzed is able to answer some history questions correctly, for example, ones concerning the dates of the death of Elizabeth I and James I. John also makes some mistakes—indeed, he misses more often than he hits the mark—and he cannot tell when he is right and when wrong. John thinks he is guessing all along. Because he thinks he is guessing, he is not inclined to believe or, we might add, to accept that his answers are correct.

Nevertheless, Radford contends we should say that John knows some history. For example, John gives the correct answer to the question concerning the year of Elizabeth's death, and so he knows the answer:

Elizabeth died in 1603. Radford bolsters this contention by asking us to suppose that John has previously learned these dates and, consequently, that the reason he gives correct answers is that he remembers them.

Must we concede that John knows that Elizabeth died in 1603, even though he does not believe or accept that this is so? We may resist the inclination to do so, if any exists, by arguing that John does not know that Elizabeth died in 1603. One strategy would be simply to deny that John *knows* the correct answer, though, to be sure, he gives the correct answer. It is, however, natural enough to say that John knows the correct answer, and, consequently, it is useful to attack the argument by means of a counterargument.

The crucial premise of such a counterargument is that, though John knows some correct answers, he does not know that these answers are correct. This is shown by the fact that he has no idea which of his answers are correct and is untrustworthy in distinguishing the correct answers from the incorrect ones. Thus, though John answers the question concerning the death of Elizabeth correctly, he does not know that his answer is correct. But what does he need to know in order to know that his answer, that Elizabeth died in 1603, is correct? To know it is correct, all he needs to know is that Elizabeth did, in fact, die in 1603. If he knew that she died in 1603, then he would also know that his answer is correct; but he does not know his answer is correct. Therefore, John does not know that Elizabeth died in 1603.

We have, from one example, elicited contradictory conclusions. Let us look at the arguments side by side. Put schematically, Radford's argument is as follows:

1. John knows the correct answer to the question.
2. The correct answer to the question is that Elizabeth died in 1603.
3. If John knows the correct answer and the correct answer is that Elizabeth died in 1603, then John knows that Elizabeth died in 1603.

Therefore,

4. John knows that Elizabeth died in 1603.

The opposing argument is as follows:

1. John does not know that his answer is correct.
2. John's answer is that Elizabeth died in 1603.

3. If John does not know that his answer is correct and John's answer is that Elizabeth died in 1603, then John does not know that Elizabeth died in 1603.

Therefore,

4. John does not know that Elizabeth died in 1603.

The second argument is equally persuasive, and, moreover, there is no equivocation in the word 'know' in the conclusions of these arguments to lessen the force of the contradiction. With such contradictory conclusions cogently defended, must we concede that the concept of knowledge is contradictory? Is knowledge impossible?

Fortunately, there is no need to concede the impossibility of knowledge. Instead, we may reject premise (3) of Radford's argument. We may say that John knows the correct answer, that Elizabeth died in 1603, but deny that John knows that Elizabeth died in 1603. To see why, consider an example in which a woman knows the correct answer to a question about the date of Elizabeth's death even though she is guessing and thus does not know that Elizabeth died in 1603. Imagine a woman, Alice, who is on a quiz programme and is asked the date of Elizabeth's death. She answers: '1603'. You, not having heard the answer, ask me, 'Did Alice know the correct answer?' To this question I could reply in the affirmative. Moreover, it might not matter whether I thought Alice was guessing or not. When the quizmaster says, 'Alice, if you know the answer to the question I am about to ask, you will win that red Ford', he does not intend to withhold the Ford if Alice guesses correctly. On the contrary, in this context to give the correct answer is to know the correct answer. When you asked, 'Did Alice know the correct answer?' I could have answered, 'Yes, but I think it was just a lucky guess'. There is no question of whether Alice knows the correct answer once she gives it. She knew. Away she drives.

Thus Alice, like John, knows the correct answer, that Elizabeth died in 1603. Alice knew just as John did, even though Alice was guessing. Though we concede that Alice knew the correct answer, we should want to insist that she did not know that Elizabeth died in 1603. A lucky guess that p is not a case of knowing that p. The preceding argument shows that there are contexts in which it would be acceptable to say that a person knows the correct answer, which is that p, but would be clearly false to say the person knows that p.

An Objection: Remembrance Without Belief

Radford has objected to the preceding argument on the grounds that the question has been begged against him.[11] In support of this, he appeals to the consideration that one may remember that *p*, and hence know that *p* from memory, when one does not know that one knows that *p*, believe that one knows that *p*, or even believe that *p*. Indeed, the example concerning John, as spelled out in detail, is one in which he has previously learned that Elizabeth died in 1603, though he has forgotten having learned it, and thus gives the right answer because he remembers what he once learned. He remembers even though he does not know or believe himself to have done so, and consequently believes he is guessing. Since John is remembering, he knows that *p*, even though he does not believe he knows, thinks he is guessing, and does not believe that *p*.

There is another quite similar example involving memory that should be considered at this juncture, for, like Radford's, it is persuasive, and the reply to both examples is quite similar. Another philosopher, E. J. Lemmon, presented the following as an example to show that a man may know that *p*, but not know that he knows that *p*.[12] A man, Alan say, who some time ago learned about the number pi when he studied geometry, is asked, 'What is the expansion of pi to four decimal places?' Alan replies, 'I don't know', and his answer is quite sincere. After a moment, he suddenly remembers and says, 'Yes I do, it is 3.1416'. Lemmon contends that when the man said, 'I don't know', he did in fact know, as is shown by his subsequent remark. So, when Alan said he did not know, he did know, but he did not know that he knew. He only knew that he knew once he remembered the expansion of pi. This example, though directed against the thesis that if a man knows that *p*, then he knows that he knows that *p*, might equally well be employed against (iB). It could be contended that Alan, when he says he does not know, does not believe that pi is 3.1416.

This example can be made to bear even more directly on (iB) by slight amendment. Suppose we have another person, Joan, and we ask her: 'Is 3.1416 the expansion of pi to four decimal places?' Joan, who studied mathematics a long time ago and is not much interested in our question anyway, might, without much reflection and with some irritation, reply, 'I don't know'. Like Alan, Joan then immediately recalls her mathematics and quickly adds, 'Oh yes, I do know, pi is 3.1416 when expanded to four decimal places and 3.141592653 when expanded to ten', and looks quite smug. In this example, it could be contended that the woman did know that 3.1416 is the expansion of pi to four decimal places when she said she did not know, as her immediately subsequent feat of memory showed. She did not believe she knew, however, nor did she believe or accept 3.1416 to be the expansion of pi to four decimal places when first she spoke. Thus, we seem here again to have a counterexample to (iB) and (iA).

Borderline Cases of Knowledge

What are we to say to these arguments against (iB) and (iA)? The most direct reply is one conceded by Radford. At one point, Radford admits that his examples are borderline cases of knowledge.[13] This is precisely the case, but what is a borderline case? To say that a case is borderline means there are considerations in favor of applying the term, and equally strong considerations in favor of not applying it. For example, if we see something that is very similar in color to many red things, so much so that this is a quite conclusive reason for saying that the object is red; but at the same time it is very similar to things that are orange and not red, so much so that this is a quite conclusive reason for saying that the thing is not red, then we have a borderline case of something red. Such cases abound.

For most terms of everyday speech, we can expect to find that the term applies without doubt or controversy in a large number of cases, and that it also clearly fails to apply in many cases. On the other hand, in between these cases there are examples of things where it is not evident whether or not the term applies, no matter how much we know about the example. Here we are very likely to conclude that the case is borderline. Debate on whether the term applies in such cases can produce arguments and profound speculation, but no one can win because the case is precisely one in which the application of the term is not fixed. As Stephan Körner has suggested, such terms are inherently inexact, and, therefore, the decision to apply or not to apply the term in borderline cases is a matter of choice.[14]

If we wish to defend (iB) and (iA) by maintaining that the cases of John, Alan, and Joan are all borderline for the application of the word 'know,' two tasks remain. First, we must show that the cases are genuinely borderline, and, second, we must justify our choice of applying epistemic terms in the manner required for the truth of (iA).

Some argument for the conclusion that John's case is a borderline case of knowledge has already been given in the earlier presentation of two persuasive arguments, one yielding the conclusion that John does not know that Elizabeth died in 1603, and the other the exact opposite. Similar argument may be offered in the cases of Alan and Joan. Since each sincerely reports and believes that they do not know, neither knows that the correct answer to the question is 3.1416 at the time of their report. In order to know that 3.1416 is the correct answer, however, all that either would have to know is that 3.1416 is the expansion of pi to four decimal places. Hence, neither person knows that 3.1416 is the expansion of pi to four decimal places when they say they do not know. This argument is in direct opposition to Lemmon's, which was that, since Joan and Alan have not learned the answer to the question between the time of their first and second remarks, each must have known all along that 3.1416 was the expansion of pi to four decimal places. Once again, there are equally persuasive arguments for contradictory conclusions. Such arguments and counterarguments concerning these examples show them to be borderline cases. It is precisely like arguing about whether something is red when it is as close to red as it is to orange; and no argument can settle that.

Knowledge Implies Acceptance

Given, as we have argued, that the cases of John, Alan, and Joan are borderline, how can we justify refusing to apply the term 'know' in such cases? The appropriate justification is theoretical, one concerning the role of acceptance and the evaluation of information in knowledge and justification. In all three cases a person may be said to possess the information that Elizabeth died in 1603 or that pi is 3.1416, but they do not, at a given time, know that the information is correct because they do not accept that it is. John possesses the information that Elizabeth died in 1603 in that it is retained in his memory. Since the information is retained in his memory, we say, when he produces an answer, that he remembered that Elizabeth died in 1603, even though he does not know that Elizabeth died in 1603. This is a case, of which there are many, where remembering that p does not logically imply knowing that p. The reason John does not know is that, though he possesses the information that p in memory, John does not know that the information is correct.

Some philosophers, Dretske, for example, have assumed that if a person receives information that p, then they know that p.[15] Others, like Radford, have assumed that if a person receives and retains the information that p, then the person knows that p. Both views have the same defect. There is an important distinction between receiving or possessing information and knowing that the received or possessed information is correct. Only when one knows that the information one receives or possesses is correct does one have knowledge.

Imagine, for example, that Mary had been told that Elizabeth died in 1603 by Peter, who is notoriously untrustworthy in such matters. Imagine further that Mary retained that report in memory only because she had accepted what Peter had told her, in spite of knowing him to be untrustworthy in such matters. It would be obvious that Mary did not know that Elizabeth died in 1603 when Peter told her because she did not know that the report she received was correct. It should be equally obvious that John does not know that Elizabeth died in 1603, when that information is retained in memory, because he does not know that the information is correct. John, unlike Mary, might have once known that Elizabeth died in 1603 because he once knew that the information was correct. Now, though the information is retained in memory, John no longer knows that the information is correct. That is why John does not know that Elizabeth died in 1603. John does not know this because he does not know that the information he possesses is correct. He does not know that the information he possesses is correct because he does not even accept it.

These reflections provide us with the basis for a perfectly general proof that knowledge implies acceptance. The proof is as follows:

1. If a person does not accept that p, then the person does not accept the information that p.
2. If a person does not accept the information that p, then the person does not know that the information that p is correct.
3. If a person does not know that the information that p is correct, then the person does not know that p.

Therefore,

4. If a person does not accept that p, then the person does not know that p.

This is equivalent to the acceptance condition,

(iA) If S knows that p, then S accepts that p

with which we began.

The premises of the argument, once made explicit, may seem so obvious as to require no proof. They do, however, reflect our concern with a kind of acceptance and knowledge consisting of the recognition of information. Acceptance of information is not a sufficient condition for knowing that the information received is correct, but it is necessary. Consequently, the failure to accept information results in failure to know that the information is correct. The problem in the cases of John, Alan, and Joan was the same. Each retained some information that p in memory, but, at a specified point in time, none accepted the information that p

and, as a result, did not know that *p*. In the case of Alan and Joan, subsequent reflection produced the acceptance of the information that pi is 3.1416, and, therefore, knowledge replaced ignorance. In short, it does not suffice for knowledge that some information is stored in memory as a result of communication or perception. One must, in addition, have the appropriate sort of access to the information and acceptance of it.

Knowledge and the Functional Role of Acceptance

The foregoing remarks may be construed as further elucidation of the kind of knowledge that is the object of our study. There may be living beings, such as a gullible child, a well as machines, such as an answering device, that receive and retain information. If we know enough about those beings and machines, they may be a source of information and knowledge for us. They, however, do not know that the information they possess, retain, and transmit is correct. We, on the contrary, not only receive and transmit information, we process it. We accept some but not all of what we receive and know that some but not all of the information is correct.

The nature and role of acceptance in knowledge requires some clarification. Acceptance is the sort of mental state that has a specific sort of role, a functional role, in thought, inference, and action. When a person accepts that *p*, he or she will draw certain inferences and perform certain actions assuming the truth of *p*. Thus, if a person accepts that *p*, then the person will be ready to affirm that *p* or to concede that *p* in the appropriate circumstances. They will also be ready to justify the claim that *p*. If they accept information received from the senses or retained in memory, they will regard such information as correct and proceed accordingly in thought and action. The reluctance of John to affirm that Elizabeth died in 1603 and the initial reluctance of Alan and Joan to affirm that pi is 3.1416 reveal an initial ignorance and lack of acceptance of the information. As a result of the appropriate processing of information retained in memory, this ignorance is replaced by acceptance and knowledge. Acceptance of *p* sometimes arises from considered judgment that *p*, but a functionally similar state of judgment may arise in other ways. To accept that *p* is to accept the information that *p*. To accept the information that *p* implies a readiness in the appropriate circumstances to think, infer, and act on the assumption that the information is correct.

The result of our argument is that we shall resolve the borderline cases of John, Alan, and Joan by saying they lack knowledge. For some purposes of everyday speech, we can afford the semantic imperfection that yields the sort of contradictory conclusions we have derived from the study of John and company, but an acceptable theory must eliminate such imperfection for the sake of consistency. We shall require that the epistemic terms in question carry the implication of acceptance, for this will enable us to extricate our employment of the terms from the contradictions noted earlier. Such a requirement leads directly to the conclusion that John, Alan, and Joan do not know that p when they say they do not know, because they then lack acceptance that p. By so doing, we are not dogmatically ruling out the possibility that some theory of knowledge might be constructed which would rule in the opposite direction. We should welcome the development of such a theory. However, as we affirmed earlier, our concern is to present a theory of knowledge and justification to explain how we are justified in accepting information as correct and claiming to know that it is. Examples of alleged knowledge in which a person does not know that the information they accept is correct may be of philosophical interest, but they fall outside the concern of knowledge that is characteristically human.

In defence of the foregoing restriction, it should be added that our decision to require the implication of acceptance of the information that p, and accompanying readiness to affirm that p in the appropriate circumstances when a person knows that p, is nothing arbitrary or idiosyncratic. It is warranted by the fact that our edifice of scientific knowledge and practical wisdom depends upon the social context in which criticism and defence determine which claims are to be employed as the postulates of scientific systems and the information for practical decisions. In such contexts, when a person admits ignorance, one is taken at one's word; for such a person is not willing to make the sort of epistemic commitments that would enable us to check their cognitive credentials. Of course, we may well be interested in their reasons, if they have any, for conjecturing what they do, but this is quite different from asking whether they are completely justified in accepting something as correct information and claiming to have knowledge. An affirmative answer to that question not only shows that the person has knowledge, it also tranfers that knowledge to those who understand the justification and apprehend its merits. Our theoretical concern with critical reasoning, and our attempt to explain how such reasoning succeeds, warrants our decision to rule that knowledge must involve the forms of acceptance cited above.

Memory Without Knowledge

At this point, we must honestly face the question, Why do all these cases seem to be examples of knowledge to the philosophers in question? The answer is that we often ascribe knowledge to others in order to explain, in a commonsense manner, why they are correct. In each of the cases considered, someone is in a position to say something, either at the time she disavows knowledge or very shortly thereafter, which warrants our concluding that the person was in a position to give the right answer. It is not just a matter of luck that she can give a correct answer. On the contrary, it is because she acquired knowledge in the past and retains information in memory that it is possible for her to come up with the correct answer now. If we suppose that the knowledge has vanished, then it seems difficult to explain how she can now be in a position to give the correct answer. For the purposes of explaining how she can now be in a position to give a correct answer, we conclude that the knowledge has not vanished. She still knows.

This very natural way of explaining correct answers is, however, highly defective. Something extremely important has been lost by the person in spite of such answers, namely, the acceptance of the information. In the absence of such acceptance, the person does not know the information retained is correct. The result is a refusal to defend a claim to know and the lack of justificatory support. The difference between the person who accepts the information that p and is ready to defend the claim that she knows, on the one hand, and a person who does not accept the information that p and thinks she is just guessing that p, on the other, is sufficiently great so that we may justifiably mark the distinction by refusing to say that the latter knows that p. By doing so, we shall in no way prevent ourselves from explaining how a person can manage to give the correct answer, that p, without knowing that p.

The latter contention is supported by the application of another argument derived from Armstrong.[16] He asks us to imagine a case in which a man, asked about the date of the death of Elizabeth, answers: 'Elizabeth died in 1306'. Now this answer, though incorrect, is sufficiently similar to the correct answer, 1603, so that we can see that it is not a mere matter of chance that he gave this answer. We cannot explain this man's answer by affirming that he knows that Elizabeth died in 1603, for, since the numbers 6 and 3 having been transposed in his memory, he does not know that Elizabeth died in 1603. (To clarify this we may even imagine that when asked, 'Are you sure it was not 1603?', the man replies that he is sure it is 1306.) Just as it would be incorrect to explain why this man gives the answer he does by affirming that he knows the date of Elizabeth's death, so explaining why John and the others are able to give a correct answer by affirming that they know, would be otiose. A theory of memory that explains how memory produces the results it does, whether correct or incorrect, does not require us to assume that a woman knows her answer is correct whenever memory enables her to produce a correct answer. To do so would be to lump together the case in which memory only functions well enough to yield a correct answer with those cases in which it produces acceptance and justification.

Our contention is that sometimes memory is good enough to give us a correct answer when it is not good enough to give us knowledge that the answer is correct. When memory does not function well enough for us to know that the information we have retained is correct, then we are not in a position either to claim to know or to justify a claim to know. Thus, we wish to distinguish sharply between those cases in which memory serves us so well that we know the information retained in memory is correct from those in which the information retained in memory is not accepted as correct and, consequently, is not known to be correct. That there is a distinction cannot be doubted, and, for the purpose of constructing a theory to explain epistemic justification, we need only count as knowledge those cases in which a person accepts the information in question and knows that the information is correct. Such cases have top value in the epistemic marketplace, and all the rest may be discounted without explanatory loss.

Introduction to the Literature

The best anthology of articles on truth is *Recent Essays on Truth and the Liar Paradox* by Robert Martin. The best single study of the subject of truth is *Truth, Vagueness and Paradox: An Essay on the Logic of Truth* by Vann McGee. The classic article on truth is by Alfred Tarski, "The Semantic Conception of Truth."

The articles with important arguments to show that knowing does not entail believing include "Knowledge—By Examples" by Colin Radford and "Other Minds" by J. L. Austin. For an important and clear discussion of the topic, see David Armstrong, "Does Knowledge Entail Belief?" The claim that knowledge consists of the receiving of information is articulated in detail by Fred Dretske in *Knowledge and the Flow of Information*.

3

The Foundation Theory:
Infallible Foundationalism

KNOWLEDGE IMPLIES completely justified acceptance. We expressed this in the condition

(iJ) If S knows that p, then S is completely justified in accepting that p.

What makes us completely justified in accepting one thing rather than another? One answer, that of the *foundation theory*, is that some beliefs, basic beliefs, are completely justified in themselves and constitute the foundation for the justification of everything else. In this chapter we shall examine the foundation theory of justification according to which all justification is based on self-justified or basic beliefs. It is traditional to formulate and discuss the foundation theory in terms of belief rather than acceptance, and we shall do so as well, but the kind of belief required for knowledge is acceptance directed at obtaining truth and avoiding error in what is accepted. We succeed in this objective when we accept something if and only if what we accept is true.

Thus, for the foundation theory to succeed, the self-justified or basic beliefs must be things we are completely justified in accepting in our quest for truth and do not depend for their justification on anything else that we accept. Everything else that we are completely justified in accepting must ultimately be based on these basic beliefs, which provide us with the foundation for the edifice of justification and knowledge. Is such a theory tenable?

We must first notice that any correct theory of justification must share at least one fundamentally important tenet of the foundation theory, to wit, that there are some things that we are completely justified in accepting without having proven or even argued that they are true. Clearly, whatever our capacity for argument, we have not, in fact, argued for the truth of everything we are completely justified in accepting. For example, no one but a few philosophers has ever argued that they have a headache or that they are thinking, but many who have never argued for such things, and would be at a loss to imagine how one might argue for them, have, nevertheless, been completely justified in accepting them. We must, therefore, agree with the foundationalist that we are completely justified in accepting some things without argument.

Infallible Versus Fallible Foundationalism

Disagreement arises when we consider answers to the question, How are we completely justified in accepting things without any argument to show that they are true? Acceptance aims at truth. If we accept something without any argument for the truth of it, how can we be completely justified in accepting it for the purpose of accepting what is true? It is to this question that the traditional foundationalist has provided an important answer, namely, that some beliefs *guarantee* their own truth. If my accepting something guarantees the truth of what I accept, then I am completely justified in accepting it for the purpose of obtaining truth and avoiding error. We are guaranteed success in our quest for truth and cannot fail. We might, therefore, call this *infallible* foundationalism. Assuming that there are beliefs that guarantee their own truth and that these suffice to justify us in accepting all that we are completely justified in accepting, infallible foundationalism provides a brilliant solution to the problem of knowledge.

We shall soon turn to a detailed examination of the merits of infallible foundationalism, but we should first note that there have been foundationalists of other sorts. There are, of course, many different possible ways to construct a foundation, and no taxonomy of foundationalist theories would do justice to them all. Without any pretensions to a complete taxonomy, it is necessary, nevertheless, to consider some other forms of foundationalism. For reasons we shall soon consider, a foundationalist might despair of finding sufficient beliefs that guarantee their own truth and settle for a more modest foundation of self-justified or basic beliefs that provide a *reason* for their acceptance but without a guarantee of their truth. Since such a reason is a fallible guide rather than a guarantee of truth, we might call a theory of this kind *fallible* foundationalism. It is characteristic of fallible foundationalism to allow that the reason a self-justified belief provides for acceptance may be overridden or defeated by other considerations, and, therefore, that the reason for acceptance is a *prima facie* reason for acceptance.[1]

The Foundation Theory in General

It is possible to give a more precise characterization of foundation theories in general by specifying the conditions that must be met for a belief to be basic. The first is that a basic belief must be self-justified rather than being justified entirely by relation to other beliefs. The second is that the justification of all justified beliefs depends on the self-justification of basic beliefs. A theory of justification with these features is one in which there are basic beliefs which are self-justified and which justify all nonbasic beliefs.

Traditionally, the doctrine of empiricism has been associated with the foundation theory. According to empiricist theories of knowledge and justification, there are some empirical statements (for example, that I see something moving or, more cautiously, that it appears to me as though I see something moving) which constitute the content of basic beliefs. The belief that such statements are true is a self-justified belief. All beliefs that are justified are so because of the justification provided by accepting the empirical statements in question. Thus, the acceptance of such empirical statements is basic. Exactly how the empirical statements are construed depends on the empiricist in question. However, the empirical statements which constitute the content of basic beliefs have always been statements to the effect that some item in sense experience has or lacks some quality or relationship discernible by means of the senses. Thus, the empirical statements are statements of observation.

Empiricists have disagreed about the objects of sense experience. The item sensed may be conceived of as a physical thing, like a chair or a meter, or it may be construed as some more subjective entity, like an appearance or a sense datum. Moreover, they have disagreed about what makes such statements self-justified and about how basic beliefs justify other statements. They do agree that there are observation statements constituting the content of basic beliefs whose acceptance justifies all that is justified and, moreover, refutes all that is refuted.

Though empiricist epistemology is most commonly associated with a foundation theory, there is no logical restriction, or, for that matter, historical limitation, of foundation theories to empiricism. Rationalistic philosophies of knowledge, for example, that of Descartes, have been foundation theories. Such a rationalist maintains that a belief may be certified by reason as having characteristics that make it basic—indubitability, for example. A strict rationalism would hold that basic beliefs, and the justification they provide for other beliefs, are certified by reason alone.[2] Similarly, a strict empiricism would hold that basic beliefs and the justification they provide for other beliefs are certified by experience alone.

Few philosophers would contend that all justification is derived solely from reason or solely from experience. That a conclusion follows from premises is ascertained by reason, and what the objects of sense experience are like is ascertained by experience. Of course, reason may play a role in the latter, and experience in the former, but it would generally be conceded that if all people were deprived of reason, then no one would be justified in believing any conclusion to be a logical consequence of a premise. Similarly, if we were all deprived of our senses, then no one would be justified in believing there to be any objects of sense experience. These are obvious truths, mentioned only to illustrate how misguided it is to conceive of epistemology as the battleground between rationalism and empiricism.

The Foundation as a Guarantee of Truth

We are adopting an entirely different approach that cuts across traditional lines. Rationalists and empiricists often share a common conception which leads to a foundation theory. They conceive of justification as being a guarantee of truth. Empiricists think that experience can guarantee the truth of basic beliefs and rationalists think that reason is the guarantee of truth. Basic beliefs are basic because they cannot be false; their truth is guaranteed. With this initial guarantee of truth in basic beliefs, the next problem is how to extend this guarantee to other beliefs.

Our earlier analysis of knowledge offers a simple explanation of why this doctrine should be held. Since one condition of knowledge is truth, it follows that no belief constitutes knowledge unless it is true. Thus, if our justification fails to guarantee the truth of what we accept, then it may leave us with a false belief. In that case, we lack knowledge, so justification sufficient to ensure us knowledge must, some foundation theorists have argued, guarantee the truth of what we accept.[3]

Another motive for the doctrine of infallible foundationalism is a consequence of our account of acceptance. If the goal of acceptance is to accept something just in case it is true, then acceptance, which guarantees its own truth, provides us with a prophylactic against accepting something false. Thus, though a fallible foundation theorist may deny that we need a guarantee for the truth of basic beliefs,[4] a central thesis of the traditional foundation theory was that basic beliefs are immune from error and refutation. If basic beliefs were erroneous and refutable, then all that was justified by basic beliefs, all that was built upon them in the edifice of justification, might be undone by error. The very foundation of all justification might prove unsound. If there is nothing to ensure that such basic beliefs are true, then, *ipso facto*, there is nothing to ensure the truth of those beliefs they justify. All justification might rest on a false foundation.

Fallible Foundations

Some recent philosophers have, nevertheless, claimed that basic beliefs are reasonable or evident in themselves without going on to claim that such beliefs guarantee their truth or are immune from refutation.[5] On such a foundation theory, the basic beliefs are justified unless there is evidence to the contrary. In other words, they are *prima facie* justified, innocent in the court of justification, unless their justification is overridden. Some foundation theorists, who have denied that the justification of basic beliefs need provide any guarantee of truth, have gone so far as to deny that such justification is connected with truth in any way at all.[6] Such theories, though philosophically important, leave us with a dilemma. Either such justification is irrelevant to the truth of basic beliefs or it is relevant. If the justification is irrelevant to the truth of basic beliefs, then it is not the sort of justification needed to justify acceptance or to yield knowledge. The acceptance required for knowledge is acceptance that aims at truth. Therefore, no justification that is irrelevant to truth is adequate to justify such acceptance.

Suppose, then, that the foundation theorist maintains that the justification of basic beliefs is relevant to the truth of those beliefs, though it does not guarantee their truth. If there is some risk of error, then the justification such basic beliefs possess must offset the risk, that is, they must make the risk worthwhile. The risk or probability of error infecting our basic beliefs must not be too high, or else we would not be justified in accepting those beliefs as our foundation. If, however, there is some risk of error in accepting a basic belief, how can we be justified in accepting the belief without confirmation that the risk of error is acceptable?

The foundation theorist may simply postulate that we are justified in accepting certain basic beliefs and give no justification for this claim. We may agree on intuitive grounds that we are justified in accepting the beliefs in question, but why do we think that the beliefs in question are justified? It is because we believe that they are sufficiently unlikely to turn out to be false or, what is the same thing, sufficiently likely to be true. We agree that we are justified in accepting the beliefs because of the probability of their truth, but why do we think the beliefs in question are so likely to be true? When one considers the candidates for such beliefs—introspective beliefs concerning one's present thoughts and sensations, or cautious perceptual beliefs about simple qualities we see directly before us—the answer is apparent. We think that our powers of introspection and perception are very unlikely to lead us into error in such simple matters.

So the justification for accepting these beliefs, if they fail to guarantee their own truth, implicitly depends on a theory we have concerning the reliability of our cognitive powers. This means, however, that the allegedly basic beliefs in question are justified by relation to other beliefs and are not genuinely basic. Such a theory is not a pure foundation theory. The allegedly basic beliefs must stand in the appropriate probability relation to other beliefs for their justification. Though the defender of a fallible foundation theory deserves a fuller hearing, it appears that only those foundation theories holding that basic beliefs guarantee their own truth are pure foundation theories. Fallible foundation theories inevitably appear tainted with a component of the coherence theory pertaining to the probability of basic beliefs.[7] For this reason, we shall now examine the merits of the stronger form of the foundation theory alleging that basic beliefs are immune from error.

Incorrigible Foundations

A foundation theory alleging that basic beliefs guarantee their truth faces two problems. The first is to show that there are some basic beliefs which can guarantee their own truth. The second is to show how basic beliefs can guarantee the truth of other beliefs. Let us consider the first problem. Philosophers have maintained that some beliefs guarantee their own truth and are thus self-justified because they are *incorrigible*. We shall now examine the tenability of this thesis. What is meant by saying that a belief is incorrigible?

Let us begin with the intuitive notion that an incorrigible belief is one such that the person who has it cannot be mistaken in believing what she does. We are immediately faced with the tricky little word 'can', a semantic chameleon. What are we to understand it to mean? We may wisely begin with a technical notion and then, should that prove insufficiently subtle, turn to some modification. Let us begin with the notion of *logical possibility*.

It is logically impossible that someone has a female brother or that some number is larger than itself. Logical impossibility is a familiar notion, though it is clear that some modal notion, possibility, for example, must be taken as primitive. So, if we assume the notion of a possible world, for example, then we can say that something is logically impossible if and only if it does not obtain in any possible world. We sometimes speak of the logical impossibility of certain sentences. For example, we might say that the sentence, 'John has a female brother,' is logically impossible. However, when we say such things we are speaking elliptically. It is what is *stated* by the sentence that is logically impossible. What the sentence 'John has a female brother' states is that John has a female brother, and that is logically impossible. This explains why the sentence is not true in any possible world and, therefore, is contradictory or analytically false. We thus come full tilt to the controversial notion of *analyticity.*

It is notoriously difficult to provide any satisfactory definition or criterion of analyticity or related notions. Some philosophers thus disregard the notion of analyticity as a philosophical relic of semantic battles lost long ago. This conclusion is premature. Some logical notion, whether that of contradictoriness, possibility, or impossibility, may be taken as basic and undefined. Once we concede that logical possibility or some other logical notion must be taken as basic and undefined, we must also admit there are going to be cases in which it is difficult to ascertain whether something is logically possible. This is partly because the distinction between logic and other areas of inquiry is not clearly drawn. Nevertheless, there are many cases in which the application of the concept will be sufficiently precise for useful employment.

A Definition of Incorrigibility

Let us now define incorrigibility in terms of the concept of logical impossibility. We can say, roughly, that a belief is incorrigible if and only if it is logically impossible for the belief to be mistaken. More formally, the definition is as follows:

The belief that p is incorrigible for S if and only if it is logically impossible that S believes that p and p is false.

Given this definition of incorrigibility, it follows immediately that if a person believes something and her belief is incorrigible, then what she believes is true. If it is impossible that she should believe that p and p should be false, then, given that she does believe that p, it follows that p is true. Hence, in one sense such beliefs guarantee their own truth.

A problem arises when we consider whether incorrigible beliefs as so defined are self-justified or, indeed, justified at all, for it is logically impossible that any person should be mistaken in believing anything which is logically necessary. By saying that something is logically necessary, we mean no more or less than that it is the denial of something logically impossible. Thus, it is logically impossible that 2 plus 7 does not equal 9 and, hence, logically necessary that 2 plus 7 equals 9. This means, however, that it is logically impossible that a person should believe that 2 plus 7 equals 9 and be mistaken in her belief. The reason is that it is logically impossible that 2 plus 7 should not equal 9.

A Counterexample

No matter how complicated or esoteric the arithmetical belief might be, it remains the case that if what is believed is logically necessary, then it is logically impossible that the belief should be false. Hence, the belief is incorrigible. For example, if a person believes that there is a one-to-one correspondence between the set of whole or natural numbers and the set of even numbers, then she believes something that is logically necessary, and her belief is incorrigible. If, however, she believes this for some foolish reason, for example, she believes that after a certain point in the series of numbers there are no more odd ones, then we would conclude that, on the basis of her reasoning, she surely could have been mistaken and was quite unjustified in her belief. It was pretty much a matter of luck that she was correct in her belief, and she certainly did not know that what she believed was true.

In this example the person could have been mistaken, even though it was logically impossible that she should have been. Thus, there appears to be some important sense of the expression, 'could not have been mistaken', that our current specification of incorrigibility fails to capture. Moreover, this demonstrates that the justification we have for believing certain necessary truths in arithmetic, mathematics, and logic is not a simple consequence of the necessity of what is believed. A person may believe something that is a necessary truth without in any way knowing that her belief is true or even being justified in her belief. This argument proves that the logical impossibility of being mistaken does not suffice for justification when what is believed is an arithmetical, mathematical, or logical truth. When it is logically necessary that p, as it is in such cases, the logical impossibility of the conjunction that S believes that p *and* it is false that p is a direct consequence of the logical impossibility of the falsity of p. That S believes that p has nothing whatever to do with the incorrigibility of her belief in these cases.[8]

An Amended Definition of Incorrigibility

The solution to this problem is a simple amendment of the definition of incorrigibility, one which will, moreover, insure that incorrigible beliefs achieve the goal of acceptance. We said that the objective of acceptance is to accept that p if and only if it is true that p. The definition of incorrigibility given above logically insures that whenever a person's acceptance of p is incorrigible, then, if a person accepts that p, it is true that p, but this is only one objective of acceptance. The other is to accept that p if it is true that p. To insure logically that incorrigible beliefs attain the objectives of acceptance, we should define incorrigibility as follows:

> The belief that p is incorrigible for S if and only if (i) it is logically necessary that if S believes that p, then it is true that p and (ii) it is logically necessary that if it is true that p, then S believes that p.

Incorrigible beliefs so defined fulfill the objectives of acceptance as a matter of logical necessity. The first condition might be called the *infallibility* condition because it requires that one cannot fail to attain truth in what one believes, and the second condition might be called the *irresistibility* condition because it requires that one cannot resist believing what is true. Beliefs that fulfill the infallibility condition will be said to be *infallible* beliefs, while those that fulfill the irresistibility condition will be said to be *irresistible* beliefs.

This definition of incorrigibility is equivalent to saying that a belief that p is incorrigible for S just in case (i) it is logically impossible that S believe that p and that it be false that p and (ii) it is logically impossible that it be true that p and that S not believe that p. The first condition, the infallibility condition, is the one that proved insufficient in consideration of necessary truths, but the addition of the second, the irresistibility condition, mends the difficulty. Though it is logically impossible that a person should believe a mathematical truth (for example, that 25 times 26 equals 650) and be in error, it is perfectly possible that a person should fail to believe such a truth. In this case the irresistibility condition is not satisfied, the belief is not irresistible. Thus, the truth that 25 times 26 equals 650 is not an incorrigible belief for a person when it is logically possible that the person not believe this because it is not an irresistible belief.

Many beliefs that a person has about herself are alleged to be incorrigible in this sense. The favorites are beliefs about conscious mental states of the moment, such as a sharp pain, the idea being that a person cannot be mistaken about what is consciously occurring in her mind at the moment it is occurring. Rather than beginning with a discussion of a belief about some mental or psychological state, though, let us go back to Descartes and consider the bare belief of a person that she exists, whatever else might be true about her.

Consider, for example, my belief that I exist. My belief that I exist cannot possibly be false, and it is plausible to affirm that I cannot possibly fail to believe it. Consider my belief that I believe something. It is logically impossible that I believe that I believe something and do not believe something. The belief is clearly infallible. Moreover, it is plausible to maintain that I cannot fail to believe that I believe something when, in fact, I do believe something and, thus, that the belief is irresistible as well. Thus, the belief that I exist and the belief that I believe something are infallible beliefs which are plausible candidates for the role of incorrigible beliefs as so defined.

Infallible Beliefs About Thoughts

The foregoing example concerning beliefs about believing something must be distinguished from a closely related one. Once it is conceded that the belief that one believes something is infallible, it might be inferred that if a person believed that he believes that so and so, then his belief that he believes that so and so is also infallible. This is doubtful, however. I cannot both believe something and be in error in believing that I believe something, but I can believe that I believe some specific thing, that my belief has some specific content, and be in error. The sort of belief that concerns us is acceptance in the interests of obtaining truth and avoiding error, and, as we noted in the last chapter, such belief is a functional state implying a readiness to infer and act in specified ways. The inferences and actions of a person may reveal that he does not accept what he sincerely says and even believes he accepts. If a man says he believes a woman is capable of performing a job as well as the man she has replaced and yet immediately infers, without investigation, that everything that goes wrong in the office is her fault, he does not really believe she is as capable as the man she replaced. His chauvinism shows that he does not accept what he says, even if he believes he does. One could offer similar arguments to show that it is logically possible for a person to be mistaken about what she hopes, fears, and wishes.

Are any mental occurrences the objects of infallible beliefs? The best candidates are thoughts and sensations. Let us consider thoughts first. We sometimes say of a person that he thinks that so and so when we are using the term 'think' to mean something very much like belief. That is not the sense of the term we shall consider now. Instead, consider the participial use of the term 'thinking' which describes an occurrent episode, for example, thinking that Mary is a colonel. Here we use the term to refer to the thoughts that are now occurring to us or our ongoing mental processes. Can a person be mistaken in his beliefs about such occurrences?

Suppose I am thinking that Bacon is the author of *Hamlet*. Suppose, secondly, that I believe that Bacon is identical with Shakespeare, that is, that the man known to us as the author, Shakespeare, is none other than Bacon. However, though I believe this identity to hold, let us also imagine that this belief is not before my mind, I am not thinking of this identity at the time at which I am thinking that Bacon is the author of *Hamlet*. Now, suppose I am asked what I was thinking. I might conclude that I was thinking that Shakespeare was the author of *Hamlet* because, believing that Bacon is Shakespeare, I also believe that thinking that Bacon is such and such is the same thing as thinking that Shakespeare is such and such. Am I correct?

The answer is no. Suppose my thinking, in this instance, consists of my talking to myself, of mulling things over in silent soliloquy, though we admit that not all thinking consists of such silent soliloquy. Nevertheless, there are some cases in which thinking consists of talking to oneself, and by focusing on such cases we shall be able to reveal the way in which a person can be mistaken about what he is thinking. Suppose that when I was thinking that Bacon is the author of *Hamlet*, my thinking consisted of saying to myself: 'Bacon is the author of *Hamlet*.' Now, it is perfectly clear that to say, 'Bacon is the author of *Hamlet*' is one thing, and to say, 'Shakespeare is the author of *Hamlet*,' another. Thus, thinking that Bacon is the author of *Hamlet* is not necessarily the same thing as thinking that Shakespeare is the author of *Hamlet*. We may, therefore, imagine that I was not thinking the latter when I was thinking the former. Thus, when I reported that I was thinking that Shakespeare is the author of *Hamlet*, and believed what I said, I was quite mistaken. Hence, believing that one is thinking such and such does not logically imply that one is thinking that.[9]

There are several objections to this line of thought which must be met. The first is that even though my thinking that Bacon is the author of *Hamlet* might, in some way, consist of my saying, 'Bacon is the author of *Hamlet*' to myself, it still does not follow that I was not thinking that Shakespeare is the author of *Hamlet* when saying to myself 'Bacon is the author of *Hamlet*'. Maybe I was thinking that Shakespeare is the author of *Hamlet*, but my so thinking did not consist of my saying 'Shakespeare is the author of *Hamlet*' to myself.

The reply to this objection is that there is no reason to say I was thinking Shakespeare was the author of *Hamlet* when I was saying something quite different to myself. My reason for saying that I was thinking Shakespeare is the author of *Hamlet* is a faulty inference. From the premise that Bacon is Shakespeare I inferred that thinking Bacon is such and such is the same thing as thinking Shakespeare is such and such. The inference is as faulty as the inference from that premise to the conclusion that saying Bacon is such and such is the same thing as saying Shakespeare is such and such. This inference is incorrect, even if the two men are identical, because I did not say that they were identical. Hence, when I said Bacon was such and such, I did not say that Shakespeare was such and such.

The argument just enunciated may be obscured by the consideration that if Bacon and Shakespeare are the same, then what I said of the one man is true if and only if what I said of the other is true. However, we can avoid this issue by assuming my belief that Bacon is Shakespeare to be false. Indeed, most scholars of Elizabethan literature do assume this. In that case, when I am saying that Shakespeare is the author of *Hamlet*, what I am saying is true, while, when I am saying that Bacon is the author of *Hamlet*, what I am saying is false. Hence, saying the one thing cannot be identical with saying the other. The same holds for thinking. If, when I am thinking that Shakespeare is the author of *Hamlet*, what I am thinking is true, while, when I am thinking that Bacon is the author of *Hamlet*, what I am thinking is false—then my thinking the first cannot be identical with my thinking the second. Hence, if I believe that I am thinking Shakespeare is the author of *Hamlet* because I believe I am thinking Bacon is the author of *Hamlet*, as was the case in the example cited, the former belief may be mistaken, even though the latter is correct.

Moreover, I can falsely believe that I am thinking Shakespeare is the author of *Hamlet* at the very same time I am actually thinking that Bacon is the author of *Hamlet*. To see that this is so, notice first of all that I can believe that I am thinking that Bacon is the author of *Hamlet* at the very time at which I am thinking that. My believing that I am thinking can coexist with the thinking and yet be quite distinct from the thinking. When a person talks to herself, she need not believe what she says. If my belief that I am thinking that Bacon is the author of *Hamlet* can exist at the same time as my thinking that, then obviously my false belief that I am thinking Shakespeare is the author of *Hamlet* can exist at the same time as my thinking Bacon is the author of *Hamlet*.

From the preceding argument we may conclude that a person can make all sorts of mistakes about what is presently going on in her mind. The preceding argument may be adopted to show that when a person believes that she is surmising that *p*, doubting that *p*, or pondering that *p*, she may be mistaken in her belief. It would be the most unforgivable pedantry to rerun the preceding argument for each of these states. Moreover, any mental state that has a specific content, the content that *p*, as an object is a state about which one can be mistaken. This should be clear from the preceding argument. Thus, we have subverted the pretentious claim of introspection to be the source of infallible belief concerning the content of even our present thoughts.

Fallible Beliefs About Sensations

Are beliefs about sensations infallible? Following a philosophical tradition, we may refer to the objects of sensory experiences as sensations whether the experience is tactile, visual, auditory, and so forth. Armstrong has argued that reports about the sensations one is having are reports that can be mistaken even though no verbal slip or other verbal confusion is involved.[10] It will be useful for our purposes to reformulate his thesis and arguments in terms of belief. The change is not fundamental. Armstrong argues that we might at some time have exceedingly good evidence both that a person was not lying or making a verbal error, and that she did not have the sensation she said she had. To this end, imagine that we have reached a level of neurological understanding beyond the present and have established that a person experiences a certain sensation when and only when in a certain brainstate, call it state 143. Let us imagine that the sensation is a visual one, for example, that sort of visual experience that a normal person has when confronted with red objects in daylight. We may call this a sensation of red.

Moreover, suppose we can give a person a drug which will make him truthful in answering questions. Now imagine we give a person such a drug, he reports a sensation of red, and we are able to observe that he is not in brain state 143. On the basis of the evidence that he is drugged, we conclude that he believes what he says. On the basis of the neurological evidence that he is not in brain state 143, we conclude that he is not having a sensation of red. This story, Armstrong would have us concede, is at least logically possible. If it is logically possible and involves no contradiction in conception, then it is logically possible that the person in question believes that he has a sensation of red when he does not have it.[11]

The basic assumption of the example is that we could have evidence which shows a person believes he is having a sensation he is not having. If it is conceded that such evidence would render it highly probable that the person is not having the sensation without thereby rendering it at least as probable that he does not believe he is having the sensation, then the argument succeeds. We know it is a theorem of probability that if evidence renders a hypothesis highly probable, then it renders any logical consequence of that hypothesis at least as probable. Let us abbreviate the hypothesis that the person is not having the sensation by 'NS' and the hypothesis that he does not believe he has the sensation by 'NB', and the evidence Armstrong mentions by 'E'. Now suppose the evidence *E* renders *NS* highly probable but does not render *NB* probable. This would show that believing one has a sensation does not logically imply having the sensation, because *NS* does not logically imply *NB*.

Nevertheless, the argument is defective. We all agree that an experimenter might have evidence which would convince her that it is highly probable that the man in the example believes that he has a sensation but does not. It would seem to her that evidence *E* renders *NS* highly probable, but fails to render *NB* equally probable. There are, however, two divergent explanations of our experimenter's attitude. One is that the evidence only seems not to render *NB* highly probable. If a person does not recognize that one hypothesis logically implies a second, then evidence that favors the first hypothesis might not seem to favor the second, even though in fact it does.

Let us consider an example in which evidence renders one hypothesis highly probable, but does not seem to render highly probable a logical consequence of it. Imagine that I see a red die on my desk, and let us suppose my sensory evidence renders it highly probable that there is a red die there. This evidence then also renders it highly probable that there is a cube on my desk, since a die is by definition a cube. Now, suppose that I do not know that it logically follows from the fact that something is a cube that it has twelve edges. In that case, though I maintain that my evidence renders it highly probable that there is a cube on my desk, I might deny that the evidence renders it highly probable that there is a twelve-edged object on my desk. Even so, the latter would be an error. The evidence that renders it highly probable that there is a cube on my desk must render it at least as probable that there is a solid object having twelve edges on my desk, for the former logically implies the latter.

The application of these considerations to the issue at hand is to illustrate two different ways of explaining the reaction of our fictitious experimenter. One is to assume what the experimenter does. The other is to assume that the experimenter simply failed to notice that believing one has a sensation logically implies that one has it. On the latter assumption she has failed to notice that her evidence renders it highly improbable that the subject believes he has a sensation. This second explanation is consistent with the infallibility of beliefs about sensations. These two ways of explaining why the experimenter thinks what she does are on exactly equal footing. We need some other argument to shake the dialectical ground beneath them.

Sensations and Incorrigibility: A Counterexample

Another argument is readily available. A person might believe that one sensation is the same as another when this belief is erroneous and, consequently, that he is having one sensation when he is having quite a different one. Let us consider an example of confusing two sensations, those of hurting and itching. Imagine that a not very enlightened man goes to his doctor and is inclined to believe what the doctor says even when her medical deliverance is somewhat preposterous. The doctor tells the man that it is not surprising that his sensation is sometimes one of pain and sometimes one of itching because itches are really pains. All itches, she says, are pains, though some are very mild. Such is the authority of the doctor, and such the credulity of the man, that her word is taken as creed. From that moment on, he never doubts that itches are pains, and, though they feel different, he firmly believes that he is in pain, even if only very slightly so, whenever he has the slightest itch. When he itches, therefore, he erroneously believes that he is in pain, even if only very slightly so. Thus, his beliefs that he is in pain are often erroneous and are by no means infallible.

It should be apparent that the man in question might have been misled by his esteemed medical sage into believing that any sensation was another when in fact it was not. He might, without understanding how such things could possibly be true, believe that they are. Hence, beliefs about sensations, like beliefs about thoughts, are fallible and corrigible. In general, very little of what we believe about our own mental and psychological states is incorrigible. Error can, as a matter of logic, insert itself stealthily between belief and what is believed in this matter as in others.

Other Alleged Counterexamples

Other counterexamples to the thesis that beliefs about sensations are incorrigible concern people who are in a more or less aberrant state. Consider a man who believes he is about to undergo some painful experience, for example, that he is about to be touched by some very hot object, though in fact the object is cold to the touch. Because he expects to feel a burning sensation, he could believe that he is feeling such a sensation during the first moment or two that the cold object is touching his flesh. This belief would then be false. The difficulty with such a counterexample is that it is problematic whether expecting to feel a burning sensation produces false beliefs or a burning sensation.

Another kind of counterexample concerns those who are mentally aberrant and undergoing hallucinations. For example, suppose that a very paranoid man complains that he is suffering excruciating pain because little green Martians are cutting into his flesh. If he then goes on to tell us that the reason he shows no sign of being in pain (he does not grimace, wince, and so forth) is that he does not want to let the Martians know they are succeeding in making him suffer, we might begin to think he believes he is in pain when he is not. The man might in fact not be undergoing any pain whatsoever, even though he does genuinely believe that he is suffering. He might later, when the aberrance has vanished, report that this is what had happened. Some philosophers might doubt that the usual concepts of belief and sensation apply in such peculiar cases as this, and others would have other doubts. Such examples may be genuine counterexamples, however.

Fallibility and Inference: Summary of the Argument

The arguments concerning the fallibility of beliefs concerning thought and sensation may be summarized as follows. Whatever one can believe as a result of introspection, one can instead believe as a result of inference, and the inference can be based on false premises. If a woman believes she is in pain as a result of feeling pain, then, of course, she will be correct in believing that she is in pain. If, however, a man believes that he is in pain because some scientific or religious authority figure tells him that he is in pain, then what he believes may well be false. In such a case, the person has accepted a premise, namely, that what the scientific or religious authority figure says is true which, together with the premise that the authority says the person is in pain, leads the person to infer and, therefore, to believe that he or she is in pain and to believe this falsely when the authority is untruthful.

Inference from the testimony of an authority is only one example of how false beliefs about one's mental states may result from inference. It may seem strange to imagine people coming to believe they have some thought or sensation as a result of inference from testimony, but this is the strangeness of the human mind, not of logic. People may believe things in ways that are quite unreasonable and mentally deranged. As a result of these mad beliefs, they may come to believe things about anything, about their very own thoughts and sensations, which they would otherwise never believe.

Nomological Infallibility

The preceding observation may be extended to refute attempts to salvage the doctrine of infallibility by replacing the notion of logical possibility with some weaker notion of possibility in the definition of incorrigibility. One might, for example, attempt to rescue the doctrine of incorrigibility by substituting a notion of *nomological necessity* or impossibility, that is, necessity or impossibility in terms of the laws of nature, for the notion of logical impossibility in the definition of in- corrigibility. This would have a beneficial consequence concerning the second condition of incorrigibility, the irresistibility condition. It is much more plausible to suppose that it is the result of a law of nature, or a law of psychology, that a person believes that she is thinking or feeling something when she is, than to suppose that this is a consequence of logical necessity.

The amendment to nomological necessity or impossibility will be to no avail for rescuing the doctrine of infallible beliefs, however. It is not only logically possible to infer false conclusions about one's thoughts and sensations from false beliefs, it is possible in terms of the laws of human nature as well. There are, for example, people belonging to religious groups who believe that pain is unreal and, therefore, that they do not have pain, though it is clear they suffer like the rest of us when injured. Some paranoid people believe they are in pain, as we noted above, when they believe they are attacked by powerful enemies. It is obvious, however, that they suffer no physical pain. The human mind provides us with no prophylactic against error, even concerning our own thoughts and sensations, as the strange beliefs of humanity, arising from hopes and fears, abundantly illustrate. There is nothing so foolish that we cannot believe it if it is repeated often enough and with enough authority. Every demagogue understands this very well.

Meaning and Belief

There is a familiar but erroneous objection against the preceding line of thought. It is that the people who hold odd beliefs really have different beliefs than they appear to have. The words they utter have a different meaning than what is customary. On this account, the man misled by his doctor does not believe he is in pain when he itches; he just attaches a different meaning to the word 'pain' so that it means 'pain or itch' and has no false beliefs about pains, though he appears to do so. Similarly, the paranoid person means something different by 'pain', as do the members of the religious cult who think there is no pain. How should we reply to this objection?

Current theories of meaning are fraught with controversy, and so it will not be possible to reply definitively by appeal to any such theory. The problem is rendered yet more difficult by argumentation, primarily due to Quine, that there is no sharp boundary between what we explain in terms of change of meaning and what we explain in terms of change of belief. Finally, a methodological principle, the principle of *charity*, exhorts us to interpret the utterances of others in such a way as to render the beliefs we ascribe to them as true as far as is charitably possible. These considerations might appear to support the objection in that, given the lack of a sharp boundary between meaning and belief, the charitable thing would be to interpret the odd remarks of the people in our examples in such a way as to ascribe true rather than false beliefs to them. To do this, we would need to suppose that the man who says he is in pain when he itches means something different by 'pain' than is customary.

The reply is simple and appeals to simplicity. We have a simple explanation as to why people say what they do that does not require the complexity involved in supposing that they have changed the meaning of the words they utter from what is customary. The simple explanation is that they acquired an odd belief, one they affirm, and that they mean what they say. The application of the principle of *charity* would, consequently, be misapplied in such cases if we were to assume they meant something different from what is customary.

Let us consider the example of the person who has come to believe that itches are mild pains. There is something in his speech behavior that might lead us to consider the hypothesis that his meaning of the word 'pain' is deviant, and, more specifically, that he means by the word 'pain' what we mean by the expression 'pain or itch'. He calls itches pains, after all, and this favors the hypothesis that his meaning is deviant, but there is evidence against this hypothesis as well. His linguistic training is altogether jejune. Describing what pain is like, he uses, as we would, words such as throbbing, stabbing, sticking, and so forth. Both these observations conflict with the hypothesis that his meaning of 'pain' is deviant and raise the question, Why does he say he is experiencing pain when he itches?

One hypothesis is that he is physiologically peculiar and hurts when we itch, but, upon questioning him, we learn the correct answer. The doctor has convinced him that itches are pains, very mild ones. He tells us that this is a very peculiar fact about itches discovered by medical research. In the light of this evidence, the simplest explanation for all his behavior is that his meaning of 'pain' is standard, but one of his beliefs about pains is peculiar. He believes that pains are itches. The crucial reason is this. The hypothesis that he means by 'pain' what we mean by the expression 'pain or itch' fails to explain what he tells us about what he learned from the doctor. For this reason, the hypothesis of meaning change must be rejected. If by 'pain' he meant 'pain or itch', then he would not consider it to be peculiar that itches are pains. That would amount to the simple tautology that itches are either pains or itches, and there is nothing peculiar about that. The simplest hypothesis to account for the total data obtained from the man, including the fact that he, too, thinks it is odd that itches are pains, is that his meaning of the word 'pain' is standard but one of his beliefs about pains is deviant.

The foregoing remarks apply with even greater clarity to the other examples of false beliefs about one's own sensations. It would be uncharitable to accept an interpretation of the meaning of what the people in the counterexamples say that would assign deviant meaning to their words in order to ascribe true beliefs about their sensations to them. To do so would render their exotically different general beliefs about the world mere tautologies. That would fail to explain why they think these beliefs are profound facts about the nature of things. It might be possible to invent some hypothesis compatible with the deviant meaning hypothesis to account for this oddity. The simplest hypothesis, however, is that the meanings of the words that people utter are standard and the beliefs they have acquired are peculiar. That is what they say, after all, so why not believe them? What could be simpler?

We may now conclude our remarks on the incorrigible. We have found almost no beliefs about contingent matters that are incorrigible in the relevant sense of the logical or nomological impossibility of error. The belief that I exist as well as the belief that I believe are infallible, but any belief about what I think or believe about any feeling or sensation, as well as other contingent matters, is fallible and subject to correction. The base of incorrigible beliefs is, therefore, inadequate to justify those beliefs we consider well enough justified to constitute knowledge. We must abandon the quest for incorrigible foundations or embrace the skeptical result.

Justification as a Logical Guarantee of Truth for Nonbasic Beliefs

Just as logical guarantees have been traditionally sought for the truth of basic beliefs by the infallible foundationalist, so it has been thought that basic beliefs must guarantee the truth of nonbasic beliefs. Though this sort of theory appears unable to provide an adequate supply of infallible basic beliefs, it is worthwhile to consider the question of whether, assuming a larger supply of basic beliefs, they could be expected to guarantee the truth of the nonbasic beliefs we take to be completely justified in accepting. There are two reasons for considering this. First, of course, we must allow for our own fallibility in argumentation. Perhaps there are more infallible basic beliefs than we have dreamt of in our philosophy. Second, and more important, some supply of fallible basic beliefs might, if true, guarantee the truth of all nonbasic beliefs we are justified in accepting. In that case, a mixed foundation theory allowing that basic beliefs be fallible but requiring that the justification of nonbasic beliefs must guarantee their truth would be acceptable.

We shall, therefore, now consider the attempt to provide a theory of the justification of nonbasic beliefs on the basis of basic beliefs which logically guarantee the truth of the nonbasic beliefs. This attempt has often led to some sort of analytically reductive theory affirming that the content of nonbasic beliefs can be reduced by logical analysis to the content of basic beliefs. One such theory, typical of analytically reductive theories, is *phenomenalism,* a modern analytic refinement of the theory of Bishop Berkeley.[12]

Phenomenalism

Berkeley held that we have immediate knowledge of our own ideas, which include the appearances of sense. Suppose beliefs concerning appearances are basic beliefs. In the opening sections of the *Principles,* Berkeley suggests that what we mean when we affirm the existence of external objects, of a tomato, for example, can be expressed in terms of what ideas we have of it, what appearances we experience (i.e., the reddish, roundish, bulgy ones), and of the appearances we would experience, if we were to undertake various courses of action. For example, we would experience squishy, wet, runny appearances if we were to undertake to strike out toward the reddish, roundish, bulgy appearances.[13] Thus, the meaning of the contents of our beliefs about physical objects or the statements expressing those contents would be equivalent in meaning in this view to statements about what ideas we have, what appearances we experience conjoined to hypothetical statements about what ideas we would have, what experiences we would experience if various conditions were fulfilled.

In modern dress, this is the doctrine of *phenomenalism* which affirms that all statements and the contents of all beliefs concerning external objects can be translated without loss of meaning into statements about what appearances we experience or would experience under various conditions; or, to adopt the terminology of sense data in place of that of appearance, about what sense data we experience or would experience under various conditions.[14] The plausibility of the doctrine can be appreciated by reflecting upon a thought experiment. Suppose that all experiences which you have or would have under any conditions are just what they would be if the external world existed but the external world has, in fact, vanished. The absence of the external world would be completely beyond detection. Now that you have imagined this, imagine that this is what, in fact, has occurred. You have no indication of your loss, of course, because all that you experience is just what you would experience if the external world had not vanished.

If you feel that this thought experiment is a verbal or semantic trick, that nothing has vanished in it, then you will understand the motivation for accepting the doctrine of phenomenalism. Phenomenalism tells us that if all the sense data we experience and would experience under any conditions are exactly the same as if the external world were to exist, then the external world *does* exist. To say that it exists just means that we do and would experience the appropriate sense data under various conditions. The imagined disappearance of the external world is a semantic illusion.

The relevance of the doctrine of phenomenalism to the foundation theory is that, if phenomenalism is true, then conjunctions of statements about what sense data we experience or would experience under various conditions, logically imply statements about the external world because they would exhaust the meaning of those statements. So conjunctions of statements about sense data would, if true, logically guarantee the truth of the statements about the external world. Put in another way, phenomenalism tells us that statements about the external world are analytically reducible to statements about sense data, and, therefore, the truth of the latter guarantee the truth of the former. Assuming sense-data statements to express the contents of basic beliefs, their truth would guarantee the truth of nonbasic beliefs about external objects. Finally, therefore, if the truth of the basic beliefs is self-guaranteed, that guarantee would extend to the nonbasic beliefs about external objects which the basic beliefs logically imply as a result of the reduction of the former to the latter.

Phenomenalism, though not commonly defended currently, is characteristic of analytically reductive theories and exhibits the relevance of such theories to the foundation theory of justification. All such theories allege that some kind of statements, the targets of the reduction, are equivalent in meaning and, therefore, logically equivalent to the statements to which they are reduced. If the latter express the contents of basic beliefs, then the reduction explains how they can guarantee the truth of the statements that are the target of the reduction. They logically imply the target statements and, assuming the truth of the basic beliefs to be guaranteed, would logically guarantee the truth of the nonbasic beliefs.

Objections to Phenomenalism

There are, however, a number of problems concerning phenomenalism that have led to its rejection. First, the language of sense data which describes the appearances one senses, or the way in which one is appeared to, leads to controversy. For example, Ayer suggested that some sense-data statements are incorrigible,[15] and we have considered the problems surrounding such a claim. Second, some philosophers doubt that the required meaning analysis of statements about external objects in terms of sense-data statements can be effected. Chisholm, for example, has argued convincingly that no statement about an external object logically implies any statement about sense data or appearances and, therefore, that the meaning equivalence fails.[16] It is possible, nevertheless, that the meaning of statements about external objects is exhausted by the meaning of statements about sense data in the sense that the latter logically imply the former, though not vice versa. The exhibition of such logical implications would yield an important kind of reduction for foundationalism. If statements about sense data, even if not incorrigible, logically imply statements about external objects, even if not vice versa, then basic beliefs about sense data, if true, can logically guarantee the truth of nonbasic beliefs about external objects.

The appeal to analytically reductive theories to support foundationalism faces a decisive problem that can be illustrated by further consideration of phenomenalism. Suppose we have a statement about an external object, E (for example, that there is a tomato in front of me) and we have a phenomenalistic analysis of E in sense-data language, consisting of a conjunction of sense-data statements $S1$, $S2$, and so forth, through Sn. For the sake of simplicity, let us refer to the statements expressing the contents of basic beliefs as basic statements and those statements expressing the content of nonbasic beliefs as nonbasic statements. Consider the statements $S1$, $S2$, and so forth, to Sn. Are these statements basic or nonbasic ones?

Some of the sense-data statements $S1$, $S2$, and so forth, to Sn which analyze or even logically imply the external object statement E must be nonbasic. We can illustrate this by appeal to the statement that there is a ripe tomato before me. Consider the sort of sense-data statements one might think are part of the analysis of this statement. Some of these statements would be about what I am sensing at the moment, for example, a reddish, roundish sense datum, and these might be basic, but they are not logically sufficient to analyze or imply logically that there is a ripe tomato before me. We would also require hypothetical, indeed, contrary-to-fact hypothetical, statements about what I would be sensing if I were to alter the circumstances, for example, by striking in the direction of the sense data with the intention of squishing the tomato. If such efforts produce no alteration, the sense data may be deceptive, the stuff of dreams and hallucinations, rather than those of a genuine ripe tomato.

In short, the hypothetical statements in question must articulate what sense data I would sense under various conditions if there were a ripe tomato before me, in order to yield the conclusion that there is a ripe tomato before me. Some of these hypothetical statements must be nonbasic, because they would have to be justified by evidence, if they are justified at all. Many of them would be contrary to fact, asserting what one would sense if certain facts were other than they are. Belief in the truth of a contrary to fact conditional, if it is justified at all, is justified on the basis of evidence. Therefore, the set of statements $S1$, $S2$, and so forth, to Sn of any plausible phenomenalistic analysis or reduction cannot all be self-justified basic beliefs about sense data. The upshot of this argument is that the sense-data statements $S1$, $S2$, and so forth, to Sn of any plausible phenomenalistic analysis or reduction of a statement E about an external object cannot all be basic. If not all the sense-data statements are basic, then the analysis or reduction does not provide us with a set of basic statements that guarantee the truth of a nonbasic statement.

The preceding argument can be extended to a variety of analytically reductive theories. Philosophers who have eschewed phenomenalism as unrealistic have often embraced some other analytically reductive theory to sustain their own version of a foundation theory. For example, some philosophers of science have regarded observation statements as basic and have proposed some reductive analysis of generalizations and theories in terms of observation statements. It was once argued, for instance, that generalizations of the form 'Anything that is $O1$ is $O2$', where '$O1$' and '$O2$' are observation terms, may be analyzed as a conjunctive statement: If $x1$ is $O1$, then $x1$ is $O2$, and if $x2$ is $O1$, then $x2$ is $O2$, and so forth. Here the difficulty mentioned above becomes obvious. Since it is clear that not all the hypothetical statements are self-justified, at least some of them must be justified, if they are justified at all, as nonbasic beliefs, that is, their justification must be based on evidence. The reason is that we shall not have observed every one of the objects $x1$, $x2$, and so forth, and, thus, even if we allow that beliefs in categorical observation statements are self-justified, not all the hypothetical statements in the analysis of the generalization are self-justified. Consequently, some of those beliefs will be nonbasic. Hence, such a reductive analysis will not show how basic observation statements guarantee the truth of nonbasic generalizations. Similar remarks apply to reductive analyses of theoretical statements in terms of observation statements. Thus, reductive analysis, though motivated by foundationalism, fails to support it because the reduction will leave us with a base of hypothetical statements in the preferred vocabulary of sense data or observation. These hypothetical statements will not, however, supply us with a foundation. We will be justified in accepting them, if we are justified at all, only on the basis of evidence, and, therefore, they are nonbasic. The objective of reduction is to reduce nonbasic statements to a collection or conjunction of basic statements. Reduction fails in this objective exactly because it leaves us with a set of different but equally nonbasic statements.

Summary

We have seen that the quest for infallible foundations is a failure. The attempt to find infallible basic beliefs that guarantee their own truth to serve as a foundation yielded the most meager results. Fallibility infects almost all our beliefs. The attempt to extend the guarantee of truth from basic to nonbasic beliefs by undertaking to reduce the content of the latter to the contents of collections or conjunctions of the former is equally unsuccessful. The reduction leaves us with different but equally nonbasic beliefs. The idea that we might construct or reconstruct the edifice of knowledge from a set of basic beliefs whose truth is guaranteed and which guarantee the truth of all the rest was of extraordinary importance in the theory of knowledge. Had it been successful, it would have provided us with a means of insuring the truth of what we accept. Like other philosophical traditions, it taught us something different from what was originally intended. The lesson is that we are fallible in what we believe and must proceed without any guarantee of our success. The quest for truth, if based on a foundation of self-justified beliefs, must be based on a fallible foundation.

Introduction to the Literature

There is an excellent discussion of foundationalism in John Pollock's *Contemporary Theories of Knowledge*, including, in Chapter 5, part 7, a defense of a kind of direct realism which resembles foundationalism though the foundational states are not beliefs. This view is an alternative to the kind of foundationalism discussed in this chapter. The traditional forms of foundationalism are exposited and defended by Panayot Butchvarov in *The Concept of Knowledge*, by Arthur Danto in *Analytical Philosophy of Knowledge*, Bertrand Russell in *The Problems of Philosophy*, and A. J. Ayer in *Foundations of Empirical Knowledge*. Roderick Chisholm defended something akin to an infallible foundation theory in his early work, *Perceiving: A Philosophical Study*. See also Carl Ginet's *Knowledge, Perception, and Memory*, and Paul Moser's *Empirical Justification*.

4

Fallible Foundations

THE PRECEDING CHAPTER has shown why a foundation theory of justification must subscribe to the doctrine that at least some basic beliefs are fallible, or else embrace skepticism. The number of infallible beliefs is far too restricted to support our commonsense claims to knowledge. Foundationalism is the doctrine that self-justified beliefs constitute the foundation of knowledge. Can the edifice of knowledge be based on a foundation without a guarantee of truth? Is it tenable for the foundation theorist to allow that beliefs which are fallible, which may be false, are, nevertheless, basic and self-justified beliefs?

Let us consider the merits and shortcomings of a fallible foundationalism advocating that knowledge rests on fallible but self-justified beliefs. Thomas Reid claimed that some beliefs, for example, perceptual beliefs concerning what we see immediately before us, are justified in themselves without need of supporting arguments, even though we have no guarantee that they are true. In short, such beliefs are self-justified because their justification is inherent. As Reid put it, they are beliefs of commonsense which have a right of ancient possession and, until this inherent right is successfully challenged, they remain justified without support from any other beliefs.[1]

Reid hit upon a critically important line of defense for the fallible foundation theory. According to him, some beliefs are worthy of our trust even if we have no guarantee that they are true much in the way in which an experienced guide is worthy of our trust, even though we have no guarantee she will bring us to our destination. Though we remain vigilant to detect errors, we may, in the customary affairs of life, rely upon the intrinsic justification that attaches as a birthright to various of our beliefs. They are completely justified in themselves without appeal to independent information. If this doctrine proves tenable, it could provide us with a set of basic but fallible beliefs. The rights of birth and ancient possession have, however, been challenged in the political sphere, and we must bring them under close scrutiny here as well.

Perceptual Belief and Independent Information

Candidates for the status of self-justified beliefs whose justification does not depend on independent information are frequently perceptual. Let us consider some promising candidates and see if we can discover any worthy of the office. Suppose I believe I see a typewriter beneath my fingers. For my belief to be justified, I must have some independent information about what I see, namely, that a thing that looks like the thing beneath my fingers is a typewriter. If I did not have that information, then I would not be justified in believing that I see a typewriter. In short, whenever I see a thing of a certain kind, my being justified in the belief that I am seeing a thing of that kind depends on independent information I have about how things of that kind look. This information justifies me in concluding that the thing I see is such an object.[2]

It is clear that a similar argument will confront us when we consider a simpler belief, for example, the belief that I see something red. It will be argued that, for me to determine that what I see is a red thing, I must have independent information about how red things look and, indeed, about how they look under various conditions. Even if we assume that for a thing to be red is just for it to look red under standard conditions to normal observers, for me to determine that what I see is red, I must know how to tell when conditions are standard and when an observer is normal. Thus, if something looks red to a person, she cannot justifiably conclude that it is red from the formula that red things look red in standard conditions to normal observers. She would also need to know that the conditions are standard and that she is normal. Independent information is, therefore, required for the justification of this perceptual belief. More generally, to be justified in accepting such a belief, one requires information about oneself and the conditions of perception.

The question to examine next is whether any more cautious perceptual belief has a justification that does not depend on independent information. A prime candidate is the belief that I see something, without specifying what sort of thing it is that I see. Here, one might think, is a belief which does not require any independent information for one to be justified in accepting it. Nonetheless, there is reason to doubt this if one construes the word 'something' in such a way as to imply that the object seen is some real thing and not, for example, something hallucinated. Once again, there is need of independent information that would enable the person in question to decide that this is a case of seeing something and not merely a case of hallucination or dreaming, or whatnot. Since one may hallucinate, one cannot justifiably conclude that one sees something as opposed to merely hallucinating unless one has information enabling one to distinguish hallucination from the real thing.

Justification and Innocent Belief

There are objections, rather standard ones, to the preceding line of thought. It might be objected, for example, that one does not need to know anything about hallucination in order justifiably to accept that one sees something. A person who never had hallucinatory or any other deceptive experiences might accept with complete justification that she sees something even though she lacks any information about deceptive experience. If it be asked how she can be so justified in her belief, even though she lacks the information to determine whether she is seeing rather than hallucinating, the answer is that such beliefs do not require the support of argument or independent information. They are justified until they are shown to be erroneous or unjustified. They are, as Reid suggested, innocent until proven guilty.[3]

No doubt, in everyday situations we allow uncritically that such beliefs are justified until they are shown to be unjustified, and no doubt in the case of the person who was innocent of hallucinatory experience, we would uncritically allow that his perceptual belief was justified. A little more critical circumspection shows that commonsense should not be allowed to run unbridled in the epistemic field, however. All sorts of perceptual beliefs, the belief that one saw a bear-print, for example, are considered justified when we have no great stake in the question of whether the belief is true or false. However, when a great deal (our personal safety, for example) hinges on the matter of whether the person saw a bear-print or something else, then we become instantly more cautious and exacting. We require a park ranger to know a bear-print when she sees one. The same applies to the typewriter and the red thing.

We are epistemically casual about the justifiability of a belief until something of practical importance or epistemic consequence rests on the question. Perceptual beliefs are considered innocent until proven guilty when we care not the least whether the belief is innocent or guilty. Once we do care, though, then we start to ask serious questions. The very first is whether the person is justified in accepting what he does in the interests of obtaining truth and avoiding error on the basis of his information. We seek to determine if the person has information which would enable him to determine whether he actually sees the thing he thinks he does. His belief is presumed to be neither innocent nor guilty but is evaluated in terms of the information he possesses. Whether he is justified in accepting what he does or not depends on the adequacy of his information.

An Objection: Reliability or Information?

It might be objected to the preceding that one does not require information to be justified in such a belief but rather a reliable competence. An externalist, who maintains that the justification of a belief is determined solely by the relation of the belief to the external world, might object that all that is required is that one's belief arise in a reliable manner.[4] To be able to tell whether one is seeing something or not is obviously essential to being justified in accepting that one is seeing something, but, it might be argued, the competence required to tell this need not involve the acquisition of information. One can have the ability to tell whether something is of a certain sort without needing any information to make such determinations. It is sufficient to respond to experience in a reliable manner.

The foregoing objection must be met squarely. A person may learn to tell whether or not he is seeing something without appealing to any premises or making any conscious inferences. Gilbert Harman has suggested we might nevertheless construe such cases as examples of unconscious inference.[5] It suffices, however, to note that a person may be said to have information he cannot present verbally and to employ such information in various ways. For example, suppose I know the shortest route from Rochester to Buffalo, though I cannot tell you the number of the road. Moreover, imagine that I am not very good at giving directions, so I cannot tell you how to get from Rochester to Buffalo. Does this show that my ability to get from Rochester to Buffalo does not depend on the information I have about how to get from Rochester to Buffalo?

Hardly. I obviously do have the information I need to get from Rochester to Buffalo, but I am very poor at conveying this information to others. That I make the trip successfully on many occasions shows that I have the required information. My reliability depends on my ability to employ information, which I might find difficult to articulate, about the route from Rochester to Buffalo. Similarly, my reliability in accepting that I see when I do, or even in accepting that I feel or think when I do, depends on my ability to employ information, which I might find difficult to articulate, about seeing, feeling, and thinking.

Any belief whatever is open to similar argument concerning the need for independent information. Indeed, even the very subjective belief, that it seems to me that I am seeing something, is one I am justified in accepting only if I have the information needed to tell whether it seems to me that I am seeing something or having some quite different experience, for example, that of wondering whether I am seeing something. I may wonder whether I am seeing something when it does not especially seem to me that I am seeing something, and unless I have the information required to tell the difference between wondering and seeming, I am not completely justified in accepting that I am in one state rather than the other. Even our most modest beliefs turn out to be ones requiring independent information to justify us in accepting them for the purposes of obtaining truth and avoiding error. The preceding argument uncovers a ubiquitous need for independent information to justify acceptance aimed at truth, and in so doing it undermines the foundation theory.

Chisholm and the Noncomparative Use of Words

The most important line of reply on behalf of the foundation theory is provided by Chisholm, who is responsible for calling our attention to the need for independent information to justify our perceptual beliefs.[6] He contends, however, that some beliefs, those articulated in noncomparative terms, do not require independent information for their justification. He distinguishes between the comparative and noncomparative uses of certain words. Ordinarily, when we apply a word, whether to our own states or to things, the application is based on a comparison we make. For example, if we say something appears red, we may be comparing the way this thing appears with the way other things appear. It is analytic or true by definition in the comparative use of 'appears red' to say that red things appear red to normal observers in daylight. In the comparative use of words, Chisholm concedes the need for independent information to justify their application.

Chisholm, however, claims that words used noncomparatively may be applied without independent information. Words used noncomparatively may be homogenized to produce a single term applying to the state of a person. As Chisholm suggests, we might speak adverbially and say that a person believes that he is being appeared-to-redly or, equivalently, that he is sensing-redly. The hyphenated term is intended to characterize the subjective state of the person in question without implying that some thing is appearing to him and without implying any comparison of this state to any other. Thus, to say that one is sensing-redly does not entail that one is sensing the way normal observers sense in daylight when they are seeing a red object. It may, of course, be true that one is sensing in that way, but it is not an analytic consequence of the term 'sensing-redly' used noncomparatively.

There is an argument to show that there must be a noncomparative use of words. To be able to describe a state in comparative terms, thus comparing it to other states, one must first be able to tell what the state is like in itself. Unless one can tell what this state is like in itself, one will be unable to compare it successfully to anything else. To be able to tell whether *A* is similar or dissimilar to *B*, one must first know what *A* is like, or any such comparison will be unreliable. Therefore, there must be a way in which one can tell what something is like, for example, a state of oneself, without comparing it to anything else. The noncomparative use of words enables one to record these noncomparative determinations.[7]

We agree with Chisholm that there is such a thing as a noncomparative use of words and ask whether this will sustain the thesis that beliefs expressed in noncomparative terms are completely justified without the need for independent information. For a person to be completely justified in believing that she is sensing in a certain way, that she is sensing-redly for example, she must have the information necessary to distinguish this manner of appearing from others. Perhaps, as Chisholm contends, the belief that one is appeared-to-redly does not entail any comparison of one's present state to any other. Nevertheless, it does entail that one's state is of a certain kind, and, to be completely justified in believing it to be of that kind, one must have the information needed to enable one to distinguish such a state from one of another kind. So we arrive at the conclusion reached earlier: to be completely justified in believing anything about a state or object or whatnot, one always requires independent information.[8]

Semantics and Justification

The preceding reflections might seem to doom the foundation theory to epistemic oblivion. We have seen that the stockpile of infallible beliefs is epistemically inadequate to provide a justificatory foundation. We have now considered the possibility that fallible beliefs might be completely justified in themselves without the need for any independent information, and we have found this proposal wanting. The latter proposal may, however, be defended with some modification. The effective modification is to claim that some beliefs are justified in themselves without need of any independent empirical information. The independent information required for such beliefs to be justified, it may be argued, is not empirical information used to justify the beliefs but semantic information required to understand the content of them. If the required information is nothing more than semantic information needed to understand the content of the belief, the need for such information does not preclude the possibility of some beliefs being justified in themselves.

Meaning and Epistemic Principles

Again, we are faced with a semantic solution to an epistemological problem. Is the solution effective? To say that it is true by virtue of semantics that beliefs of a certain kind of content are justified in themselves is equivalent to saying that the epistemic principles according to which beliefs of that kind are self-justified are semantic principles or meaning postulates.[9]

Typical meaning postulates are principles such as the following:

All red things are colored things.

Any two things identical to a third thing are identical to each other.

Such principles are true by virtue of the meaning of the words contained therein. Thus, the claim that certain beliefs are justified as a result of meaning postulates is equivalent to saying that an understanding of the content of the belief is sufficient to know that the beliefs are justified in themselves, just as an understanding of something being red is sufficient to know that it is colored. This is a consequence of semantic foundationalism.

Meaning and Skepticism

Is the thesis true? A skeptic might claim that no beliefs are justified or, more modestly, that the alleged basic beliefs are not justified. She may share most of our beliefs, but she does not share our epistemic convictions concerning what is evident, certain, justified, and so forth. If our fundamental question is to be answered in the affirmative, then appeal to semantics, to the meaning of words, must suffice to refute the skeptic. Let us consider whether the meanings of words are sufficient to untie the skeptical knot.

If a person should claim that something is red but not colored, we would conclude that he was contradicting himself or else using the words in question in some peculiar way to mean something different from what is ordinarily meant. Should we conclude that the skeptic is using the word 'justified' in some peculiar way to mean something different from the rest of us when she claims that simple perceptual beliefs or beliefs about how things appear are not justified beliefs? Must the skeptic mean something different by epistemic terms simply because she speaks with a skeptical tongue? The answer to this question, happily for the skeptic, is that she need not mean anything different by these terms from the rest of us. The systematic difference in what she says from what the rest of us say may suggest that she means something different, but the conclusion cannot be forced upon her.

We noted in the last chapter that there are two ways to account for the fact that others regularly say different things from what we say in the same situations. One way is to suppose that the words they utter mean something quite different when uttered by them. The other is to suppose that the words mean nothing different, but they differ from us in what they believe. When the skeptic utters epistemic words, we may either suppose that she means something different from the rest of us, or we may suppose that her beliefs differ from ours. How can we show which supposition is true?

The situation is like the one in the previous chapter. Suppose the skeptic provides us with an explanation of why she speaks the way she does in terms of her beliefs about justification. For example, suppose she holds the view that only beliefs whose truth is guaranteed are justified and denies that the beliefs in question are ones whose truth is guaranteed. Her conclusion that such beliefs are not justified is most simply explained by these background beliefs and does not permit us to attribute semantic deviance to her remarks.

There may be no evidence of semantic deviance based, for example, on the way the skeptic understands the semantic relations between epistemic terms, such as 'know', 'certain', 'evident', and 'justified', comprising what John Lyons and Adrienne Lehrer consider a semantic field.[10] Agreement about semantic relations between terms in a semantic field is a mark, if not a proof, of agreement in the meaning of terms. Moreover, there is nothing contradictory in our skeptic's skeptical claims. Nothing she says contradicts itself or anything else she says. The skeptic is consistently odd. The simplest explanation for the oddity of her remarks is that she believes that no one is completely justified in believing what they do unless they have some guarantee of the truth of the belief. That is what she says and that is what she means. We should take her at her word.

Self-justification and Necessary Truth

We have said that the skeptic is not contradicting herself, not affirming anything necessarily false, when she denies that alleged basic beliefs are justified. Can we give some argument to refute the claim of a foundation theorist who affirms, to the contrary, that it is true by virtue of the meaning of words that certain beliefs are self-justified, and contradictory to deny this? There is little credibility in the idea that when the skeptic says that any belief is not completely justified she is thereby saying something contradictory. Compare the skeptic's claim with the claim that there is a red object that is not colored. The latter, if taken literally, is impossible. There is no logically possible way in which an object can be red but not colored. The suggestion is logically incoherent. By contrast, the claim that a belief, any belief, is not completely justified, however contrary to our convictions, is logically coherent. We can understand how it is possible, for example, if there are no completely justified beliefs. The skeptic does not contradict herself. It would be plainly dogmatic and unwarranted to pin the label of inconsistency upon her pronouncements.

Justification and Necessity

We can, moreover, go beyond general skeptical argumentation to refute the claim that the meaning of words sustains self-justification. At the same time, we can refute the related claim that principles of self-justification, those telling us that some kinds of beliefs are self-justified (simple perceptual beliefs for example) are justified in themselves. We noted above that the justification of alleged basic beliefs depends on possessing independent information that enables one to discern the difference between one state or thing and others. Suppose that a person believes that she sees a red thing, but lacks the information enabling her to tell the difference between a red thing and a green one. Then she is not completely justified.

We can easily generalize this consideration. Put formally, suppose someone claims that for any S,

(*a*) S believes that x is F

necessarily or semantically implies, that is, entails

(*b*) S is completely justified in believing that x is F.

There is a recipe for constructing counterexamples that even a novice can follow. Suppose that

(*c*) S lacks the information needed to tell whether something is an F or not and believes that he or she is incompetent to tell the difference.

The conjunction of (*a*) and (*c*) obviously does not entail (*b*). A person who believes that *x* is *F* but lacks the information needed to tell whether something is an *F* or not and, moreover, believes he or she is unable to tell the difference, is obviously not completely justified in believing that *x* is *F*. If, however, the conjunction of (*a*) and (*c*) does not entail that (*b*), then (*a*) alone does not entail that (*b*). This is a consequence of the general principle that if a premise entails a conclusion, then the premise conjoined to anything else also entails the conclusion.

Necessity and Prima Facie Justification

There are two foundationalist replies to this argument. One is that the justification semantically implied by belief is a *prima facie* justification only. A second is to abandon the semantic strategy and admit that justification is not semantically implied but only contingently implied. Let us consider the first line of reply. What does it mean? It means that it is semantically or necessarily true that if a person believes that *p*, then the person is justified in believing that *p* unless the justification is undermined. The class of beliefs of this sort would most naturally be specified in terms of the content of what is believed. Beliefs about one's present thoughts and feelings, or beliefs about some object or quality one sees directly before one, are plausible candidates.

There are two objections to this line of thought. The first is already familiar. A skeptic who claims that no belief is ever justified and hence that the alleged basic beliefs are not *prima facie* justified, appears to be perfectly consistent. If, however, it is consistent to deny that alleged basic beliefs are not *prima facie* justified, then it is not true by virtue of the meaning of words or necessarily true that the beliefs are *prima facie* justified. Moreover, if we insist that it is a semantic truth that the beliefs are *prima facie* justified, the skeptic may simply reformulate her objection in other words. She may object that we do not really believe the things in question but only appear to do so, and that it is not semantically true that apparent beliefs are beliefs.

Moreover, the claim that certain kinds of beliefs are *prima facie* justified naturally leads to dogmatism concerning what beliefs are justified. Suppose, for example, that I, being a partisan of the theory of paranormal phenomena, claim that if one person believes he has communicated with another person telepathically, then the person is *prima facie* justified in this belief. You might retort that people have such beliefs all the time, and that they are more often erroneous than correct. You might add, moreover, that people lack the information to tell whether or not they have communicated with another telepathically and, as a result, are incompetent to tell whether such communication has occurred.

Suppose I reply that such considerations override the *prima facie* justification of such telepathic beliefs but fail to show that the beliefs are not *prima facie* justified. How could you reply? You will find it difficult, and the difficulty exposes the emptiness of the claim. Any argument to show that a belief is not *prima facie* justified may be interpreted as merely showing how the *prima facie* justification of the belief can be overridden. Any claim of *prima facie* justification can be rendered untestable and invulnerable to criticism but, alas, only at the cost of rendering it vacuous. If all reasons for denying that a belief is justified are construed as merely showing that the *prima facie* justification is overridden, then any claim that any belief is *prima facie* justified is rendered trivial. In this way, all beliefs, as well as beliefs of their denials, may be trivially affirmed to be *prima facie* justified. No epistemology flows through an empty pipe.

In summary, the claim that alleged basic beliefs are necessarily *prima facie* justified is either vacuous or false. If the claim is not vacuous, then the possibility of a person lacking the information enabling him or her to tell whether the alleged basic belief is true or false, suffices to refute the contention that it is necessarily true that the belief is *prima facie* justified. Cognitive incompetence based on ignorance of necessary information does not override *prima facie* justification, it excludes justification in the first instance.

Contingent Self-justification

At this point, the fallible foundation theorist may retreat from semantics to the claim that the self-justified beliefs are self-justified as a contingent matter of fact. There is something plausible to the proposal that some beliefs are justified in themselves, that they are, so to speak, the first premises of inference. There are some beliefs that are justified without being consciously inferred from any other. When I see a red object, I believe I see something red without consciously inferring that from anything else. When, however, we ask why that belief is justified, the answer reveals a dependence on independent information, as we noted above, and shows that the belief, though justified without conscious inference, is not self-justified in the sense required by the foundation theory. The justification of the belief depends on other information, to wit, information rendering me competent to discern truth in such matters, in this case, competence to tell something red when I see it.

These considerations might lead us to doubt the tenability of even a modest fallible foundationalism, affirming that, as a matter of contingent fact, some beliefs are justified in themselves independently of other information and belief. It appears that the justification for accepting anything we believe depends on other information, general information that enables us to obtain truth and avoid error. Alston and Van Cleve have argued, however, that self-justified basic beliefs may provide the basis for justifying general beliefs which, in turn, may be used to explain why the basic beliefs are self-justified.[11] We infer that the basic beliefs are almost always true and thereby obtain the means to explain why we are justified in accepting the basic beliefs in the interests of obtaining truth and avoiding error.

The question for the foundation theorist, however, is whether the justification of our basic beliefs depends, at the time at which they originally arise, on our beliefs about our competence to tell what is true and what is not in such matters, or upon the information on which such competence is based. I believe that I see something red. Someone alleges the belief to be basic. It may well be that I have not consciously inferred this belief from any other, but the justification for accepting the belief seems to depend on the assumption, and on my assumption, that I can tell a red thing when I see one. If I have no idea whether I can tell a red thing when I see one, then, even if I can, my belief that I see something red lacks the sort of justification required for knowledge.

To become convinced of this, suppose that I am asked to try to distinguish real diamonds from fakes by looking at them through a magnifier. Imagine that, though I have no idea that it is so, all my identifications are correct. Real diamonds look different to me than zircons and other imitations, and so, when I believe I see a diamond with the magnifier, I do indeed see a diamond. I have never had my judgments checked, however, and I really have no idea that I always see a diamond with the magnifier when I believe I do or that I have the competence to tell a real diamond from a fake. I am not completely justified in accepting my belief that I see a real diamond through the magnifier, even if I do, because I have no evidence that any of my identifications are correct.

If, on the other hand, I have evidence, from checking my identifications against an authoritative list, that I have the special competence to tell a real diamond from a fake in terms of some noted difference in their appearance when viewed though a magnifier, I might justifiably accept that I have the competence to identify a real diamond in this way. On that assumption, when I next identify something as a diamond in this way, I am justified in believing that I see a diamond. Once I have justified the belief about my competence in identifying diamonds, I may come to believe that I see a diamond through the magnifier without inferring this from the information about my competence. I may simply form the habit of believing that I see a diamond when I identify something as a diamond with the magnifier. The justification for my belief that I see a diamond depends, nevertheless, on my background information that I have the special competence to identify a diamond with a magnifier when I see one. Similarly, when I believe that I see something red, the justification I have for accepting that belief in the interests of obtaining truth and avoiding error depends on my justified background belief that I have the competence to tell a red thing when I see one, though I do not *infer* that I see a red thing from that background belief. I may, at first, infer that I see a diamond or a red thing from a premise about my competence in diamond or red-thing identification, but, subsequently, a habit of belief replaces inference. Nevertheless, my justification for accepting these beliefs depends on background information about my competence to obtain truth and avoid error in my doxastic commitments.

The moral of the story about basic beliefs was suggested at the beginning of our examination of the foundation theory. If alleged basic beliefs do not guarantee their truth, then the justification for accepting those beliefs in the quest for truth must depend on other information or beliefs. The alleged basic beliefs will fail to be self-justified. All justified acceptance of beliefs, with the possible exception of a small number of infallible beliefs, will depend on some background information about our competence to determine whether the contents of the beliefs are true or false, and our knowledge depends on this as well.

Probability and Justification: Fallibilistic Foundationalism

We also noted at the outset that if our beliefs are fallible and do not guarantee their own truth, then such beliefs entail some risk of error. If such beliefs carry a risk of error, then assuming we seek truth and eschew error, we must be assured that the risk is worth taking. The risk of error is the probability of error. The fallible foundationalist allows that there is a risk of error, but this risk, or *probability*, of a belief being erroneous must not be too great or we shall not be justified in accepting the belief for the purposes of obtaining truth and avoiding error. Thus, any belief we are justified in accepting, whether basic or nonbasic, must have a sufficiently high degree of probability to justify acceptance.

The preceding formulation of the problem takes us to the most fundamental issue, one concerning the probability of truth. We suppose the fallible foundation theorist to have given up the attempt to find any guarantee of truth in the justification of basic or nonbasic beliefs. For the foundation theory to succeed, the basic beliefs of the theory must be highly probable and must render nonbasic beliefs highly probable as well. If the evidence formulated in self-justified basic beliefs is to justify completely nonbasic beliefs, then the truth of nonbasic beliefs must be highly probable on the evidence of the basic ones. Nonbasic beliefs are, therefore, justified in the requisite sense only if they are at least highly probable on the evidence of basic beliefs.[12]

Three Concepts of Probability

Philosophers and logicians have distinguished a number of different conceptions of probability.[13] Among these are the frequency concept, the logical concept, and the subjective concept. We shall consider them all and ask what application each concept has to the problem of the justification of nonbasic beliefs. First, we consider the frequency concept. A frequency probability statement expresses the numerical frequency with which members of class *A* are also members of class *B*, for example, the frequency with which smokers are people who suffer heart disease. What exact interpretation is given to such statements is controversial. Some philosophers have interpreted such statements as expressing the limit of the relative frequency in an infinite series. Other philosophers have interpreted the frequency statement as expressing a propensity of members of one class to be members of a second class.

However, the crucial feature of such statements for the purposes of our discussion is that all such statements turn out to be very general contingent statements about the world. Consequently, if such probability statements enter into the justification of our beliefs, whether basic or nonbasic, the question arises of whether we must be justified in accepting the frequency statements and, if so, how we can be justified in accepting them in terms of fallible foundationalism. Are they basic beliefs? If so, how can they be self-justified? If they are not basic, what basic beliefs justify them?

Frequencies and Justification: An Objection

To appreciate the problems associated with frequency probabilities and the justification of nonbasic beliefs on the evidence of basic beliefs, let us return to the special case of justifying statements about external objects on the basis of sense-data statements, for example, the belief about there being a tomato in front of me on the evidence of the reddish, roundish, bulgy sense data. We noted that this evidence by itself does not logically guarantee the truth of the claim about the tomato, but a fallible foundationalist might argue that the evidence renders the claim about the tomato highly probable in a frequency sense of probability.

The frequency with which tomatoes accompany sense data of this sort is very high.

There is a classical objection to the strategy of employing frequency probabilities to justify statements about external objects on the evidence of sense-data statements. It is that, in order to determine the truth of the probability statement concerning the frequency with which some special variety of sense data are accompanied by the existence of external objects of a specified kind, we would already have to have determined the frequency with which the special variety of sense data were accompanied by the specified kind of external objects in a fair sample of observed cases. By analogy, to determine that smokers get heart disease thirty percent of the time, one would have had to determine the frequency with which smokers get heart disease in a fair sample of cases.

To know the frequency of the presence of external objects (tomatoes, for example) in the sense-data sample, however, one would have to know precisely what the frequency probability statement was supposed to enable us to know, namely, that beliefs about the external objects, the tomatoes, are true. The attempt to justify statements about external objects by appeal to frequency statements is, therefore, futile. It presupposes that we already know and are already justified in believing exactly those statements, the ones concerning external objects, that the frequency probabilities were supposed to enable us to justify. That is the classical argument.

It is a plausible argument, indeed. If we grant that the only method we have of knowing that a frequency statement is true is by inference from what we know in a sample, and that the frequency statement must be known for the truth of it to sustain the justification of the nonbasic beliefs, then the argument is decisive. It is most natural to make just this assumption, for how else are we to know that the frequency statement is true except by appeal to a sample of the relevant sort? And if we do not know that it is true, how can it completely justify any belief? How can a statement, even a true one, of which we are ignorant, justify us in believing anything?

Truth Frequency and Externalism

There are two distinct lines of reply. A fallible foundationalist influenced by externalist theories might reply that frequencies suffice to yield justification and knowledge even when we are totally ignorant of them. In terms of our example, the mere high frequency with which reddish, roundish, bulgy sense data correlate to the existence of tomatoes suffices to justify our belief in the existence of the external object, the tomato, on the evidence of the sense data—even when we are ignorant of the frequency. It is, on this view, the frequency rather than our knowledge or justified acceptance of it which enables our basic beliefs to yield completely justified nonbasic ones. Indeed, such a foundationalist enthralled with the advantages of externalism might even go on to claim that the justification of basic beliefs is the result of their truth frequency rather than of any information we have about such frequencies. Truth frequency itself greases the slide of justification.

A detailed account of externalism will occur in a later chapter, but it is easy enough to see why traditional foundationalists have not been seduced by the ease of this solution of their problem. We have already considered the critical rejoinder in the example of the person who, without knowing it, succeeds in correctly identifying diamonds with a magnifier. The person might notice some special appearance of some of the stones she examines, a special lustre, for example, and believe that the stones with this appearance are the diamonds. If she happens, as luck would have it, to be correct, then the truth frequency of her beliefs about which stones are diamonds will be high, though she will be ignorant of this fact. But since she is ignorant of the fact that the appearance she notices is the appearance of the diamond, ignorant, that is, that this is the way diamonds appear, the truth frequency leaves her without justification for believing that the stones that appear in the way she notices are diamonds. Her beliefs about which stones are diamonds are correct, but she is not completely justified in accepting them, nor does she know that they are true. Ignorance of the frequencies, however high, is the sticking spot on the slide.

A foundationalist, who acknowledges that frequencies of which we are totally ignorant yield neither justification nor knowledge, might reply instead that at least some such frequency statements are basic, for example, ones we are completely justified in believing without being justified by any other statements. A philosopher willing to defend the foundation theory by arguing that the frequency statements needed for basic statements to justify nonbasic ones are themselves basic statements, may avoid the need to justify the frequency statements by appeal to anything else. Being self-justified, the beliefs about frequency probabilities can bridge the justificatory gap between basic beliefs about sense data and nonbasic beliefs about external objects.

A skeptic might claim that such a foundation theory begs the question against skepticism. Empiricists might protest that if the frequency statements are assumed to be basic, then such a foundation theory abandons empiricism by supposing that general statements, the frequency statements, are justified without the confirmation of particular observations. These objections have no force against a foundation theorist who is willing to accept the inadequacy of skepticism and empiricism, however.

There is, however, no internal inconsistency in the attempt to employ frequency probabilities to explain how nonbasic statements of a foundation theory are justified by basic beliefs, provided that we are willing to adopt beliefs about frequencies as basic. Is it tenable to solve the problems of foundationalism in this way?

Unfortunately not. The defect in the proposed solution becomes apparent when we consider the question, Why are we justified in accepting basic beliefs about the frequencies? When the beliefs about the frequencies are held to be basic beliefs by the fallible foundationalist, the only answer is that such beliefs are self-justified. This answer has the twin disadvantages of being unenlightening and incorrect. We posed the question to find out why we are justified in accepting beliefs about the frequencies. The answer, that the beliefs are basic, amounts to saying that we just are justified and that is all there is to be said about it. Since it is not at all obvious why such beliefs should be justified in themselves, the answer is unenlightening.

The answer, in addition to being unenlightening, also is obviously incorrect. We are convinced that there is a better answer, namely, that we have evidence from past experience of the frequency of truth. The reason that we are justified in accepting that we see tomatoes, chairs, doors, hands, and other familiar perceptual objects on the evidence of how they appear to us is that such appearances have rarely led us to error. We are justified in accepting such perceptual beliefs on the basis of appearances because such beliefs are almost always correct and almost never in error. That is why cautious perceptual beliefs about seeing tomatoes on a table directly in front of us are completely justified, while more speculative ones about seeing water on a highway far away are not. The appearances of the former almost always produce true beliefs about the presence of tomatoes, while the appearances of the latter frequently produce false beliefs. The claim that beliefs about such frequencies are basic is in error. They are justified, when they are, by the evidence of our past successes and failures.

Logical Probabilities and Justification

It is, therefore, worthwhile to ask whether some other conception of probability, the logical or subjective conception, is better designed to supply a bridge of probability between basic and nonbasic beliefs. In fact, both the logical and subjective conception at first appear better adapted to this purpose than the frequency conception. We cannot undertake a detailed examination of either, but a rough description will suffice to convey the idea of each and the similarity between them.

The logical probabilities are formed by considering the basic logical alternatives and assigning probabilities to them. A standard example

would be that of a normal six-sided die. From a simple description of
the die and prior to having observed it being thrown, one would assign
a prior or antecedent probability of 1/6 to a face turning up on a normal
throw of the die. Why? Logic alone tells us that there are six sides, and,
in the absence of any empirical information about how the die behaves
when thrown, we regard them as equally likely to turn up. You might
be inclined to think that some empirical information about the behavior
of our die is influencing this assignment of probability. Suppose, on the
other hand, that you were ignorant of such empirical information. With
only logic to guide you, would you not assign the probabilities in the
manner indicated?

That is the idea behind the logical conception which may, moreover,
be applied on a global scale. Consider the basic, logically alternative
ways one might describe the world and assign probabilities to these
alternatives. From that assignment, one may define a conception of
probability, a logical conception sufficient to define all probabilities. That
is the theory; all you need is logic and definitions. The probabilities are
all consequences of the definitions.

You might, of course, object that all the probabilities will depend on
how we assign them to the basic alternatives. It might seem obvious
enough that we should assign equal probabilities to various faces of the
die turning up when the die falls on one of the faces, but must we
assign equal probabilities to the various total descriptions we might give
of the universe? And might there not be different ways of providing
total descriptions resulting in different ways of assigning probabilities?
In fact, logicians have shown that there are infinitely many different
ways of assigning logical probabilities.[14] This diversity provides a motive
for the subjective theory.

Subjective Probabilities and Gambles

One is left by the logical theory with many possible ways of assigning
the initial or prior probabilities which are all consistent with the basic
postulates of probability theory, and the choice between them appears
subjective. The subjectivist simply embraces the result. We may assign
prior probabilities as we choose so long as the assignment is consistent
with our own behavior and our behavior is rational. What sort of
behavior is connected with the assignment of probabilities? Our choices
and, most importantly, our betting choices.

Consider a bet in a game of chance in which a person must pay
$.75 for a gamble in which the person receives $1.00 if they win and
nothing if they lose. Imagine you are offered the chance to take the
bet, that is, pay $.75 for the gamble, receiving $1.00 if you win or

nothing if you lose, or give the bet to someone else, that is, receive $.75 and pay the other $1.00 if they win or nothing if they lose. (The gamble might be a draw from an ordinary deck of cards with the stipulation that you lose if a heart is drawn but win otherwise.) Suppose you find that you are indifferent to taking the bet or giving it. In that case, your behavior is rational just in case you assign a probability of .75 to winning the gamble. If you assign a higher probability, you should rationally choose to take the bet, and if you assign a lower probability, you should rationally choose to give the bet. If you are indifferent, you should rationally consider the bet fair, that is, the probability of winning to be exactly .75.

In general, the subjectivist allows any assignment of probabilities that is consistent with rational choice. It turns out interestingly enough, that your assignment of probabilities will be consistent with the postulates of the theory of probability if and only if using your probabilities for betting would not allow someone betting with you and knowing your probabilities to bet in such a way as to be certain of winning money from you regardless of the outcome of the gambles. If someone could be certain of winning money from you by betting with you on the basis of the probabilities you used to determine fair bets without knowing the outcome of the gambles, then your probability assignment is incoherent and irrational.

One simple way for this to occur would be if you assigned two different probabilities to the same thing, for example, .75 and .65 to winning the gamble considered above. In that case, someone betting with you could give you $.65 for the gamble, receiving $1.00 if she wins and nothing if she loses, since that is fair if the probability of winning is .65, as you said it was, and, at the same time, demand $.75 of you for the gamble, giving you $1.00 if you win and nothing if you lose, since that is fair if the probability of winning is .75, which you also said it was. Whatever the outcome of the gamble, whether a heart is drawn or not, she will have gained $.10 and you will have lost $.10. Your assignment of probabilities results in irrational behavior when they are used as a betting quotient. On the contrary, if they do result in rational behavior when they are used as a fair betting quotient, they are coherent and consistent with the theory of probability. That is all a subjectivist thinks it is reasonable to require of a probability assignment.

Logical and Subjective Probabilities: Advantages and Objections

What are the advantages of a logical or subjective conception of probability? You can ascertain logical or subjective probabilities by mere reflection without determining any frequencies. Thus, the information concerning such probabilities does not lead directly to the impasse we noticed with respect to information concerning frequency probability statements, to wit, that the employment of such information to justify nonbasic beliefs on the evidence of basic beliefs presupposes that we already know and are justified in accepting nonbasic beliefs to be true. Logical and subjective probability statements can be known without knowing anything about frequencies because they do not tell us anything about frequencies. It might thus seem that a fallible foundationalist should avail himself of these nonfrequency probabilities to span the justification gap between basic and nonbasic beliefs.

Nevertheless, the encouragement offered by these probabilities has a hidden defect. Since there is an infinite number of ways in which we might assign such probabilities, all of which are coherent and consistent with the theory of probability, we face the problem of establishing a connection between probability and truth. There may, after all, be none. Granting that our nonbasic beliefs are highly probable on the evidence of our basic beliefs, a detractor may query, How can your assigning a high probability to a nonbasic belief on the evidence of a basic belief justify us in accepting the nonbasic belief as true when there are a myriad of other ways of assigning probabilities under which the same nonbasic belief would have a low probability on the evidence of the same basic beliefs?

One reply to such a query is that the logical or subjective probability assigned is our *estimate* of truth frequency, but this reply, as it stands, is inadequate. The question remains whether it is a reasonable estimate. The answer must be that it is a basic, self-justified belief that the probabilities in question are reasonable estimates of truth frequencies because only then will the probabilities become appropriate to the objective of justification, to wit, accepting something if and only if it is true. Here we encounter a strategy similar to the one employed in the defense of the use of frequency probability statements in the justification of nonbasic beliefs by basic ones. We close a gap in the justification by filling it with a basic belief concerning frequencies.

We are back to where we stood when we considered the frequency conception of probability. There the problem was to explain how we are to ascertain that such frequency probability statements are true, for, if they are true, they establish a frequency relation between the truth of basic and nonbasic beliefs. In the case of logical and subjective probabilities, the problem of ascertaining probabilities can be solved by reflection and calculation alone. Though the problem of ascertaining probabilities is less, however, we are confronted with the problem of relevance. That is to say, here we must show that probability is relevant to the truth of the nonbasic statements, and, more specifically, to the frequency with which nonbasic beliefs of a specified kind are true when basic beliefs of a certain sort are true.

If there is no correlation between the high logical or subjective probability of a nonbasic belief on the evidence of a basic one and the truth of the nonbasic belief on the evidence of the truth of the basic belief, then such high probability is irrelevant for the purpose of justifying nonbasic beliefs on the evidence of basic ones. Thus, in the case of both logical and subjective probability, we need additional information about the correlation between these probabilities and truth frequencies to render them relevant to justification aimed at obtaining truth and avoiding error. Our information about the correlation presupposes information about the frequencies which, for the reasons we noted when considering the frequency conception of probability, must be assumed to be basic. We are, therefore, no better off with logical or subjective probabilities than with frequency probabilities. The problem is the same: the foundationalist must postulate that beliefs about the frequencies are basic, that is, self-justified, and such postulation, as we noted, seems as incorrect as it is unenlightening.

Probability, Truth, and Basic Belief

The conclusion is that whatever conception of probability we adopt, to render the probability relevant to justification of the required sort, we need the assumption that probability is a guide to truth. If we are justified in accepting such an assumption on a foundationalist theory, it must be because it is a basic belief. The underlying problem is like the one we uncovered in considering the justification of basic beliefs, to wit, that the justification of nonbasic beliefs, like the justification of basic beliefs, depends on some general information that tells us when our particular beliefs are a trustworthy guide to truth and when they are not.

In the case of basic beliefs, we require independent general information about when our basic beliefs are a trustworthy guide to their own truth. In the case of nonbasic beliefs, we require independent general information about when basic beliefs are a trustworthy guide to the truth of nonbasic beliefs. In both cases, the foundationalist must regard the independent general information as basic belief. This device raises serious problems, as we have noted.

First of all, how are we to avoid the charge of being arbitrary in what is claimed to be basic? The foundation theory was to provide a safe structure of justification where everything was based on a foundation of self-justified basic beliefs. Now we see that in order to construct this edifice—indeed, in order to lay the first foundation stone, as well as to lay the second upon the first—we need to assume as basic a justificatory superstructure of general information concerning the truth frequency of basic and nonbasic beliefs. The foundation, rather than consisting of particular beliefs that run a minimal risk of error, consists of general beliefs that suffer all the hazards of speculation about general conceptions.

Finally, as we have noted concerning frequencies, it is difficult to believe that such general beliefs are not justified by other particular beliefs. Within a foundation theory, these general beliefs cannot be justified by particular beliefs without arguing in a circle. But the particular beliefs cannot be justified by those general beliefs without arguing in a circle, either. This suggests, contrary to the foundation theory, that the justification of both kinds of statements may be reciprocal, that each justifies the other as a result of cohering with a system of beliefs containing particular beliefs about what we experience, as well as general beliefs about our competence to discern truth from error and the frequency of our success in so doing. To concede this, however, is to give up the foundation theory and embrace the coherence theory instead. We shall turn to such a theory in subsequent chapters after summarizing our discussion of the fallible foundation theory.

Summary: Competence, Success, and Coherence

The fallible foundationalist does not require that justification guarantee truth, but must accept that it is correlated with truth. Acceptance of the correlation is indispensable because the very purpose of justification is the attainment of truth. To ensure the truth correlation for the justification of nonbasic beliefs, we found need for general information concerning the frequency correlation between the truth of basic beliefs and the truth of the nonbasic beliefs they justify. The beliefs concerning such a correlation will turn out to be basic on a foundation theory, but this proposal appears incorrect.

To ensure the truth correlation for the justification of basic beliefs, we found need for independent information about the competence of the person to discern truth from error in the subject matter of those beliefs. As a result, the alleged beliefs turned out not to be basic. They depended for their justification on independent information about the competence of the person. To say that the person is competent to discern truth from error in some subject matter implies that the person will be successful with a high frequency in accepting what is true and avoiding accepting what is false in that subject matter. So, again in the case of basic beliefs, what turns out to be basic is not the particular beliefs about what we see and think and feel but a general belief about the frequency of success in believing what is true and avoiding believing what is false. The fallible foundationalist must assume justified acceptance of a general truth correlation, and the only way for him to obtain it is to postulate it as basic. Such postulation may provide us with an account of the justification of both basic and nonbasic beliefs and, therefore, satisfy a desire for parsimony. There is something more important in philosophy than parsimony, namely, understanding. It is here that such postulation of justified acceptance of the truth correlation as basic fails us.

Why are we justified in accepting that our beliefs about our thoughts, feelings, and simple perceptions are almost always true while other kinds of beliefs are more frequently in error? Why are we justified in accepting that some nonbasic beliefs are almost always true, given the evidence of basic beliefs, while other beliefs are more frequently in error? A foundationalist cannot provide an enlightening answer to such questions when he postulates that the beliefs about such frequencies are basic. Postulating that the general belief about our competence, trustworthiness, or success is basic is a refusal to answer the questions about why we are competent, trustworthy, and successful in our quest for truth.

Our legitimate hunger for philosophical explanation remains unsatisfied. How can it be satisfied? With few exceptions, justified acceptance of the sort required for knowledge depends upon information concerning our competence, trustworthiness, and, in short, success frequency in discerning truth and detecting error. What we are justified in accepting about such success frequency appears not to be a basic belief, however, contrary to what the fallible foundationalist must aver. Our justification for what we accept about our success frequency depends instead on our information about our successes and failures in the quest for truth. In this way, justified acceptance of any belief will depend on a background system of information about our competency and incompetency, about successes and failures, in our attempt to find truth and elude error in what we accept about the world and our relation to it. That is the thesis of the coherence theory to which we shall now turn.

Introduction to the Literature

Mark Pastin presents fallible foundationalism in "Modest Foundationalism and Self-Warrant," and similar theories are articulated and discussed by Ernest Sosa in "Epistemic Presupposition" and William Alston in "Two Types of Foundationalism." An account of how epistemic principles might be justified on a foundation theory is contained in James Van Cleve's important "Foundationalism, Epistemic Principles, and the Cartesian Circle." See also Richard Foley's important discussion of foundationalism in *The Theory of Epistemic Rationality*. The most distinguished defender of the foundation theory is Roderick Chisholm in his various books, including *Theory of Knowledge*, 3rd ed. A good introduction to the subjective or personalist theory of probability is to be found in Richard Jeffrey, *The Logic of Decision*.

5

The Explanatory
Coherence Theory

WE SHALL NOW CONSIDER an alternative theory of justification, according to which justification is a reciprocal relation of *coherence* among beliefs belonging to a system. A coherence theory affirms that a belief is completely justified if and only if it coheres with a system of beliefs. The following is a schema for a coherence theory of justification:

S is completely justified in accepting that p if and only if the belief that p coheres with other beliefs belonging to a system C of beliefs of kind k.

This schema raises one question immediately and a second is hardly concealed. The first question concerns the relation of coherence. What is coherence? In what way must a belief *cohere* with other beliefs belonging to a system of beliefs in order to be completely justified? The second is: What kind of system is kind k? That is, what sort of system of beliefs makes a belief completely justified when the belief coheres with others in that system? Definite answers to these questions are needed to convert our schema into a substantive theory.

The Regress or the Circle

Before attempting to answer these questions, however, an objection to any sort of coherence theory must be considered. It has been argued that no coherence theory is feasible. The argument purports to demonstrate the unavoidability of basic beliefs, and hence of a foundation theory, for an adequate theory of justification. It affirms that unless some beliefs are basic, the justification of all beliefs must inevitably lead either to an infinite regress or to a circular argument. Its conclusion is that either consequence is epistemically intolerable. Thus is it inferred that we must uphold the foundation theory.

This argument needs more precise articulation. If a person is completely justified in a belief on the basis of evidence, then appeal to that evidence would constitute a correct answer to the question, 'How do you know?' Now suppose no beliefs are basic. Then, every completely justified belief is so justified by appeal to evidence, but evidence must itself be completely justified belief and, therefore, must also be justified by appeal to evidence. This means that every completely justified belief must be justified by some other, thus leading either to an infinite regress or to a justificatory circle. If both those alternatives are unacceptable, then there must be some basic beliefs.

This argument must be met, or the project of constructing a coherence theory will be doomed from the outset. Fortunately for the coherence theorist, the argument is defective despite its distinguished credentials. Not all completely justified beliefs need to be justified by *appeal to evidence*. Appealing to evidence is an activity or process that occurs over time. Being completely justified in believing something is a state that exists at a time and need not result from the activity or process that occurs over time. Being beautiful is a state that exists at a time and need not result from the activity or process of beautification. A belief may be completely justified for a person because of some relation of the belief to a system to which it belongs, the way it coheres with the system, just as a nose may be beautiful because of some relation of the nose to a face, the way it fits with the face. One may justify a belief by appeal to evidence, but many beliefs are completely justified without such appeal, just as one may beautify a nose by appeal to surgery, but many noses are beautiful without such appeal.

It may yet be objected that if a belief is completely justified when no belief is self-justified, then a person must be able, at least in principle, to carry out the justification completely. That is, she must be able to justify the belief by appeal to evidence, and to justify her belief in that evidence by appeal to other evidence, and to justify her belief in that evidence by appeal to still other evidence, and so forth. One reply to this objection is that a person might in principle be able to carry out each step of this justification without being able to carry out the entire process. As an analogy, a person might be able to add three to each number without being able to carry out the whole process. It would be mistaken to infer that there is some number to which a person is unable to add three from the fact that she is actually unable to carry out the infinite task of adding three to each number. Similarly, it would be a mistake to conclude that a person is not completely justified in any belief from the fact that she is unable to carry out the infinite task of justifying every belief to another. Hence, the regress argument fails.

Nevertheless, it is only fair to point out one further objection to the foregoing. Some beliefs surely appear to be such that, though they are completely justified, one cannot justify them by appeal to evidence. For example, a person might justify her belief that she sees an apple by appeal to the evidence that there is an object before her that looks red and apple-shaped, and she might justify her belief that the object before her looks this way by appeal to the evidence that she *thinks* that there is an object that looks this way; but, eventually, she must reach the point where no further evidence can be elicited. We would thus come to some completely justified belief that the person would be unable to justify by appeal to evidence. This objection takes us to the heart of the argument.

The reply to the objection is twofold. First, it must be noted that justification is ordinarily justification to someone else, and whether a justification given to someone shall suffice will depend on what that person is willing to grant. If he is willing to grant that the object in the distance is Argile Hill if it looks like the hill in a picture, one need only show him that the object looks like the one in the picture to justify one's belief that the object is Argile Hill. If, on the other hand, he doubts that the object in the picture is Argile Hill, then justification will have to be extended. Hence, there is a pragmatic element in justification depending on the epistemic qualification of the person to whom the justification is directed.[1] If a person is asked, 'How do you know?', her answer may satisfy one person and fail to satisfy another.

The second reply is more fundamental. Even when no further evidence can be elicited on behalf of a belief, the relation of the belief to some system of beliefs may account for the justification of the belief. For example, a system of beliefs may imply that if a person believes that something looks red to her, then, unless there is some unusual condition or circumstance, the explanation for why the person believes something looks red to her is that something *does* look red to her. It might be strange for a person to appeal to such a consideration as evidence that something looks red to her, but it might be such an explanatory relationship of her belief to her background system of beliefs that makes her completely justified in believing that something looks red to her, nonetheless. This does not make the belief self-justified, however, even though it may be noninferential. The belief is not justified independently of relations to other beliefs. It is justified because of the way it coheres with other beliefs belonging to a system of beliefs.

The foregoing reflections show that a coherence theory is not impossible and a foundation theory not necessary. We have yet to explain what coherence is or with what sort of a system a belief must cohere to become justified. We now turn to answer these questions.

The Traditional Answer: Coherence as Implication

Let us begin with the relation of coherence. Some defenders of the coherence theory conceived of the relationship of coherence as a relation of necessary connection.[2] Thus, a belief that p coheres with other beliefs of a system C if and only if p either necessarily implies or is necessarily implied by every other belief in C. Suppose, however, that we have a system of beliefs that is logically consistent, contains some logically contingent statements, and is such that every statement in the system either necessarily implies or is necessarily implied by every other statement. We can easily form another system having these same characteristics by taking the contingent statements in C, negating them, and forming a new system containing the negations of the contingent statements in C, together with whatever noncontingent statements may have been contained in C. This new system will be consistent if C was, and it will be such that every statement in the new system either necessarily implies or is necessarily implied by every other statement. The new system, though just as coherent as the old in terms of the necessary connections between statements, will tell us exactly the opposite about the world. Every contingent statement in one system is negated in the other. Thus, if we were to assume that such coherence was sufficient for complete justification, we should have to admit that any contingent statement a person is completely justified in accepting is such that he is also completely justified in accepting the denial of that statement.

Logical coherence is not, moreover, necessary for complete justification. Take any two observation statements describing observations of different and unrelated objects. Neither of these necessarily implies the other, but we can be completely justified in accepting both of them. Similarly, consider any two laws, one about stars and the other about mice. These may also be such that neither necessarily implies the other, but we may be completely justified in accepting both of them. The two laws or the two observation statements may be related in some way: they may be consequences of some more general law, but they are not necessary consequences of each other.

These objections are decisive. The question is, how can a coherence theory avoid such difficulties? First, we must keep distinct the two questions raised above, namely, what is coherence? and, second, what kind of a system is required? We shall not obtain a satisfactory coherence theory of justification by answering only the first question. In defending a belief or knowledge claim by arguing that it coheres with certain other beliefs, we must be prepared to explain why coherence with those beliefs provides complete justification. Hence, to articulate a satisfactory coherence theory, we must answer the second question as well. We must say what kind of system provides complete justification for those beliefs that cohere with the system.

Coherence as Explanation

A coherence theory of justification may affirm that the kind of coherence required for justification is explanatory coherence. Wilfrid Sellars has propounded such a view, and Gilbert Harman has argued at some length that whether a belief is justified depends on the way in which it fits into the best overall explanatory account.[3] The question of whether a belief is justified cannot be decided, according to such a theory, in isolation from a system of beliefs. It is in relation to other beliefs belonging to a system of beliefs that the justification of a belief must be decided. Moreover, the system of beliefs determining justification must be one in which we explain as much as we can and leave as little unexplained as we must. A system having a maximum of explanatory coherence confers justification on beliefs within it.

If the kind of coherence required for justification is explanatory, then it is the function of a belief in explanation that justifies it. There are two ways in which a belief can so function. It can either explain or be part of what explains something, or it can be explained or be part of what is explained. To have explanatory coherence, one must both have something to explain and something to explain it.

Bertrand Russell once remarked that, though we do not know of the existence of physical objects, we may reasonably infer the existence of such objects because the hypothesis of their existence is the simplest and best explanation of why we experience the sense data we do.[4] A defender of the explanatory coherence theory of justification could reply that Russell does not go as far as explanation would warrant. The hypothesis that physical objects exist is such a good explanation of our experience of the sense data in question that we are completely justified in accepting and claiming to know of the existence of such objects. The traditional problem of the justification of perceptual claims on the basis of sense-data statements appears solved by the explanatory coherence theory.

Moreover, the problem of the justification of our claims about the mental states of others seems amenable to comparable treatment. If I see a man behaving just as I would were I in a certain mental state, then, one could argue, the best explanation I have for why he behaves that way is that he is in that mental state. Suppose, for example, that I see an injured man before me writhing, moaning, and otherwise behaving as I know I would if I were experiencing intense pain. The best explanation for why he behaves as he does is that he is feeling pain. To see that this is so, consider the problems one encounters with any hypothesis denying that the man is in pain. First, I must explain why the man is behaving in this way if he does not feel pain. Even if, however, my hypothesis does explain this, to obtain a satisfactory overall explanatory account, I must explain more. In explaining his behavior in some alternative way, I shall either assume that, though this man feels no pain, others in such circumstances would, in which case I must explain why this man does not feel pain when others would. Otherwise, I shall assume that others generally fail to feel pain in such circumstances, in which case I must explain why I do feel pain when others do not. In either case, I am left with an unsolved explanatory problem that would be avoided by hypothesizing that others generally, the man in question included, feel pain as I do under these conditions. From the standpoint of overall explanatory coherence, the latter hypothesis is obviously advantageous.[5]

As we proceed from perceptual claims and claims about the mental states of others to statements about distant times and places and, finally, to statements about theoretical states and objects, the appeal to explanation becomes more obvious and familiar. We might think it odd to justify the claim that we see our bodies or that our friends are suffering by arguing that it is best from the standpoint of explanation to suppose that these things are so, but it is commonplace to argue that hypotheses about the past, the physically remote, and the theoretically unobservable are completely justified by the way they explain what we seek to understand.

On the Justification of What Is Explained

The thesis that hypotheses are completely justified because of what they explain is most plausible, but how are we justified in accepting those things that are explained? If we claim that what is explained consists of basic facts and beliefs, we shall merely appeal to explanation to justify the inference from basic beliefs to nonbasic ones. We are now considering a more radical departure from the foundation theory. According to the coherence theory under consideration, there are no basic beliefs. All beliefs are justified by their explanatory role. To explain, however, one must have something to explain as well as a hypothesis to explain it. What justifies those beliefs that provide the matter to explain?

The answer is that if some beliefs are justified because of what they explain, others are justified because they are explained. Moreover, it is plausible to suppose that some beliefs are justified because they are so well explained. Suppose I look at a streak in a cloud chamber and conjecture that the streak is the path of an alpha particle. If I do not understand how an alpha particle could make such a streak, I may not be completely justified in my belief. Once it is explained to me how the alpha particle causes condensation, I may become completely justified in accepting that the streak is the path of the particle. It is no rare event in science or everyday life to have some doubt concerning a fact removed by some explanation of it. Such explanations may change dubious beliefs into completely justified ones.

Moreover, a belief may be justified *both* because it explains *and* because it is explained. That a chair supports me may explain why, in my present posture, I do not fall to the floor; and that the chair supports me may be explained, given my position on it, by the rigidity, and so forth, of the chair. Similarly, the path of the alpha particle may explain why we see what we do and may be explained within atomic theory. The same belief may be both explaining and explanatory, and it may derive justification from both roles. It is those beliefs that both explain and are explained whose justification seems most adequate. Indeed, explained unexplainers, such as sense-data statements, have been epistemically controversial, as have unexplained explainers, such as statements concerning the supernatural. Recently, philosophers of empiricist leanings have tended to construe the fundamental empirical statements as perceptual claims concerning physical objects rather than reports concerning sense data. The underlying reason for this tendency may be an unrecognized desire to settle on some empirical statements that are *both* explained and explanatory. Perceptual statements both explain sense experience and are explained by theories of perception.

Explanatory Coherence and Justification: An Analysis

The foregoing considerations substantiate the suggestion that completely justified beliefs are ones that explain or are explained, or both. Explanatory coherence thus appears to determine justification. We shall now attempt to offer a precise analysis of such justification. Let us reconsider the formula for coherence theories introduced earlier.

S is completely justified in accepting that p if and only if the belief that p coheres with other beliefs belonging to a system C of beliefs of kind k.

To offer a coherence theory of justification, we must offer an account of coherence and of the kind of system with which a belief must cohere. Let us first consider the question of what kind of system of beliefs is required. Sellars suggests that our choice of a system should be one that yields a maximum of explanatory coherence, but a problem of interpretation arises immediately. A number of systems of beliefs compete for the status of having a maximum of explanatory coherence, and some of these systems might be ones that any given person could hardly conceive. Are we to require that for a person to be completely justified in what he believes, his belief must cohere with a system of beliefs of which he could not conceive?

One answer is that the required system be the one with a maximum of explanatory coherence of all those of which S could conceive. The other alternative is to require that his belief must cohere with that system having a maximum of explanatory coherence, whether he could conceive of it or not. Both answers present difficulties. One problem with the first answer is that a person might turn out to be completely justified in accepting something because of his inability to conceive of the system having a maximum of explanatory coherence with which his belief fails to cohere. One drawback of the second answer is that according to it a person might be completely justified in accepting something, even though it fails to cohere with systems he understands: his belief may cohere with a system of beliefs having a maximum of explanatory coherence which he is unable to comprehend. Of the two difficulties, the latter appears the more severe. Hence, we shall suppose that the system of kind k is the one having a maximum of explanatory coherence among those systems of beliefs understood by S. We shall be able to elucidate further the concept of *maximal* explanatory coherence when we have clarified the notion of coherence.

Explanatory Coherence

Now, let us consider the concept of coherence. One ingredient in coherence is consistency. A belief logically inconsistent with others fails to cohere with them. Consistency is not sufficient, however, when the kind of coherence required is explanatory. To explicate this kind of coherence, we shall take the concepts of explanation and of *better* explanation as primitive, that is, undefined. It is agreed that these concepts are themselves in need of clarification. We shall consider the problems surrounding such clarification subsequently.

To cohere with the beliefs belonging to a system, a belief must fill an explanatory role, but what sort? It would be too restrictive to require that the belief explain or be explained by *all* beliefs belonging to the system. We may, however, require that it be an essential part of an explanation of some beliefs belonging to the system or part of what is explained by such beliefs. We shall speak of beliefs that are explanatory in this way as explaining something relative to system k, and of beliefs explained in this way as something explained in relation to system k. Can we say that a belief coheres with a system of beliefs if and only if it is consistent with the system and either explains or is explained in relation to the system? No. A general belief may explain some belief within a system of the required sort, but fail to be completely justified because some other general belief explains that belief better. Two contradictory general statements may each explain what is believed to be a fact, when one explains better than the other. Obviously, a person cannot be completely justified in accepting both hypotheses. Some additional restriction is needed.

We must require that a belief cohering with a system either explain or be explained in relation to the system better than anything which contradicts it. Contradiction must be made relative to the system. Two mutually consistent statements may be such that a system of beliefs entails that they cannot both be true. We shall speak of such beliefs contradicting each other and thus employ a relativized concept of contradiction. With this stipulation, the preceding problem is easily solved. A belief coheres with a system of beliefs if and only if the belief is consistent with the system and either explains something in relation to the system not explained better by any belief that contradicts it, or the belief is better explained by something in relation to the system, and nothing that contradicts it is explained better.

We thus obtain the sought-after notion of coherence needed to provide a coherence theory of justification as follows:

> S is completely justified in accepting that p if and only if the belief of S that p is consistent with that system C of beliefs having a maximum of explanatory coherence among those systems of beliefs understood by S, and the belief that p either explains something relative to C which is not explained better by anything which contradicts p or the belief that p is explained by something relative to C and nothing which contradicts it is explained better relative to C.

Let us now reconsider the concept of a system having a maximum of explanatory coherence. The preceding discussion suggests the way to elucidate this concept. If the beliefs belonging to one system explain better and are better explained than the beliefs belonging to a second system, then the first system has greater explanatory coherence than the second. A system *C1* has greater explanatory coherence than *C2* if and only if *C1* is logically consistent and *C2* is not, or both are consistent but more is explained in *C1* than *C2*, or both explain the same things but some things are explained better in *C1* than *C2*. We then adopt the following analysis of maximal explanatory coherence which provides the sort of system of beliefs we sought at the outset:

> A system *C* has a maximum of explanatory coherence among those systems of beliefs understood by *S* if and only if there is no system having greater explanatory coherence among those systems.

This condition together with the preceding one constitutes a theory of justification in terms of explanatory coherence in which we have taken for granted the concepts of explanation, better explanation, and the usual logical notions.

On Explanation

The conception of explanation is, unfortunately, so interwoven with epistemic notions that we could not expect to explicate the idea of one explanation being better than another without at least covertly appealing to some epistemic notion. For example, one explanation is often said to be better than another solely because the first is more likely to be true from what we *know* than the second. Such considerations lead us in a small circle.

This difficulty can best be elaborated if we consider the concept of explanation *simpliciter*. There is an immense literature on this topic of considerable linguistic and formal sophistication. This literature illustrates most clearly the futility of hoping to find an explication of explanation to which we can fruitfully appeal in our articulation of the explanatory coherence theory. Consider first the deductive model of explanation admirably articulated by Carl Hempel.[6] With various refinements, this model of explanation tells us that *F* is explained by a statement of boundary conditions *B* and law *L* if and only if *F* is deducible from *B* and *L* in such a way that *B* and *L* are both essential to the deduction. Such analyses are wont to lead to implausible conclusions, the most notable of which is that almost any law can be used to explain almost any statement.[7] Moreover, the qualifications needed to eliminate such untoward consequences often appear to be entirely *ad hoc*. The more important objections to such analyses from the standpoint of the explanatory coherence theory rest on counterexamples.

Consider the following example which is a modification of one proposed by Sylvain Bromberger.[8] Imagine that I am standing with my toe next to a mouse that is three feet from a four-foot-high flagpole with an owl sitting on top. From this information concerning boundary conditions, and the Pythagorean theorem, which we here construe as an empirical law, we can deduce that the mouse is five feet from the owl. Moreover, all the premises are essential to the derivation. Thus, in the proposed analysis, the boundary conditions, together with the law, explain why the mouse is five feet from the owl. Nonetheless, this deduction does not explain why the mouse is at that distance from the owl at all. If you have any doubts about whether this is an explanation, imagine that you *know* that the distance from the top of the flagpole to where you stand is five feet and that you have asked why the mouse is five feet from the owl. An answer to this question based on the boundary conditions cited and the Pythagorean theorem would not be explanatory. Receiving such an answer, you would, perhaps, apprehend how to deduce that the mouse is five feet from the owl from some premises, but those premises do not explain why the mouse is five feet from the owl. And, moreover, the matter requires explanation—owls eat mice!

An Epistemic Analysis of Explanation

The sort of amendment required, according to Bromberger, is epistemic. An explanation supplies the right answer to a question, when the person to whom the matter is explained does not know the answer and, indeed, would rule out any answer she could think of on the basis of what she does know. Such a person lacks understanding, and the understanding lacking is supplied by the explanation. These considerations lead Bromberger to offer an analysis of explanation consisting of an explication of sentences of the form, SEBW, where S and B take expressions referring to persons as values, E takes some form of the verb 'to explain' and W takes some question.[9] Thus, one instance of the formula would be: Hempel explained to Lehrer why the mouse is five feet from the owl. One truth condition of this sentence is that Lehrer at first does not understand or know why the mouse is five feet from the owl. A second truth condition is that what Hempel communicates to Lehrer gives Lehrer knowledge of why the mouse is five feet from the owl.

The sort of analysis of explanation that Bromberger offers, however plausible and significant it may be, cannot be exploited here without rendering the explanatory coherence analysis of knowledge immediately circular. Knowledge would be analysed in terms of explanatory coherence, which would be analysed in terms of explanation, which would be analysed in terms of knowledge. Moreover, if we assume that Bromberger is correct, or very nearly correct, in his analysis, then it seems reasonable to conclude that if an analysis of knowledge is based on the concept of explanation, the latter concept should be taken as primitive in our analysis. This is the proper moral of the story.

Hempel has a reply to the preceding objection that we shall consider briefly.[10] He argues that the conception of explanation appealed to above, being relative to a subject and what he knows, is not the one he was attempting to explicate. The conception of explanation that Hempel claims to be explicating is an objective logical relation between the law and what is subsumed under it. The question is whether the objective logical relation between a law and what is subsumed under it is a relation of explanation. For the purpose of explicating the logical structure of scientific theories, laws, and singular statements subsumed under them, it may not matter whether or not the relation of subsumption is that of explanation. For our purposes, however, it is crucial. The sort of counterexample considered above is conclusive here: the subsumption relation may fail to be explanatory.

The preceding remarks are not offered as a refutation of Hempel's claim. They are, instead, a defense of our strategy of taking as primitive the conception of explanation, and of one explanation being better than another, in our discussion of the explanatory coherence theory. If we attempt to explicate the relation of explanation as an objective deductive relation of subsumption, we shall find that the relation fails to explicate why the premises of the deduction explain the conclusion. As we noted in the example of the owl and the mouse, sometimes the deduction is nonexplanatory. To distinguish adequately those deductions that are explanatory from those that are not, and to explicate what makes some deductions explanatory, we would have to appeal, as Bromberger contends, to epistemic considerations, to what we do and do not know. Such an appeal would render the analysis of knowledge circular. Instead, we shall take our explanatory conceptions as primitive. No thoroughly satisfactory nonepistemic analysis of explanation has been proposed, and, consequently, our remarks concerning theories of justification based on the concept of explanatory coherence must rely on an undefined notion of explanation. Yet, we can find arguments against the explanatory form of the coherence theory strong enough to warrant abandoning it.

Objections and Replies to Coherence as Explanation

The first problem raised by our explanatory theory of complete justification concerns comparing systems with respect to explanatory coherence. Our theory tells us that one system has greater explanatory coherence than a second if the first leaves less unexplained or explains better what it does explain than does the second. Even so, one system may leave less unexplained and explain better what it does explain by containing less to be explained. One system may admit statements of unexplained facts which the other excludes. To reduce what is unexplained, one may refuse to concede the truth of those statements that need explanation. Explanation involves those statements that do the explaining, on the one hand, and those that describe what is to be explained, on the other. One can increase the explanatory coherence of a system either by adding statements that explain or by subtracting statements to be explained. The method of increasing the explanatory coherence of a system by decreasing what is to be explained must be limited. Otherwise, we may obtain a maximum of coherence only by securing a minimum of content.

The foregoing remarks may be illustrated with a very simple formal example. Compare any system of beliefs within science to the following. Take a language with one observation predicate 'Ox' and one theoretical predicate 'Tx'. Then, adopt a system affirming that everything is T, that everything T is O, hence, that everything is O. Let the system contain only these sentences. We can now get a maximum of coherence by adding just those observation sentences to our system that fit with our one empirical law. More concretely, if we wish to have the law affirming that all dragons breathe fire, we may then add the 'observation' sentences that object one is a fire-breathing dragon, object two is a fire-breathing dragon, and so forth. The coherence between the law and observation statement will be perfect, and the absurdity of the system will be manifest. To avoid this sort of implausibility, philosophers have imposed further limitations on what kinds of statements may belong to a justificatory system.

Explanatory Coherence and Observation Statements

Both Quine and Sellars suggest conditioned responses as one determinant of whether a statement is epistemically qualified.[11] Of course, this amounts to abandoning the theory of justification under consideration, for whether we are completely justified in accepting some observation statement to be true will then depend not only on its explanatory coherence with other statements but also on the existence of certain patterns of conditioned responses to sensory stimuli.

Both Quine and Sellars advance theories of meaning according to which the meaning of terms and statements depends on the relations of those terms and statements to other terms and statements. Sellars would not identify the meaning of an observation statement with the pattern of conditioned responses in terms of which one responds, with such a statement to sensory stimuli. Nevertheless, both authors consider such patterns to constitute the link between language and sensory experience. Hence, whether we are completely justified in accepting some observation statement to be true depends on how that statement is linked to sensory experience by such patterns. These patterns accordingly constitute some restraint on the way in which we may eliminate observation statements from the system to save ourselves explanatory labor.

Observation Statements and Conditioned Responses

Clearly, some amendment of the explanatory coherence theory is needed to preserve an explanatory base. Let us consider whether the present modification yields a satisfactory theory of justification. Consider the view that what makes a person completely justified in accepting some observation statement to be true depends, at least in part, on certain patterns of conditioned responses associated with the sentence. Of course, *action*, and not *belief*, is usually required as a response to episodes of belief acquisition. There is a defect in this proposal that is easy to appreciate and which infects sophisticated modifications. It is that a person may be conditioned to respond with erroneous beliefs.

Experiments regarding perceptual beliefs concerning the size of coins show that a poor person will respond with erroneous beliefs much more frequently than one who is not. Let the experiment be one in which a person is shown a coin, then shown a disc, and is asked to report whether they are the same size, or whether one is larger than the other. The poor person will frequently judge the coin to be larger than it is. Is she completely justified in her belief? Of course not. What this shows is that conditioned responses can regularly produce erroneous as well as correct belief. Conditioning in and by itself is neutral with respect to truth and error.

The preceding remarks are not intended to refute the proposal that a person might be fortunate enough to be completely justified in accepting some observation statement whenever her belief is a conditioned response to a certain kind of stimulus. It may be true, just as it may be true that she is completely justified in accepting an observation statement whenever she is in a brain state of some special kind. Even if such beliefs happen to be completely justified, however, it is not the conditioning or the brain state that *makes* them completely justified. If people happen to be so conditioned that what they believe is completely justified, that is fortunate. Still, they could equally well have been so conditioned that what they believe would not be completely justified. It may be that I am conditioned to believe that an object is red when I am confronted with a red object in certain circumstances, but I could equally well have been conditioned to believe that such an object is yellow. The latter belief would not have been completely justified. What makes the belief justified is not the conditioning, even if the completely justified belief is a response to a conditioned stimulus.

The foregoing argument applies against any theory affirming that what makes a belief completely justified ever depends on the belief being a conditioned response to a stimulus of a certain kind. What a person is conditioned to believe is one thing, and what she is completely justified in accepting is another, even if the two happen to coincide. Of course, we condition a child to have beliefs which we think are completely justified and discourage beliefs we think are completely unjustified. Nevertheless, it is not her being so conditioned that makes her belief completely justified.

Observation and Spontaneity

Another attempt to solve the problem of accounting for observation, suggested by Bonjour, would be simply to impose an observation requirement to the effect that various beliefs that occur spontaneously are reliable or likely to be true.[12] There are two objections to this technique. First of all, it does not seem to be the spontaneity of the beliefs that accounts for their justification but rather their content. It is because observation beliefs are about what we observe that they are justified, not because they are spontaneous. What a person spontaneously believes is one thing, what she is completely justified in believing is quite another. A person given to having spontaneous beliefs about demons and monsters would not be completely justified in such beliefs. The most critical objection to imposing such a requirement, however, is that it must be either arbitrary or unnecessary. If our system of beliefs gives us no justification for accepting that beliefs about what we observe are reliable, then the requirement is arbitrary. If, on the other hand, our system of beliefs does give us a justification for accepting that such beliefs are reliable, then the requirement is unnecessary.

Observation and Natural Selection

Yet another way of saving observation statements, by appeal to the theory of natural selection, is equally faulty for similar reasons. To argue that beliefs about what we observe must be completely justified because they have survival value in the process of natural selection will leave one epistemically bankrupt. First, the form of survival theory that currently appears most tenable is one recognizing that many factors bear little weight in the struggle for survival and, consequently, may be retained even though they have almost no survival value. Hence, one cannot argue directly from the existence of beliefs to their survival value. Second, and more important, even if this inference is allowed, the epistemic leap to the conclusion that such beliefs are completely justified is totally unwarranted. Beliefs that are neither true nor completely justified may have considerable survival value. Perhaps the truth would destroy us.

An Ethical Analogy

One final argument. Consider briefly the parallel between ethics and epistemology.[13] Chisholm, following Lewis, has argued that a theory of justification provides a criterion of evidence and justification just as a theory of ethics provides criteria of right and wrong. Imagine a person arguing that an action he performed was right because he was conditioned to perform that action or because the performance of such actions has not been extinguished through the process of natural selection. The latter contention is absurd on the face of it. The flaw in the former is less clear.

If we believed that a person was conditioned to perform a certain action, we might conclude that he could not help but perform it, that he was responding to a kind of compulsion, and thus refuse to condemn him. However, if the action was one intentionally aimed at producing wanton pain and suffering in others, we would not condone the action as right. The action was not right even if the person could not help but perform it. The claim that a person is completely justified in accepting something because it is a conditional response to sensory stimulation is no better warranted than the claim that a person is right in performing an action because it is such a response. Conditioned responses fail to justify our beliefs. Justification must emanate from another source.

We conclude that the appeal to conditioned responses, however interesting psychologically, will not suffice as the basis of a supply of completely justified observation statements to be explained within an explanatory system. Moreover, as we noticed earlier, the appeal to conditioned responses amounts to introducing an additional factor into the explanatory coherence theory. Is there any way of preventing the wholesale depletion of observation statements from our system of beliefs without abandoning the theory of justification as explanatory coherence? In fact, there is a way.

Self-explanatory Beliefs

One could maintain that observation statements are self-explanatory and, hence, that a gain of explanatory coherence results from the inclusion of such statements within the system.[14] How can a statement be self-explanatory? When the truth of p explains why the person believes that p. For example, suppose I believe I see blood on my shoe. How is my belief to be explained? One explanation of why I *believe* that I *see* blood on my shoe is that I *do* see blood on my shoe. According to Bromberger, this explanation appeals to an *exceptive* principle.[15] In answering the question of why I believe that I see blood on my shoe, we are presupposing a principle affirming that no one believes that he sees blood on his shoe *except* when he does see blood on his shoe, or when he incorrectly takes what is on his shoe for blood, or when he is hallucinating, and so forth. If I believe that none of the other alternatives is correct and such beliefs cohere with my system of beliefs, then the statement that I see blood on my shoe explains, at least in part, why I believe that I see blood on my shoe. As a consequence, my belief is justified.

The preceding argument shows how a belief could be justified by being self-explanatory. If what is believed is true, then the truth of the belief explains, at least in part, the existence of the belief. Of course, a fuller explanation should be forthcoming, for instance, one explaining how I happen to see blood on my shoe, perhaps because my bruised foot is bleeding, and so forth. Though the explanation is incomplete, it is acceptable as far as it goes. Moreover, those beliefs most plausibly taken to be self-explanatory in this way seem to coincide with perceptual beliefs. Hence, this sort of justification promises to provide a base of completely justified observation statements. Memory statements seem amenable to comparable treatment.

Before turning to a critical examination of this theory, it is useful to notice its virtues. It offers the possibility of providing justified perceptual beliefs within the context of an explanatory coherence theory without dragging in some nonexplanatory feature to account for their justification. Such beliefs are justified because the truth of the belief explains the existence of the belief, that is, the statement that a person believes what he does is explained by the statement that what he believes is true. Moreover, this explanation depends on the *system* of beliefs a person has, and, consequently, on other beliefs in that system, for example, those that exclude alternative explanations for the existence of the belief. The self-explanatory justification is, therefore, not a form of self-justification. The self-explanatory character of perceptual beliefs depends on explanatory coherence within a system of beliefs.

Self-explanation: An Evaluation

The proposal that justification can be obtained through self-explanation in a system of beliefs, though promising, evokes criticism appropriate to the explanatory coherence theory as a whole. It may be doubted whether the purported self-explanation is explanation at all, and it may be affirmed that the justification obtained does not depend on explanation. We shall examine these objections as they apply to the theory of justification through self-explanation and then to the more general form of the theory of justification by explanation.

First, it might be objected that the general principles involved in self-explanation, *exceptive* principles, are trivially true, and, consequently, no explanation can be based upon them. The principle that no one believes he sees something *except* when he does see it, or when he erroneously takes something else for it, or when he is hallucinating, and so forth, has the appearance of a tautology. It tells us no more than that no one believes that he sees something except when he sees it or when he erroneously believes that he sees it. This, it might be objected, is not a principle of explanation, but rather the barest of tautologies. Moreover, people sometimes see things they do not believe they see just as they sometimes believe they see things when they do not. If the spot on my shoe is nail polish, not blood, then I may not believe that I see a spot of nail polish on my shoe though I do, and I may believe that I see blood on my shoe though I do not. Thus, we lack any explanatory law, exceptive or otherwise, to provide an explanatory link between what a person believes she sees and her seeing that object.

Second, it might be contended that if a person believes that she sees something immediately before herself, the existence of this belief justifies us in accepting that she sees it, at least when one has no reason to doubt that she sees what she believes she does. If her belief justifies *us* in concluding that she sees the object in question, then her belief must also justify her. Thus, the example illustrates a self-justified belief, but it does not depend on explanatory considerations. That a person believes that she sees something provides justification for concluding that she does see it without explaining or being explained by any other belief or statement. That is the objection.

One might defend the explanatory coherence theory against such objections either by rejecting the doctrine of self-explanatory beliefs or by maintaining that such explanation is genuine. We cannot offer any decisive argument against the possibility of sustaining these alternatives, but neither seems tenable. Of course, these remarks are no defense of a foundation theory against a coherence theory. The way in which perceptual beliefs cohere with a system of beliefs may render them completely justified even though the coherence is not explanatory. Coherence may be explicated in some other manner. We now turn to other criticisms of the explanatory coherence theory which point in that direction.

Justification Without Explanation: Some Examples

The first example of a completely justified belief whose justification does not depend on explanatory considerations was presented above. It is the example in which a person deduces from the Pythagorean theorem and boundary conditions that the mouse is five feet from the owl, even though he has no explanation of why this is so. The belief is completely justified, but the justification of the belief does not depend on explanatory relations. It is enough that the person knows the Pythagorean theorem, the distance to the pole, and the height of the pole, and deduces the conclusion. He is then completely justified in his belief that the mouse is five feet from the owl, even if he has no idea how to explain that nor any idea about how to explain anything else in terms of that belief.

For a second example, suppose that David Hume in eighteenth century Edinburgh sees a dead man before him. If asked whether the dead man was sexually conceived, Hume would reply that he was and would be justified in his belief because he would be justified in accepting that all who die are conceived. Death, however, does not explain conception any more than conception explains death.[16] The constant conjunction Hume observed between conception and death did not indicate a causal connection. Conception does not cause death any more than death causes conception. Neither explains the other. Moreover, the observed conjunction will cease to hold in our century and is no law when some die who were laboratory artifacts. Hume was justified in accepting that the dead man was once sexually conceived, nonetheless.

These are two examples of completely justified beliefs whose justification does not depend on explanatory relations to other beliefs. They may be neither explained nor explanatory, but are justified because they cohere, in some way independent of explanatory function, with the other beliefs within a system of beliefs. Because the beliefs that the mouse is five feet from the owl and that the dead man was once conceived cohere with other beliefs, they are completely justified, but the coherence is not explanatory.

A defender of the explanatory coherence theory could reply to these objections that we have ignored the way in which the conclusions and premises in question function in the overall explanatory system. She might argue that those beliefs are only completely justified because of the explanatory relations of those beliefs within an overall system having a maximum of explanatory coherence. She could also claim that the Pythagorean theorem and the general principle concerning how people come to exist are themselves completely justified because of their systematic explanatory role. Finally, she could say that such general beliefs within an overall system having a maximum of explanatory coherence are what make our conclusions justified.

It is difficult to comment on this reply without indulging in simple counterassertion. However, with some imagination we may, I believe, construct something of an argument. Imagine a group of people who, perhaps because of their religious beliefs, meticulously avoid asking for explanations of what they observe. They are anti-explanationists. Anti-explanationists ask not why or how things happen but are content to observe the way things happen and rely on such observations without seeking explanations. They pride themselves in their intellectual humility. Such people might arrive at the Pythagorean theorem from observation. They may not inquire as to why it is true and they may not have deduced it from more general axioms. Nonetheless, they might be completely justified in accepting what they derive from it, for example, that the mouse is five feet from the owl, whether or not the theorem or the conclusion derived from it contributes to the explanatory coherence of some overall system of beliefs. It would be most peculiar to affirm that what made them completely justified in accepting what they did on these matters was the explanatory role of such beliefs within the system of their beliefs. They might be wholly oblivious to such explanatory virtues, and, indeed, would be indifferent or perhaps even hostile to receiving suggestions concerning the explanatory merits of what they believed. What makes them completely justified in accepting what they do has something to do with the way in which these beliefs cohere with a system of beliefs they have, but the coherence involved is not explanatory. Thus, explanatory coherence is not necessary for complete justification.

It might be objected that the anti-explanationists are simply ignorant of what *makes* their beliefs justified. What makes their beliefs justified is the explanatory coherence of their system of beliefs, even though they have no idea that this is so. Suppose, however, that their system of beliefs based on observation, empirical generalization, and deduction from those generalizations is not sufficient to insure that anything is explained. It might, nevertheless, suffice for justification.

Some Final Objections:
Weak Explanations and Competing Systems

There remain two related objections which shall be mentioned because they illustrate some problems to be solved by any satisfactory form of the coherence theory, explanatory or not. First, suppose that some hypothesis provides a better explanation of other beliefs within a system having a maximum of explanatory coherence, even though the explanation is not fully adequate. Imagine, for example, that a man has been shot and that the maid is the prime suspect. Her fingerprints are on the gun and she admits the deed. Moreover, suppose that she has a motive. Nevertheless, imagine that she has never fired a gun previously, the spot from which she would have had to fire the gun was a good distance from the victim, and moreover, there are footprints outside the window and in the room where the crime took place, made by boots which clearly were not worn by the maid. Even if the maid avows that she made the footprints with boots to turn suspicion away from herself and then destroyed the boots, we may have our doubts. They hypothesis that she shot the victim may be the best explanation because we can conceive of no better one. In this situation, we would not claim to know; there is too much in doubt for that; and, even if we do believe that the maid is the killer, we would not be completely justified in accepting this. We would not think we were that well justified, nor would others.

Following the justificatory theory offered above, we would be completely justified in accepting that the maid is the killer. This suggests that we must require that a hypothesis not only explain better than any alternative we can conceive but also be a comparatively good explanation, good enough so that we are completely justified in accepting it. More generally, beliefs must cohere in some comparatively *strong* way with other beliefs within a system for such coherence, however it is explicated, to yield complete justification.

Our final objection to the explanatory coherence theory is that it has a defect characteristic of coherence theories, to wit, inconsistent statements turn out to be completely justified. Two systems of beliefs may each have a maximum of explanatory coherence and yet be inconsistent with each other. There may be two or more systems of beliefs each having a maximum of explanatory coherence. Each may be such that no other consistent system of beliefs leaves less unexplained, and none explains what it does explain better. Consequently, a belief may cohere with one system of beliefs having a maximum of explanatory coherence while the contradictory of that belief coheres with another system of beliefs having a maximum of explanatory coherence. In the current account both beliefs would be completely justified.

One might attempt to meet this objection by (i) requiring that there be *one* system which is, from the standpoint of explanation, the best, or (ii) requiring that the concept of complete justification be made relative to a system. Both these maneuvers fail. The first fails because we have no reason to believe that there is *one* best system from the standpoint of explanation. There are always conflicting theories concerning some aspect of experience that are equally satisfactory from the standpoint of explanation. Hence, if it is required that there be a best overall system before any belief is completely justified, we shall never be completely justified.

As for the second suggestion that complete justification be made relative to a system of beliefs, there remain two objections. First, and perhaps most important, the question of whether a person is completely justified in accepting that *p* is not answered by the announcement that he is completely justified in accepting it relative to a system *B*. We must ask whether a person who is completely justified in his belief relative to system *B* is completely justified in his belief. In other words, is system *B* a system to which a man may appeal to justify his beliefs completely? If *B* is but one of a set of systems having maximal explanatory coherence which are inconsistent with each other, then we have no way of answering this question.

We are left with the problem of inconsistent *systems* of beliefs having a maximum of explanatory coherence, and, consequently, inconsistent beliefs being completely justified by such systems. It is interesting to notice that the very defect of idealistic coherence theories, the inconsistency of equally coherent theories, is also a defect of the theory of explanatory coherence. Moreover, the difficulty is not hard to discern. No relation between statements suffices for complete justification. In addition to relations between statements, some other feature must be an ingredient of justification.

Simplicity and Conservation

Some philosophers, such as Sellars, Quine, and Harman, for example, have appealed to the simplicity of the overall system to supply the needed additional ingredients.[17] Of two systems both of which have a maximum of explanatory coherence, the simpler of the two is the one providing complete justification for beliefs within it. There are some objections to this strategy. First, simplicity is both obscure and complex. The complexity of simplicity results from the different ways in which one system can be simpler than another and from a certain stress between these modes of simplicity. One system may be simpler than another in terms of the postulates of the system; in terms of the basic concepts of the system; or, in terms of the ontology of the system. We have, at least, postulational, conceptual, and ontological simplicity to consider, and these modes of simplicity may conflict. We sometimes purchase conceptual simplicity at the cost of multiplying entities in our ontology. Moreover, the notion of simplicity is hardly pellucid. It is difficult, even on intuitive grounds, to judge when one system is simpler than another. When a philosopher says his system is simpler than another, one may fairly suspect him of special pleading for the sort of system he prefers. Perhaps there is some common feature of such preferred systems. Or maybe such preferences are shaped by the cognitive fashions of the decade. No matter, we may reasonably doubt whether there is any sufficiently articulate conception of simplicity to which impartial appeal could be made in choosing between explanatory systems.

Even if we were to grant, however, that there is some serviceable conception of simplicity, this would fail to resolve the problem before us. There may be two systems that are not only maximal with respect to explanatory coherence but are also minimal with respect to complexity. If we have two systems that are equally coherent and equally simple, we shall have no way of deciding which system provides complete justification for the beliefs within it. Moreover, we actually complicate matters by introducing the concept of simplicity. Now we must balance simplicity against coherence when, for example, one system is slightly more coherent and leaves more unexplained, while the other is slightly simpler and presupposes a smaller ontology.

Finally, the appeal to simplicity exacerbates a problem we left unsolved above, namely, that we may justify beliefs by depleting a system of statements to be explained. By rejecting concepts and entities, we can obtain a simpler system as well as a more coherent one. If we seek both simplicity and coherence, we shall have the very strongest motive for rejecting observation statements for the purpose of reducing what needs to be explained, thereby obtaining greater explanatory coherence and simplicity. We again confront the sterile simplicity of a system confined to one theory, one law, and one set of confirming singular statements. Everything else may be hygienically disposed of, to avoid explanatory untidiness, and thus keep the system clean and neat.

The authors cited appeal to a principle of conservation in an effort to escape the unwanted diminishment of the system. Sellars stresses the need to conserve observation statements.[18] Quine and Harman refer to a principle of conservativeness or laziness in the general retention of beliefs.[19] If we apply their remarks to the problem before us, it is proposed that if two systems are equal in explanatory coherence and simplicity, and all others are less coherent and less simple, then that system provides complete justification for beliefs within it which conserves what we believe, at least among statements of a specified variety.

The primary problem with this proposal is simply that it is a principle of epistemic conservatism, a precept to conserve accepted opinion. Sometimes, such a precept may provide good counsel, but often it will not. The overthrow of accepted opinion and the dictates of commonsense are often essential to epistemic advance. Moreover, an epistemic adventurer may arrive at beliefs that are not only new and revelatory but also better *justified* than those more comfortably held by others. The principle of the conservation of accepted opinion is a roadblock to inquiry and, consequently, it must be removed.

The preceding remarks are less than argument. Moreover, this principle of conservation, though wide of the mark, embodies at least one important insight, to wit, that whether a person is completely justified in accepting something depends on her actual beliefs. Indeed, the fact of belief itself, the subjective reality of conviction, provides the basis for a satisfactory coherence theory of justification. Such a coherence theory of justification based on the existence of belief and upon the comparative degree of such beliefs will find maxims of conservation and stability unnecessary and unwarranted. On the contrary, such a theory contains within it an explication of the way in which shifts and changes of belief, however radical, bring with them changes in what a person is completely justified in accepting. Before turning to the development of these ideas, however, it will be useful to have a summary of the results of this chapter before us.

Summary

We have found three major reasons for rejecting the explanatory coherence theory of justification developed at the beginning of the chapter. First, the explanatory coherence of a system could be increased by decreasing what needs explanation. We thus reduce the problem of explanation by systematically denying the truth of those statements describing whatever is unexplained until we obtain a very simple system in which everything is perfectly explained because there is almost nothing to explain. No explanatory function or role of statements suffices to prevent this artificial manipulation of explanatory systems. Second, we found examples of statements and beliefs that were completely justified by general statements within a system, such as the conclusion derived from the Pythagorean theorem, quite independently of any explanatory role or function of such statements. Finally, systems may tie for the award of being the system with a maximum of explanatory coherence. A statement completely justified with respect to one such system is not justified with respect to another. Indeed, some statement inconsistent with the first may be completely justified in another equally maximal system.

All these difficulties spring from the same source. Having abandoned a foundation theory in which justification is built upon self-justified basic beliefs, we are led by the explanatory coherence theory to build justification on the explanatory relations between statements. Such explanatory relations will not suffice, however. Explanatory relations between statements fail to pick out a *unique* set of completely justified beliefs, because we may, with sufficient imagination, concoct a myriad of different systems of statements in which such explanatory relations hold. Explanatory relationships *can* yield complete justifications—in this the theory is correct—but there must also be some other ingredient determining what needs to be explained in the first place. Here one might be tempted to waver and return to the theory for a supply of basic beliefs in need of explanation. But that way is closed. We must proceed without a signpost guaranteeing the way to truth. There is nothing other than the coherence among our beliefs on which to rely.

The element needed to produce a sound coherence theory has been constantly before us. The goal of acceptance, acceptance being the sort of belief required to yield justification, is to obtain truth and avoid error. This is why the objective of maximizing coherence is neither necessary nor sufficient for the sort of justification we have been seeking. We may aim at truth without aiming at explanation, and we may aim at explanation without aiming at truth.[20] We need not seek any guarantee for the truth of what we believe, nor need we appeal to explanatory relations among beliefs to provide a justification. A set of beliefs which arise from the quest to accept what is true and avoid accepting what is false can provide complete justification to deserving beliefs among its membership without appeal to explanation, simplicity or conservation, while those that arise from an interest in other matters may prove epistemically impotent. Let us consider what sort of justification may be obtained simply from fidelity to the goal of accepting something just in case it is true.

Introduction to the Literature

The traditional defender of the explanatory coherence theory is Wilfrid Sellars in *Science, Perception and Reality*. Bruce Aune carried on the tradition in *Knowledge, Mind and Nature*. Gilbert Harman has written two very readable books, *Thought* and, more recently, *Change in View*. The former is, perhaps, the most accessible formulation of the explanatory coherence theory. See also Alan Goldman's, *Empirical Knowledge*, William Lycan's, *Judgement and Justification*, and Jay Rosenberg's, *Our World and Our Knowledge of It*. For a single article applying the explanatory coherence theory to the problem of other minds, see Paul Ziff's "The Simplicity of Other Minds."

6

Internal Coherence
and Personal Justification

JUSTIFICATION IS COHERENCE with a background system. In the preceding chapter, we considered a theory according to which justification consists of explanatory relations within a system of beliefs. The objectives of accepting what is true and avoiding accepting what is false are best served, according to that theory, by maximizing explanatory coherence. A principle can serve the purposes of truth, however, while lacking explanatory merit. The Pythagorean theorem suffices to obtain the truth about distances whatever its explanatory limitations. We shall correct the defect in the explanatory coherence theory by giving truth its due. To this end, we emphasize acceptance as the central notion. It is what we accept in the interests of obtaining truth and avoiding error, our *acceptance system*, that constitutes the relevant background system. Coherence with our acceptance system is determined by what it is reasonable to accept based on this system. A concern for truth and nothing but the truth drives the engine of justification.

We shall begin with what we accept. From what we accept, we shall generate a notion of subjective or personal justification. Why begin, subjectively, with acceptance? Not because we have any guarantee of truth in that domain. We err about the character of our own mental states as we do about the external world. Indeed, our capacity for precise observation of the external world of objects and properties is more refined than our capacity for observing the internal world of thoughts and sensations. We start with what we accept for lack of another alternative. One might protest that we should begin with experience, with the prick of sense. The stimulation of our senses raises the question of what we should accept, however, rather than answering it. Our senses may give rise to some conception or belief about what is transpiring in our sensory neighborhood. How are we to decide, though, whether what is suggested to us by our senses is true and accurate rather than false and illusory? We must consult information about the matter. What is this information? It is what we have accepted in the quest for truth. It is our background system of accepted information. The evaluation of all claims to truth, whether those of our senses, of reasoning, of memory, or of the testimony of others, must be based on our acceptance system, which contains our conception of the world and our access to it. There is no exit from the circle of what we accept. Acceptance is the fuel for the engine.

Acceptance and Belief Reconsidered

How does an acceptance system generate justification? It does so by telling us how reasonable it is to accept something in the quest for truth. Our acceptance system tells us it is more reasonable to accept one thing than another and more reasonable to accept something on one assumption than on another when we seek truth, that is, seek to accept something if and only if it is true. Consider the distinction between acceptance and belief that we propounded in Chapter 2. Many false ideas are presented to us in attractive ways and may, as a result, be believed when we know they are false. A politician may convince you of the truth of what he says when you know that he is untrustworthy. You know he will say whatever is needed to obtain your vote with practiced persuasiveness. You can see it in his ambitious eyes. But you want to believe him. You want to believe that the economy is stronger, that you are economically secure, especially when the objective measures are alarming. He is warm, human, and comforting, while the data are cold, mathematical, and distressing. How can you resist? You do believe him, but you know that the economy is slipping.

How are we to account for this conflict between knowledge and belief? We are divided into separate systems. One is truth-seeking, and it contains what we accept in the interests of obtaining truth and avoiding error, of accepting something just in case it is true. The other system is the yield of habit, instinct, and need. Often the two coincide. For the most part, what we believe is also something we accept in the interests of obtaining truth and avoiding error, and what we accept in this way is also something we believe. Sometimes the ways divide, however. Sometimes the voice of truth speaks against the more ancient tongue of belief. We do not accept what the politician tells us as the *bona fide* truth even if we cannot help but believe him.

Take another example. We look at the stars on a summer night and believe that they all exist somewhere far away from us in the heavens. As we look, we cannot help but believe that these bright objects now exist. Yet, science tells us that some of them have long since disappeared and only the light traveling through space is reaching us after an astronomic delay. Science, not our eyes, is to be trusted, and so we do not accept what our eyes tell us. An ancient system of perceptual belief conflicts with the scientific system of acceptance. Traditional philosophers spoke of a conflict between reason and belief, while modern philosophers may be more inclined to speak of a conflict between a central system capable of ratiocination and some more automatic input system. Whether we prefer a traditional or modern construction, one system, the acceptance system, acts as judge of the other to obtain truth and avoid error.

Justification and Reasonable Acceptance

An acceptance system yields justification by informing us that it is more reasonable to accept some things than others, but how does it do this? The answer should be clear from what has gone before. An acceptance system tells us when we should trust our sources of information, when we should trust our senses and when not, when we should trust our memory and when not, when we should trust the testimony of another and when not, when we should trust some method of science and when not.

My acceptance system tells me that if I see what looks like a handbag on my dining table in the front room, it is more reasonable to trust my eyes and accept that it is a handbag than to accept that it is not. By contrast, if I see what looks like a handbag in a plastic case, in an art museum with the label reading, "Marilyn Levine, Ceramic Object," my acceptance system tells me it is more reasonable for me to accept that the object is not a handbag but a ceramic sculpture of one. I may be wrong in both instances. My wife may have purchased a ceramic work of art and put it on our dining table, or Marilyn Levine may have put a leather handbag in the plastic case to construct a work of conceptual art with a misleading label. My acceptance system is fallible, naturally, but it is the instrument I must use at this moment to decide what to accept on the basis of the information I now possess. In deciding whether to accept something or not at the present moment, reason requires the use of the relevant information I have accumulated in the quest for truth. That information is contained in my acceptance system.

My acceptance system changes in response to new data and further ratiocination, but at any moment it represents the outcome of my efforts, however brilliant or ineffectual, to distinguish truth from error. I may be justly criticized for not having done better in sorting truth from error in the past, but I cannot be faulted for judging now on the basis of my present acceptance system. I confront the question of whether or not to accept some information that I receive, that the economy is improving, or that a star exists. My acceptance system answers the question by telling me how reasonable it is to accept the information in comparison to other competing considerations. If, on the basis of my acceptance system, the information is more trustworthy considered in terms of source and circumstance than conflicting or undermining objections, then it is more reasonable for me to accept the information on the basis of that system because of the way it coheres with that system. That is the way coherence yields justification.

Justification, Reasonableness, and Coherence

We are now in a position to give an account of coherence and justification based on the notion of an acceptance system. We began with the schema

S is justified in accepting that p at t if and only if p coheres with system X of S at t

and noted that it was necessary to specify a system and a relation of coherence in order to complete the account. We have indicated that we are going to begin by giving an account of personal or subjective justification, and the appropriate system for explicating such justification is the acceptance system of S at t. We may, therefore, fill in the reference to a system, noting at the same time the restriction to an account of personal justification, as follows:

S is personally justified in accepting that p at t if and only if p coheres with the acceptance system of S at t.

Personal justification will provide us with a first component in an adequate account of complete justification. Because of the entirely subjective character of the notion of an acceptance system, our account of personal justification must be combined with an objective constraint to yield complete justification. The problem immediately before us, however, is to analyze the notion of coherence in the schema above. We can execute this analysis by appeal to what it is reasonable to accept on the basis of an acceptance system.

Let us begin by assuming that we are able to tell when it is more reasonable to accept one thing than another on the basis of our own acceptance system. Proceeding subjectively, I can dispense with certain skeptical proposals in short order. Consider the skeptical suggestion that I might at this very moment be hallucinating, deceived by some powerful demon, or having my disembodied brain stimulated electronically by some scientist.[1] On the basis of my acceptance system, it is more reasonable for me to accept that I see a cat before me than that I am hallucinating. Why? I accept that I can tell when I am not hallucinating. I accept that I have refrained from ingesting hallucinogenic substances, and that there is no indication in my experience of hallucination. I may not be able to say how I can tell that I am not hallucinating at the moment, but I accept my trustworthiness in the matter. This is not, of course, a refutation of the skeptic. It is a statement of the consequences of what I accept.

Similarly, I accept that I can tell that I am not now deceived by a powerful demon or a powerful scientist, though, again, I may not be able to say how I can tell that these things are so. Suppose some skeptic suggests that everything that I accept is the result of the mind washing efforts of a Cartesian demon powerful enough to determine completely what I accept. With a twisted grin, the skeptic might note that I might be completely alone in the world with the exception of the undisclosed demon and not have a single external object on which to sit in my epistemic desperation. I have two possiblities. I can accept what the skeptic says. In that case I shall become demented, and there is no cure for that in epistemology. Or I can reject what the skeptic says while admitting the logical consistency of the skeptical fantasy. I accept the trustworthiness of my senses and reason while admitting the logical consistency of the skeptical oddity. On the basis of what I thus accept, it is more reasonable for me to accept the existence of others and of the objects of the external world than to accept the existence of the deceptive demon. In general, how reasonable it is for me to accept something will depend on the information I accept about my trustworthiness in the matter. When I have no reason to trust some source of information, then my acceptance system fails to provide any basis for considering it more reasonable to accept the information I receive from that source than to reject it.

These remarks, cursory as they are, reveal a connection between coherence with an acceptance system and the reasonableness of accepting something. Some claims conflict with others, as my claim that I see a cat conflicts with the skeptical claim that I am hallucinating. If it is more reasonable for me to accept one of these conflicting claims than the other on the basis of my acceptance system, then that claim fits better or coheres better with my acceptance system. The claim that I see a cat coheres with my acceptance system while the conflicting claim that I am hallucinating does not cohere with that system. My acceptance system does not supply me with the original conviction that I am seeing a cat; perception does that. On the other hand, my acceptance system adjudicates in favor of the conviction against those with which it conflicts and justifies me in accepting the conviction. Thus, what I accept coheres with my acceptance system if that system favors what I accept over competing claims, those of a skeptic, for example.

The foregoing reflections suggest the following preliminary definition:

> p coheres with the acceptance system of S at t if and only if it is more reasonable for S to accept p than to accept any competing claim on the basis of the acceptance system of S at t.

The notion of an acceptance system and of competition have been informally explained but should now be defined; first, we define the notion of an acceptance system:

> The acceptance system of S at t may be defined as the set of statements of the form—S accepts that p—attributing to S just those things S accepts at t with the objective of obtaining truth and avoiding error with respect to the content accepted, that is, with respect to the content that p.

Competition Defined

The notion of competition is more problematic. One might think that competitors of a given claim are those claims that contradict it. Claims that contradict a given claim do compete with it, but some claims that do not contradict the claim also may compete with it. The example of hallucination was such an example. The claim that I see a cat is not contradicted by the claim that I am hallucinating, for it is logically possible for a person to actually see a cat even though he is hallucinating. The claim that I am hallucinating does not logically conflict with the claim that I see a cat, but the assumption that I am hallucinating would make it less reasonable for me to accept that I am seeing a cat than the opposite assumption. If I am hallucinating, then I am less trustworthy about what I see than if I am not hallucinating. The desired notion of competition may be defined in terms of a comparative conception of reasonableness on an assumption as follows:

> c competes with p for S on system X at t if and only if it is less reasonable for S to accept that p on the assumption that c is true

than on the assumption that c is false on the basis of the system X at t.

The foregoing definition contains a variable X that may be replaced by reference to the acceptance system of S to obtain the required notion of competition on the basis of an acceptance system. The defnition is given in this general form so that we may avail ourselves of the definition in order to define competition on the basis of other systems later. The definition of competition on the basis of acceptance obtained from the foregoing is as follows:

> c competes with p for S on the basis of the acceptance system of S at t if and only if it is less reasonable for S to accept that p on the assumption that c is true than on the assumption that c is false on the basis of the acceptance system of S at t.

Having defined competition in this way, we must now reconsider whether our definition of justification in terms of coherence is adequate. If it is more reasonable to accept something than to accept any of its competitors, it is natural to think of it as *beating* its competitors. The notion of *beating* may be defined as follows:

> p beats c for S on X at t if and only if c competes with p for S at t and it is more reasonable for S to accept that p than to accept that c on X at t.

These definitions suggest that a person is personally justified in accepting something just in case it coheres with the acceptance system of the person in the sense of beating all competition on the basis of the acceptance system. Therefore, we might define personal justification as follows:

> S is personally justified in accepting that p at t if and only if p beats everything that competes with p on the basis of the acceptance system of S at t.

We shall attempt to clarify the implications of this definition with some examples and then note a defect that requires some amendment of it.

The Justification Game: Replying to a Skeptic

How are we to decide whether something that competes with a given claim is beaten? It is not necessary that a person have reflected on the competitor for the competitor to be beaten, but it is necessary that the acceptance system of the person imply that it is more reasonable to accept the claim than the competitor. If the acceptance system of a person implies that it is more reasonable to accept that p than to accept that c, then the person must be in a state to think and reason as though this were true. We can determine that this is so by imagining how a person would respond to skeptical questions. We imagine a game a person plays with a skeptic to show that she is personally justified in accepting what she does. Let us refer to the game as the *justification game.*

The justification game is played in the following way. The claimant presents something she accepts as true. The skeptic may then raise any objection in the form of a competitor of what the claimant presents. If what the claimant accepts is something that is more reasonable for her to accept than the skeptical objection, that is, if the competitor cited by the skeptic is beaten, then the claimant wins the round. If all the competitors raised by the skeptic are beaten, then the claimant wins the game. If she wins the game, she is personally justified in accepting what she presented; if not, she is not personally justified. The game is a heuristic device for understanding the considerations that make a person justified in accepting something rather than a psychological model of mental processes.

Let us consider a few rounds of the justification game played by an imaginative skeptic with me as the claimant. In this game, the skeptic objects to a claim of mine. The claim may be considered as a statement of something I accept, or, to give a little added vivacity to the game, to something I claim to know. In earlier chapters, we noted that our justification for what we accept depends on background information. This information is contained in the acceptance system and accounts for the reasonableness of the reply to the skeptic. It is what makes it more reasonable for me to accept what I do than the competitors presented by the skeptic.

Imagine that I am at the Edinburgh Zoo looking at a zebra. The animal is a paradigm example of a zebra and the sign before me says 'zebra'. I would claim to know that I see a zebra. So I enter that as the claimant in the justification game.

Claimant: I see a zebra.
Skeptic: You are asleep and dreaming that you see a zebra.

Claimant: It is more reasonable for me to accept that I see a zebra than that I am asleep and dreaming that I see a zebra. (I can tell that I am awake and not asleep and dreaming now. My experience does not feel at all like a dream and I have a distinct memory of what preceded my present experience, leaving my hotel, taking the cab to the zoo, buying a ticket, all of which is trustworthy information that I am now at the zoo looking at a zebra and not asleep and dreaming.)

Skeptic: You are awake but hallucinating a zebra.

Claimant: It is more reasonable for me to accept that I see a zebra than that I am hallucinating a zebra. (There is nothing in my experience that would lead me to think that I am hallucinating, nor does my memory of the past indicate that there is any reason to think that I might be hallucinating now. There is no indication that I am hallucinating and trustworthy evidence that I am not.)

Skeptic: You are seeing a mule painted with stripes to look like a zebra.

Claimant: It is more reasonable for me to accept that I see a zebra than that I see a mule painted with stripes to look like a zebra. (Though I have no specific information about the stripes, I have no reason to believe that the Edinburgh Zoo would paint a mule to look like a zebra and identify it as a zebra, or be deceived by somebody else doing so. The Scots are known for their honesty. So my perceptual evidence is trustworthy information that the animal is a zebra.)

Skeptic: You are generally deceived in a systematic way and see nothing. You are either a disembodied mind deceived by a Cartesian demon or disembodied brain lying in a vat deceived by electrical information supplied to the brain by a scientist.

Claimant: It is more reasonable for me to accept that I see a zebra than that I am generally deceived in a systematic way and see nothing. (I have no reason to think that I am deceived in a systematic way and, though it would be impossible to detect such a systematic deception, the hypothesis is totally improbable. By contrast, the information that I have that I see a zebra is trustworthy and renders it very improbable that I am deceived.)

The justification game played to the point reached above leaves the claimant the victor in each round. There is no pretension that the claimant has refuted the skeptic. The claimant's replies are, however, adequate replies for the purposes of exhibiting personal justification. The parenthetical remarks illustrate the sense in which coherence with my acceptance system is what personally justifies me in accepting what I do, that I see a zebra. Each challenge of the skeptic is rejected on the grounds that it does not cohere with what I accept, as the parenthetical remarks indicate, while my claim that I see a zebra does cohere with that system. The parenthetical remarks are part of my acceptance system. They are a brief summary of my relevant information.

A Foundationalist Objection

One traditional foundationalist objection arises and must be met, however. A detractor will point out that the parenthetical remarks might be unjustified, even subjectively. How, she might inquire, can I be justified in accepting that I see a zebra on the basis of things that I accept but am not justified in accepting? The fundamental reply is that each of the things that I accept may be claims that I am justified in accepting because of other information I accept. Still, the foundationalist might persist, suppose that you only accepted one thing, then it would cohere with itself, and surely that is not the sort of justification required for knowledge. Moreover, even if a person accepts many things, it is possible that one claim stands in isolation from everything else. Again, since that one thing coheres with itself, the person will, unfortunately, turn out to be personally justified in accepting that one claim as a simple result of accepting it.

How are we to reply to the foundationalist? First of all, mere acceptance of something by itself does not suffice to yield the result that it is more reasonable to accept it than its competitors, and the objection fails for that reason. If mere acceptance does not suffice, what does? From the short justification game played above, the answer should be apparent. It is not enough that one accept something for it to be more reasonable than its competitors on the basis of one's acceptance system. One must have some information that such acceptance is a trustworthy guide to truth. The objective of acceptance is to obtain truth and avoid error in the specific thing accepted. For it to be reasonable to think one has succeeded, one must have information to meet the objections of a skeptic in the justification game. If I put forth the claim that I see a zebra and the skeptic counters with the claim that I do not, it is no answer to the skeptic to say that I accept that I see a zebra. I must have reason to think that I can tell a zebra when I see one in circumstances like those I am in at the moment and, consequently, am trustworthy in such matters.

The Principle of Trustworthiness

The foregoing answer leads to the final dialectical move. The foundationalist will surely note that everything depends now on the claim that my acceptance is a trustworthy guide to truth and that I am trustworthy as I aver. She will inquire how that claim is itself justified. The claim that I am trustworthy in any particular matter under any special set of circumstances may be justified on the basis of the other things that I accept; I accept that I have had success in reaching the truth about similar matters in similar circumstances in the past and that the present circumstances do not differ in any relevant way from past circumstances when I was correct. There is, however, more to the issue. I may accept that my faculties, perception, memory, reasoning, and so forth are trustworthy guides to truth in circumstances of the sort that I find myself in when I accept some claim of those faculties. I must accept, however, that I am trustworthy as well: that when I accept something, that is a good enough reason for thinking it to be true, so that it is at least more reasonable for me to accept it than to accept its denial.

Thus, there is one special principle of an acceptance system, to wit, that one is trustworthy in matters of obtaining truth and avoiding error. This amounts to the following principle formulated in the first person:

T. Whatever I accept with the objective of accepting something just
in case it is true, I accept in a trustworthy manner.

If someone else accepts that I am trustworthy in this way, then my accepting something will be a reason for her to accept it. Similarly, if I accept that I am trustworthy in this way, then my accepting something will be a reason for me to accept it. Another person might be confronted with some other considerations that cast enough doubt on whether what I accept is true, even granting my trustworthiness, so that my accepting something, though providing a reason for her accepting it, does not justify her in accepting what I do. My accepting something when I am confronted with similar considerations casting doubt on whether what I accept is true, would not justify me in accepting it when I do either.

Trustworthiness as a Principle of Detachment

The consequence of adding principle (T) to my acceptance system is that whatever I accept is more reasonable for me to accept than its denial. It has the effect of permitting me to detach the content of what I accept from my acceptance of the content. My acceptance system tells me that I accept that p, accept that q, and so forth. Suppose I wish to justify accepting that p on the basis of my acceptance system telling me that I accept that p. How am I to detach the conclusion that p from my acceptance system? The information that I accept that p, which is included in my acceptance system, does not justify detaching p from my acceptance of it in order to obtain truth and avoid error. I need the additional information that my accepting that p is a trustworthy guide to these ends. Principle (T) supplies that information and, therefore, functions as a principle of detachment. It is the rule that enables me to detach the conclusion that p from my acceptance of p.

The manner in which we trust what we accept indicates that we do accept that we are trustworthy. The mark of our regarding a person as trustworthy is that we trust them, and this applies to ourselves as well. The acceptance of (T) is, perhaps, the result of our nature and universal among people, but this is by no means certain. Some more restricted principle may supplant it in a reflective person, forcing her to arrive at the conclusion that she is trustworthy in some domains but not others. She might accept that she is not trustworthy in some domains, for, despite her best efforts not to accept things without adequate evidence, she often commits a kind of doxastic *akrasia* and accepts some things without adequate reason. For example she might be attracted to particularly elegant mathematical principles and, as a result, accept some principles as theorems because of their elegance, without adequate consideration of the proofs offered for them.

If, however, a person does accept (T) in full generality, then her acceptance of (T) itself will have the result that it is more reasonable to accept (T) than its denial. For, of course, the principle applies to itself. It yields the results that if she accepts (T) with the objective of accepting it just in case it is true, then she does so in a trustworthy way. Thus, principle (T) not only provides for the detachment of other things we accept from our acceptance of them, it provides for the detachment of itself as well. To avoid the paradoxes discussed in Chapter 2, we might avail ourselves of various technical strategies.

It is, however, more natural simply to regard a person as applying principle (T) to itself. As such, it can play a special role. Just as the addition of the principle has the result that other things we accept are things it is more reasonable for us to accept than their denials, so the addition has the result that it is more reasonable for us to accept (T) than its denial. To borrow an analogy from Re'd, just as light, in revealing the illuminated object, at the same time reveals itself, so the principle, in rendering the acceptance of other things more reasonable than not, at the same time renders the acceptance of itself more reasonable than not.[2]

This does not entail, as the foundationalist might wish, that we are personally justified in accepting the principle, only that it is more reasonable to accept it than to accept its denial. Some competitor of it might not be beaten. One such competitor is the fallibilistic claim that we are sometimes in error in what we accept. To meet such a competitor, we need more information about the sort of circumstances in which we err and those in which we do not. Thus, even in the case of principle (*T*), we require some background information in order to be personally justified in accepting the principle. If, however, the foundationalists are incorrect in arguing that there are basic beliefs that justify themselves, they are right in thinking that there are some beliefs that may contribute along with other beliefs to their own justification.

Neutralizing Competitors

There is another objection to the theory of personal justification that is more difficult to meet. It is that some objections a skeptic might raise cannot be expected to be beaten in cases in which a person is personally justified in accepting something and, indeed, knows that what he thus accepts is true. The reason is that some things that compete with a claim may do so only very indirectly and may, as a result, be very reasonable to accept. Let us return to the justification game between myself as the claimant and the skeptic. Consider the zebra example again.

> *Claimant:* I see a zebra.
> *Skeptic:* People sometimes dream that they see zebras.

Suppose that I remember having had a very strange dream full of strange episodes, not at all like everyday life, in which I dreamt I saw a zebra. Though I have not the least doubt about whether I am dreaming at the moment, that is, I am sure that I am at the Edinburgh Zoo looking at a zebra, I must concede that the skeptic has presented a competitor. Let us compare the following two assumptions:

> *A.* People sometimes dream that they see zebras.
> *NA.* People never dream that they see zebras.

It is more reasonable for me to accept that I see a zebra on the assumption that (*NA*) is true than on the assumption that (*A*) is true. Why? If people sometimes dream that they see zebras, which they do, then they might be misled into accepting that they see zebras when they are only dreaming that they do: while if they never dream that they see zebras, then they will not be misled in this way. If people are misled in this way, then, of course, I might be misled in this way.

It is clear what the reply should be, namely, that (*A*) is irrelevant because I am not dreaming. Thus, I should be allowed a step in the game which, though it does not consist of beating the competitor offered by the skeptic, does neutralize the skeptic's objection. Thus, I should be allowed to proceed in the game as follows:

Claimant: I see a zebra.
Skeptic: People sometimes dream that they see zebras.
Claimant: I am not dreaming.

Under what conditions, though, should neutralizing replies like the last be allowed?

The answer depends on the reasonableness of accepting the neutralizer in conjunction with the competitor. If it is as reasonable for me to accept the competitor together with the neutralizer as to accept the competitor alone, then I may use the neutralizer as a reply to the skeptic in the justification game. Compare the following two statements:

C. People sometimes dream that they see zebras.

C&N. People sometimes dream that they see zebras but I am not dreaming.

On the basis of my acceptance system, it is as reasonable for me to accept the latter statement as to accept the former. There is, of course, some additional risk of error added to the latter, but the objective of accepting what is true supplements the objective of avoiding error. Put another way, (C) gives us less of the relevant truth about dreaming and seeing zebras that (C&N) does. The skeptical claim in the justification game outlined above is true, but it is misleading in the context because it suggests that I might be dreaming that I see a zebra. The neutralizing claim that I am not dreaming corrects this misleading suggestion. It successfully neutralizes the skeptical move. The conjunction (C&N) is, therefore, as reasonable for me to accept as (C) alone. We may define the notion of neutralization as follows:

n neutralizes *c* as a competitor of *p* for *S* on *X* at *t* if and only if *c* competes with *p* for *S* on *X* at *t*, but the conjunction of *c* and *n* does not compete with *p* for *S* on *X* at *t*, and it is as reasonable for *S* to accept the conjunction of *c* and *n* as to accept *c* alone on *X* at *t*.

The justification game should be amended to allow that the claimant be in a position either to beat or neutralize a competitor introduced as a move by the skeptic. A competitor may be neutralized by conjoining a neutralizer to the competitor and noting that the conjunction is as reasonable to accept as the competitor.

The Justification Game and
the Definition of Personal Justification

Reformulating the justification game to conform to this format, it would run as follows:

Claimant: I see a zebra.
Skeptic: People sometimes dream that they see zebras.
Claimant: It is as reasonable for me to accept both that people sometimes dream that they see zebras *and* that I am not dreaming as to accept the former alone. (My information that I am not dreaming is trustworthy and the information that people sometimes dream that they see zebras is misleading with respect to the question of whether I see a zebra. Conjoining that I am not dreaming produces a result that does not compete with my claim that I see a zebra.)

A claimant wins a round in the justification game just in case she can beat or neutralize the competitor produced by the skeptic. A claimant wins the justification game, showing that she is justified in accepting that p, just in case she wins every round in the justification game starting with the claim that p. We may put this more formally in terms of a general definition of justification as follows:

S is justified in accepting that p at t if and only if everything that competes with p for S on X at t is either beaten or neutralized for S on X at t.

Personal justification based on the acceptance system of a person may then be defined as follows:

S is personally justified in accepting that p at t if and only if everything that competes with p for S on the basis of the acceptance system of S at t is beaten or neutralized on the basis of the acceptance system of S at t.

This completes our account of personal justification.

Reasonableness and Probability

Coherence and personal justification have been defined in terms of reasonableness and acceptance directed at obtaining truth and avoiding error. Reasonableness has been taken as primitive. This has two constructive advantages. First of all, we acknowledge the normative aspect of justification. One ought not to accept something, if one is epistemically rational, when it is more reasonable to accept its denial. At the same time, we leave open the question of whether this notion of reasonableness is reducible to some naturalistic or nonnormative conception. Second, we allow for a plurality of factors to influence the normative evaluation. We have left it open what considerations might make it more reasonable to accept one thing rather than another in the quest for truth on the basis of one's acceptance system. We leave open the question of what sort of factors are relevant to obtaining truth and avoiding error. Most of the defenders of the coherence theory, Quine, Sellars, Harman, Aune, Rosenberg, and Bonjour have, in one way or another proposed that multiple factors determine whether a belief coheres with some system.[3] They have, however, differed among themselves as to what factors are relevant.

Is some naturalistic reduction of reasonableness possible? The simplest reduction would be to equate reasonableness with probability. For such an account to be naturalistic, we would have to be sure that the notion of probability was itself free from normative definition. This condition is not satisfied in those notions of probability which impose normative constraints on the assignment of probabilities. The equation of reasonableness with probability fails for other reasons, however. One needs to consider more than probability to decide whether it is more reasonable for a person to accept one thing than another. Since the equation of reasonableness with probability has so much intuitive lure and traditional backing, it is worth considering briefly why it should be rejected.

The basic reason for rejecting the equation of probability and reasonableness is that probability is only one factor relevant to deciding what is reasonable to accept in the interests of obtaining truth and avoiding error. One can see this from a simple example. Compare the following two claims:

It looks to me as though there is a computer in front of me.

There is a computer in front of me.

How would one compare the reasonableness of accepting each of these statements with the objective of obtaining truth and avoiding error? The first statement is less risky, but it tells us less. The second statement is a bit more risky, but it is more informative. As a result, we can say that the risk of error is greater in accepting the second than the first, but the gain in obtaining truth is greater in accepting the second than the first. This example reveals that the objectives of obtaining truth and avoiding error are distinct and may pull in opposite directions. The more informative a statement is, the more it tells us about the world, the greater our gain in accepting it if it is true and the greater our risk of error. The probability of a statement tells us what our risk of error is, but it tells us nothing about how much we gain in accepting it when it is true.

Major scientific claims, those concerning galaxies, genes, and electrons, for example, though among the most important things we accept and claim to know, are less probable than either of the cautious claims articulated above. The reasonableness of accepting such claims is influenced by our interest in accepting claims which, if true, are important general truths about ourselves and our universe. Given the past history of scientific claims, even those put forth by scientists of great genius, we must concede that the risk of error, the probability that these claims are false, is far from negligible. We can easily see that the interest in accepting what is true and the interest in avoiding accepting what is false may pull in opposite directions by considering the results of aiming at one to the exclusion of the other. If a person were only interested in avoiding error and indifferent to accepting truths, total success could be attained by accepting nothing at all. If, on the other hand, a person were only interested in accepting everything that is true and indifferent to accepting falsehoods, total success could be attained by accepting everything. The problem is to accept what is true while at the same time seeking to avoid error.

Reasonableness and Expected Utility

The foregoing ideas can be summarized in a simple mathematical representation. Suppose that we could specify what value or, more technically, the positive utility we assign to accepting some specific hypothesis, h, if h is true, and represent that by '$Ut(h)$', and, similarly, the negative utility we assign to accepting h, if h is false, and represent that by '$Uf(h)$'. Now, if we ask ourselves how reasonable it is to accept h in the interests of accepting what is true and avoiding accepting what is false, we must take into account the values of both $Ut(h)$ and $Uf(h)$. There are just two outcomes of accepting h, that h is true and that h is false, and we must take into account what value we attach to each of those outcomes. There is, however, another factor to consider, namely, how probable each of those outcomes is. So, if we let '$r(h)$' represent the degree of reasonableness of accepting *h*, and '*p(h)*' represent the probability of *h* being true and '*p(−h)*' as the probability of *h* being false, we obtain the following formula for computing the reasonableness of accepting *h:*

$$r(h) = p(h)Ut(h) + p(-h)Uf(h).^4$$

The reasonableness of accepting *h*, *r(h)*, the sum of two products, may be called the epistemic expected utility of accepting *h*. It is equal to the sum of one's positive expectation of accepting *h* when *h* is true and one's negative expectation of accepting *h* when *h* is false.

This formula clarifies precisely the consequences of identifying probability and reasonableness. To do so is mathematically equivalent to assigning a value of one to $Ut(h)$ and a value of zero to $Uf(h)$, no matter what *h* is. In that case, no matter what claim *h* might be, $r(h) = p(h)$. It is absurd, however, to regard all truths as equally worth accepting. Some truths are more valuable than others measured strictly in terms of obtaining truth about the world because, as we have noted, some truths tell us much more about the world than others. Therefore, the equation of reasonableness and probability must be rejected. Its rejection does not, of course, mean that probability is irrelevant to reasonableness. On the contrary, we can see that if the utilities of accepting two claims are the same, then the comparative reasonableness of accepting one in comparison to the other will be determined solely by the probabilities. This is more important than it might at first seem, because some competing claims satisfy the constraint of having the same utilities.

The Lottery Paradox

To see the importance of the preceding observation, consider the lottery paradox due to Kyburg.[5] The paradox proceeds from the assumption that some probability less than unity is sufficient for justified acceptance. Suppose that we pick a probability of .99 as sufficient. Consider, then, a lottery we know to be fair with one hundred tickets such that the winner has been drawn. In that case, any one of us could argue in the following manner: I am justified in accepting that the ticket number one has not won because the probability of its winning is only .01 and, therefore, the probability of its not winning is .99 as required. By the same argument, I am justified in accepting that each ticket has not won, for the probability of each ticket winning is .01 and of not winning is .99. The assumption that .99 is sufficient for justified acceptance will not permit me to argue that the conjunction of all these individual conclusions that I am thus justified in accepting is something that I am also justified in accepting. The set of conclusions I am justified in accepting to the effect that each of the tickets will not win is, however, logically inconsistent with my knowledge that one of them has won.

Though it may be improbable that a given ticket has won, there is a simple argument to the effect that I do not know that it has not won and, hence, that I would not be justified in claiming to know, or accepting, that it has not won. It is that I know that exactly the same reasoning is available to 'justify' accepting that the winning ticket has not won. The definition of justification given above, when combined with the formula for reasonable acceptance, yields the correct result that I am not justified in accepting that the number one ticket has not won. Consider the following move in the justification game:

Claimant: The number one ticket has not won.
Skeptic: The number two ticket has not won.

The skeptic has produced a competitor to my claim because, by definition, c competes with p just in case it is more reasonable to accept that p on the assumption that c is false than on the assumption that c is true. If what she has claimed is false and the number two ticket has won, then my claim must be true. On the other hand, on the assumption that what she has claimed is true, the probability of my claim is reduced to 98/99 because the number of potential winners is reduced to 99. In this case, the utilities of accepting the two claims, mine and the skeptic's, are obviously the same, and, therefore, the comparative reasonableness of the two claims is the same. Consequently, the skeptic's claim is not beaten, it is as reasonable as mine, and it cannot be neutralized either.

The Advantages of Truth

We have noted that the utility of accepting h when h is true depends on how much h tells us, on how informative h is. Therefore, the reasonableness or expected utility of accepting h is a function of the informativeness of h as well as of the probability of h. This observation sustains our earlier contention in the justification game that it may be as reasonable to accept some conjunction, that people sometimes dream they see zebras *and* I am not dreaming, as to accept only the first skeptical conjunct, that people sometimes dream they see zebras. The conjunction is less probable than the one conjunct because there is greater risk of error, but the conjunction is more informative and, given that the risk of error is negligible in either case, it is just as reasonable to accept the conjunction as the single conjunct.

This illustrates that it can be of greater advantage to accept one truth than another, depending on the characteristics of the truth, on its informativeness, for example. Other philosophers have insisted on other advantages of accepting a truth. They have insisted on the advantages of explanatory power, of simplicity, of pragmatic value, and even of conserving what one has already accepted, as we noted in the last chapter. Any of these factors may be relevant to the utility and expected utility of accepting something and, therefore, to the reasonableness of acceptance. It is, however, the truth of what is accepted that is paramount. Consequently, there is a barrier of risk below which we should not fall. No matter how much explaining we may accomplish by accepting *h*, no matter how simple or informative *h* may be, we cannot reasonably expect to gain anything in our attempt to obtain truth and avoid error when the risk of error is too great. Accepting a false explanation explains nothing. Accepting a simple hypothesis that is false may be nothing but an error of oversimplification. Accepting something of great informational content when it is false is only to accept a great amount of misinformation. The advantages of conserving error are minimal. Though we may value the other advantages of accepting a truth, it is the truth of what we accept which produces those advantages. Spices may enhance the flavor of good ingredients, but if the ingredients are spoiled, enhancing the flavor increases the risk of our consuming food that is dangerous to our health. Explanation, simplicity, and informativeness are but the spices of truth.

Introduction to the Literature

The most important recent books defending the sort of view contained in this chapter are Laurence BonJour's *The Structure of Empirical Knowledge* and the precursor of the present book, Keith Lehrer's *Knowledge*. The theories of Lehrer and BonJour are discussed by a number of authors with replies by Lehrer and BonJour in *The Current State of the Coherence Theory* by John W. Bender. For another article critical of Lehrer's theory, see John W. Bender's "Knowledge, Justification and Lehrer's Theory of Coherence." Also see Nicholas Rescher, *The Coherence Theory of Truth*, for another version of the coherence theory. The application of decision theory to epistemic problems was developed by Carl G. Hempel in "Deductive-Nomological vs. Statistical Explanation" and by Isaac Levi in *Gambling with Truth*, both difficult but readable works for those unafraid of symbols.

7

Coherence, Truth, and Undefeated Justification

SHOULD WE SAY that a person is completely justified in accepting everything that she is personally justified in accepting? Having reflected on the importance of truth, we must confront the objection that the acceptance system of a person could be mostly in error. As a result, we shall in this chapter construct a theory of how personal justification may be converted into complete and, indeed, undefeated justification which does not depend on error. To accomplish this, we need only amend the justification game we introduced in the last chapter to allow the skeptic greater advantage. Our account of undefeated justification arises from a technical problem, but the solution has more general implications. It will, as we shall see at the end of this chapter, allow us to reduce knowledge to undefeated justification. Finally, our analysis has the consequence, which we shall consider in subsequent chapters, that skepticism is in error.

The Uncharitable Possibility of Error

Some authors, most notably Davidson, deny the possibility that what we accept could be mostly in error.[1] That claim, if correct, would simplify our task, and so we begin by consideration of his argument. Davidson claims that a principle of charity in interpreting the beliefs of others requires that we interpret them in such a way as to make them turn out to be mostly true. Since charity begins at home, we are committed to the supposition that our beliefs, at least what we accept in the quest for truth, are mostly true. Assuming the principle of charity as a principle of interpreting the content of our beliefs, we must suppose that our beliefs are mostly true and the problem of acceptance systems wherein most of what is accepted is false would not arise. In that case, personal justification would coincide with complete justification. Thus, Davidson's proposed principle of charity is congenial to the account of justification offered here.

Unfortunately, the principle does not itself appear to be true. We may be in a position where it would be uncharitable or at least doxastically imperialistic to interpret the beliefs of another in such a way that they are mostly true. Suppose I am a nominalist. I confront someone who is such a devout platonist that he is careful to couch the content of every belief of his in platonistic terms and to reject everything not couched in such terms. When I believe that water is wet, he believes that water exemplifies the universal wetness and, indeed, rejects the simple claim that water is wet on the grounds that this is a deplatonized and hence erroneous description of the platonistic fact of exemplification. We have a similar difference of opinion about all matters of fact. When I believe that x is f, he believes that x exemplifies *Fness* and rejects the simple claim that x is f on grounds of the platonistic inadequacy of the description. He tells me, moreover, why he restricts his beliefs in this way. It is because of his devout commitment to platonism. On the basis of what I have thus discovered about his platonism, I would conclude from the perspective of a nominalist that he has succeeded in formulating all his categorical beliefs about the world in such a way that they are false. They all imply that something exemplifies some universal when, nominalism being true, nothing exemplifies a universal. Error dominates in his acceptance system.

Application of the principle of charity would require that I interpret as many of his beliefs as possible as true. To conform to this principle, I would need to interpret his beliefs in a deplatonized manner. I would have to interpret him as a nominalist. It is not clear how I should proceed to do this, and such an interpretation would be absurd in any case. Such examples show that the principle of charity is at best a defeasible method for interpreting the beliefs of others and, by extrapolation, our own beliefs as well. There is, unfortunately, no conceptual absurdity or necessary falsehood involved in supposing that most of what a person believes is false. Thus, any person, like our platonist, may turn out to have a prodigiously large collection of false beliefs. Personal justification does not automatically convert to complete justification as a result of the necessity of interpreting most of the acceptance system of a person as true, for there is no such necessity.

Personal justification is the basis of complete justification and, indeed, of undefeated justification. No one can be completely justified in accepting anything that he is not personally justified in accepting, but someone can fail to be completely justified in accepting something that he is personally justified in accepting. Anyone familiar with those who accept astrology as the basis of predicting the future or who accept the claim that the universe was created by God a few thousand years ago can illustrate the point. The latter sort of person may provide a reinterpretation of the data concerning the age of the universe by claiming that when God created the universe a few thousand years ago it was created in such way as to provide evidence of much more ancient existence, perhaps as a test of faith. An opponent might well need to concede that such a person is personally justified in accepting that the Alps have only existed for a few thousand years, but such an opponent would be disinclined to concede that his adversary is completely justified in accepting that the Alps are of such recent origin, particularly an opponent from geology.

Moreover, the reason for denying that the fundamentalist is completely justified cannot be that he or she is ignoring the evidence. On the contrary, we might suppose that the fundamentalist is also a geologist, one who takes special pleasure in observing that God has created the world in such a way that even the most precise scientific examination of geologists will not provide a clue as to the true origin of the universe. That is revealed through faith, not science. If such a person is not completely justified in accepting that the Alps are only a few thousand years old, this is not due to any lack of scientific acumen but to the falsity of a basic assumption and the consequences thereof. It is lack of truth, not lack of science, to which a critic must appeal.

Verific Justification

The foregoing suggests that complete justification is personal justification that is not based on error. If we agree that a person is personally justified in accepting something and also that the independent information cited in the justification game is correct information, then we should also agree that she is completely justified. This suggests a technical notion of justification based on what remains of the acceptance system of a person when all error is deleted. Consider the subsystem of the acceptance system when all error is deleted by dropping every member—S accepts that p—when p is false. The resulting subsystem of the acceptance system, which might be verified by an omniscient critic, we shall call the *verific system* of the person. We can then define a technical notion of verific justification as follows:

S is verifically justified in accepting that *p* at *t* if and only if S is justified in accepting that *p* on the basis of the verific system of S at *t*.

We may then combine justification and verific justification to obtain complete justification as follows:

S is completely justified in accepting that *p* if and only if S is personally and verifically justified in accepting that *p* at *t*.

In short, if a person is personally justified in accepting that *p* and would remain so if all errors in her acceptance system were eliminated, then the person is completely justified in accepting that *p*.

The Verific Justification Game and the Gettier Problem

We may illustrate the role of verific justification by considering the justification game amended to produce the verific justification game. The rules are the same with one exception. We assume the skeptic to be supplied with a list of what the claimant accepts with the truth or falsity of each item indicated. If the claimant appeals to anything false in a move, the skeptic in the verific justification game is allowed to disqualify the move by the claimant. The skeptic disqualifies a move by denying the false claim of the claimant following it with an exclamation mark and thereby wins the round. As an example of the verific justification game, consider the kind of counterexample Gettier raised against the claim that knowledge is justified true belief.[2] The claim is that someone in my class owns a Ferrari. Someone I know to be in my class, Mr. Nogot, says to me that he owns a Ferrari, shows me papers stating that he owns a Ferrari, and drives a Ferrari. I conclude that Mr. Nogot owns a Ferrari and, therefore, that someone in my class owns a Ferrari. In fact, another student in my class, Mr. Havit, owns a Ferrari, though I am entirely ignorant of this. The student I take to own a Ferrari, Mr. Nogot, does not own a Ferrari. He has lied to me, forged the papers, and so forth. Consider the following justification game:

Claimant: Someone in my class owns a Ferrari.
Skeptic: None of the students in your class who appear to own Ferraris actually own Ferraris.
Claimant: It is more reasonable for me to accept that at least one student in my class who appears to own a Ferrari does own a Ferrari than to accept that none of the students in my class who appear to own Ferraris actually own Ferraris. (Mr. Nogot owns

a Ferrari. He is also a student in my class. He has told me that
he owns a Ferrari, has shown me papers stating that he owns
a Ferrari, and he drives a Ferrari.)

Though the claimant wins the round understood as a round in the
original justification game, he loses the round understood as a round
in the verific justification game because the skeptic can disqualify the
claimant's last move. Thus, the final move in the verific justification
game would be a move of the skeptic indicating the false claim made
by the claimant as follows:

Skeptic: Mr. Nogot does not own a Ferrari!

The skeptic wins the round.

Does the foregoing loss of the round to the skeptic show that the
Gettier problem has been solved by denying that I am completely justified
in accepting that some student in my class owns a Ferrari? The example
in which my justification of this claim depends on my acceptance of
the claim that Mr. Nogot owns a Ferrari may be dealt with in terms
of the failure of the claimant to win the verific justification game. That
does not mean that the Gettier problem is solved, however. Gettier
noted that the justification of my claim that some student in my class
owns a Ferrari need not be based on acceptance of the false claim that
Mr. Nogot owns a Ferrari but might, instead, be based on the true
claims that Mr. Nogot told me he owns a Ferrari, showed me papers
stating he owns a Ferrari, and drives a Ferrari.[3] In this case, the second
move of the claimant in the justification game above would be as follows:

Claimant: It is more reasonable for me to accept that at least one
student in my class who appears to own a Ferrari does own a
Ferrari than to accept that none of the students in my class who
appear to own Ferraris actually own Ferraris. (Mr. Nogot is a
student in my class. He has told me that he owns a Ferrari, has
shown me papers stating that he owns a Ferrari, and he drives
a Ferrari.)

Here the claimant wins the round in the verific justification game,
for there is nothing false in what he claims, and, consequently, he may
win the game as well. This confirms Gettier's basic contention that
completely justified true belief may fall short of knowledge. We shall
find that a person's justification may depend on a false claim which
defeats the justification even though the person does not accept that
false claim. When the person does not accept the false claim, that Mr.

Nogot owns a Ferrari, for example, it will not appear in the verific justification game. So, it will not lead to the disqualification of any move of the claimant. We shall, consequently, need to seek a solution to the Gettier problem. We shall do so by adding an account of *undefeated* justification to our analysis of justification.

Some Inadequate Solutions

The most obvious solutions to the Gettier problem are, in fact, inadequate. For example, some philosophers aver that the problem is solved by requiring that for a person to know, her justification must not involve inference from a false premise.[4] Inference from a false premise, however, need not be involved, though it was in the original example.

Moreover, the justification that a person has for accepting a true statement may be noninferential, even though the justification is defeated by some false statement. An example from Chisholm, which we have already considered in another context, illustrates this quite clearly.[5] Suppose I see an object in a field that looks exactly like a sheep and I, in fact, take it for a sheep. If I have considerable experience with sheep, I may be justified in accepting that I see a sheep. Imagine that I also see another object at the same time which does not look like a sheep, though it is one, and which I do not take for one. If the object I thus take to be a sheep is not one, then I do not know that I see a sheep, even though I am justified in accepting, and do accept, that I see one. Since the second object I see actually is a sheep, it is true that I see a sheep. I have a justified true belief, but I do not know that I see a sheep because what I take for a sheep is not a sheep, and the sheep I see I do not take to be one. Here we do not have an inference in the example at all. It is a simple case of mistaking one thing for another. It is an example of noninferential perceptual error.

Such examples lead some philosophers to demand that what justifies a person in accepting something must not justify her in accepting any false statement at all. Nevertheless, it may well be that whatever justifies us in accepting anything also justifies us in accepting at least some false statements. Other philosophers have suggested that for a person to know something, she must not only be justified in accepting it, her justification must not contain any false statements or beliefs. This suggestion is, however, also inadequate.

A Harmless Error

Let us consider a small modification of the earlier example where Mr. Havit is replaced by a Mr. Knewit of whose Ferrari ownership I am knowledgeable. Suppose there are two men, Mr. Nogot and Mr. Knewit, each of whom I see before me with others in the room. Imagine that, from what I accept about Mr. Nogot, I am justified in accepting that he owns a Ferrari. Moreover, imagine that because of this, in response to the question of whether I know whether anyone in the room owns a Ferrari, I reply that I know that at least one person owns a Ferrari. Again, it seems that, if Mr. Nogot does not own a Ferrari but someone else in the room does, though I would have a justified true belief that at least one person in the room owns a Ferrari, I would not know this to be true. What justifies me in accepting this is my false belief that Mr. Nogot owns a Ferrari. Suppose, however, I am justified on independent grounds in accepting that Mr. Knewit owns a Ferrari, and, indeed, Mr. Knewit does own a Ferrari. In this case, though part of what justifies me in accepting that at least one person in the room owns a Ferrari is my false belief that Mr. Nogot owns a Ferrari, I have a justification that does not depend on this false belief. It is based on my completely justified and correct belief that Mr. Knewit owns a Ferrari.[6]

The Knowledge of Falsity

The foregoing illustrates why we have formulated condition (*iv*) in the analysis of knowledge as follows:

(iv) If S knows that p, then S is completely justified in accepting that p in some way that does not depend on any false statement

or, equivalently formulated in terms of defeasibility,

If S knows that p, then S is completely justified in accepting that p in some way that is not defeated by any false statement.

We require only that S has *some* justification that does not depend on any false statement or is not defeated by any false statement. We have yet to explain what it means to say that a justification depends on or is defeated by a statement. A proposal advanced independently by Klein and Hilpinen is relevant to the explication of dependency.[7] In our terminology, they propose that the complete justification that a person S has for accepting that p depends on the false statement q if and only if S would not be justified in accepting that p if S knew q to be false. If I knew it to be false in the original Nogot and Havit case that Nogot owns a Ferrari, then I would not be justified in accepting that someone in my class owns a Ferrari. If I knew it to be false that what I take to be a sheep is a sheep, then I would not be justified in accepting that I see a sheep. On the other hand, in the last case considered concerning

Nogot and Knewit, if I knew it to be false that Mr. Nogot owns a Ferrari, I would be completely justified in accepting that at least one person in my class owns a Ferrari because I am completely justified in accepting that Mr. Knewit owns one.

The Grabit Example

Nevertheless, the proposal is defective. In these cases, there is some false statement which misleads one, and knowing the statement to be false would clarify matters. This is a special feature of these examples. There are situations in which knowing some statement to be false would be misleading rather than clarifying. Another example from the literature illustrates this.[8] Suppose I see a man, Tom Grabit, with whom I am acquainted and have seen often before, standing a few yards from me in the library. I observe him take a book off the shelf and leave the library. I am completely justified in accepting that Tom Grabit took a book, and, assuming he did take it, I know that he did. Imagine, however, that Tom Grabit's father has, quite unknown to me, told someone that Tom was not in town today, but his identical twin brother, John, who he himself often confuses with Tom, is in town at the library getting a book. Had I known that Tom's father said this, I would not have been justified in accepting that I saw Tom Grabit take the book, for if Mr. Grabit confuses Tom for John, as he says, then I might surely have done so, too. Under the Klein and Hilpinen proposal, I do not know that Tom Grabit took the book.

But do I lack knowledge? Notice that I originally have no reason to accept that Mr. Grabit said what he did. Suppose, moreover, that Mr. Grabit made the remarks about John Grabit while raving alone in his room in a mental hospital. The truth is that Tom's thieving ways have driven his father quite mad and caused him to form the delusion that Tom has a twin, John, who performs the thefts which are actually the work of Tom. Mr. Grabit thus protects his wish that Tom is honest. I know none of this, but I did see Tom Grabit take the book. Mr. Grabit's remarks, of which I am totally ignorant, are completely misleading. We should, therefore, not deny that I know that Tom Grabit took the book because of the ravings of his father, of which I am fortunately ignorant. I know Tom Grabit took the book just as I know other people do the things I see them do. I accept nothing, moreover, concerning Tom's father and what he might or might not have said. Given these two features, I may be said to know that Tom Grabit took the book despite the fact that, had I known what his father said without knowing about his madness, I would not know whether it was Tom who took it.

The Newspaper Example

The Tom Grabit example is to be distinguished from one suggested by Harman to illustrate how a person may lack knowledge, even though her belief is justified entirely by true statements.[9] Suppose a person reads in a newspaper that a civil-rights leader has been assassinated. The story is written by a dependable reporter who in fact witnessed and accurately reported the event. The reader of the story accepts this and is completely justified in accepting that the civil-rights leader was assassinated. However, for the sake of avoiding a racial explosion, all other eye-witnesses to the event have agreed to deny that the assassination occurred and affirm that the civil-rights leader is in good health. Imagine, finally, that all who surround the person in question have, in addition to reading the story, heard the repeated denials of the assassination and thus do not know what to accept. Could we say that the one person who, by accident, has not heard the denials, knows that the civil-rights leader was assassinated? The answer appears to be that she does not know.

If we agree to this, the obvious problem is to explain the difference between this case and the case of Tom Grabit. In both cases, there is some misleading information which, were it possessed, the person in question would not know. In the newspaper case, when a person lacks this information, we still deny that she knows that the civil-rights leader was assassinated, while in the case of Tom Grabit, we affirm that the person knows that Tom Grabit took the book. What is the difference? In the Grabit example, no beliefs of mine concerning Tom's father or what he might have said serve to justify me in accepting that Tom took the book. In the newspaper example, though this is unstated, part of what justifies the person in accepting that the civil-rights leader has been assassinated is her belief that the newspaper story is generally considered to be a reliable source of information about the assassination. The person's justification for accepting that the civil-rights leader has been assassinated depends on her false belief that others accept the story, but my belief that Tom Grabit took the book does not depend on any false belief about what Tom's father did or did not say. Anyone doubting this should reflect on how the newspaper case is altered if it occurs to the reader that other eyewitnesses might deny the success of the assassination, and, because she completely trusts the reporter, resolve not to let the doubts of others shake her confidence. With this modification, I suggest that we would say that the person does know that the civil-rights leader was assassinated. She has placed her confidence in the right place.

A Solution: Defeat and
the Ultra Justification Game

The proper solution to these problems may be formulated by a modification of the original justification game. Suppose that we supply the skeptic with a list like that supplied in the verific justification game which includes everything accepted by the claimant marked as to the truth or falsity of the thing accepted. The skeptic is then allowed a new sort of move in the justification game. She may require the claimant to eliminate anything the claimant accepts that is false, and the claimant must eliminate the specified item from his acceptance system and at the same time eliminate anything he accepts that logically implies the eliminated item. Or the skeptic may require the claimant to replace anything the claimant accepts that is false with the acceptance of its denial and at the same time replace anything that logically implies the replaced item with acceptance of its denial. The skeptic may then cite a competitor that must be beaten or neutralized after the claimant makes the required alteration of the claimant's acceptance system. The justification of the claimant is undefeated by any false statement just in case she wins this justification game, the ultra justification game, against the skeptic.

Let us see how this works in the examples we have considered. Consider the original Gettier counterexample concerning Nogot and Havit and the resulting ultra justification game.

Claimant: Someone in my class owns a Ferrari.
Skeptic: Replace 'Nogot owns a Ferrari' with 'Nogot does not own a Ferrari'. No one in your class owns a Ferrari.

The claimant cannot win this round because, once the replacement is made, the competitor cited by the skeptic cannot be beaten or neutralized because the claimant has no information to support the claim that someone in her class owns a Ferrari. The claimant's justification is defeated.

Consider next the example in which the claimant is justified in accepting that Mr. Nogot owns a Ferrari, which is false, but is also justified in accepting that Mr. Knewit owns a Ferrari, which is true, and knows that Mr. Nogot and Mr. Knewit are students in her class.

Claimant: Someone in my class owns a Ferrari.
Skeptic: Replace 'Mr. Nogot owns a Ferrari' with 'Mr. Nogot does not own a Ferrari'. No one in your class owns a Ferrari.

Claimant: It is more reasonable for me to accept that someone in my class owns a Ferrari than to accept that no one in my class owns a Ferrari. (Though Mr. Nogot does not own a Ferrari, Mr. Knewit does, as my information about him shows.)

This round is won by the claimant, and the claimant will remain victorious in the ultra justification game showing the claimant to be justified in accepting that someone in her class owns a Ferrari in a way that is undefeated by any false statement.

The example, which is like the original Nogot and Havit example except that the conclusion, someone in my class owns a Ferrari, rather than being inferred from the statement that Nogot owns a Ferrari, is, instead, inferred from the statements of evidence for accepting that Nogot owns a Ferrari, is more difficult. The reason is that the statements of evidence in question may all be true. Given our account of acceptance as a mental state having a certain functional role in inference, we may say that the claimant accepts the hypothetical to the effect that *if* the statements of evidence are true, then Nogot owns a Ferrari, even if, for some reason, she does not accept the conclusion that Nogot owns a Ferrari. The reason for ascribing acceptance of the hypothetical to the claimant is that the inference from the evidence to the conclusion that someone in her class owns a Ferrari rests on the acceptance of the hypothetical linking the evidence to that conclusion. Hence we can envisage the following ultra justification game:

Claimant: Someone in my class owns a Ferrari.
Skeptic: Replace 'If the evidence I have that Nogot owns a Ferrari is true, then Nogot owns a Ferrari' with 'The evidence I have that Nogot owns a Ferrari is true, but Nogot does not own a Ferrari'. No one in your class owns a Ferrari.

The claimant loses the round because after the replacement the competitor cited by the skeptic cannot be beaten or neutralized. The justification is defeated.

The construction of the remaining ultra justification games to deal with other examples is left to the reader. In the case of Grabit, the claimant will win because there is nothing false that I accept which is relevant to the example, while in the case of the sheep I falsely accept that what I take to be a sheep is a sheep and in the case of the assassination the person falsely accepts that the newspaper report is generally considered to be trustworthy. These errors allow the skeptic to win the ultra justification game showing that the justifications are defeated.

One might worry that the skeptic in the ultra justification games imagined above is merely a useless fiction because no one will actually be in a position to play the role of the skeptic. This objection is, however, unwarranted. I may know enough about what another person accepts to play the winning role of a skeptic against him. A person does not need to know the truth about everything a person accepts in order to know that some specific justification of his depends on accepting some false claim, for example, that Nogot owns a Ferrari. Since Nogot knows that Nogot does not own a Ferrari, he can play the winning role of the skeptic against me, the claimant, in the original example concerning Nogot and Havit. Thus, we are often in a position to know that another person will lose the ultra justification game. In this way, the ultra justification game is a useful tool for the evaluation of the knowledge claims of others.

Truth Connection and the Isolation Objection

The appeal to the ultra justification game provides a reply to the most familiar objection to coherence theories. The objection is that coherence among a set of propositions or, in terms of the theory developed here, among members of the acceptance system, might fail to provide any connection with reality. The acceptance system and all that coheres with it could occur in a mind completely isolated from the external world. Internal coherence is not enough.

We may agree with the conclusion of the objection, while replying that undefeated justification reaches beyond internal coherence to truth. Undefeated justification provides a truth connection between the mind and the world, between acceptance and reality. In fact, we may easily supply an argument that no form of the isolation objection can succeed against our theory. We may call it the *transformation argument*. Suppose that someone claims something about the world, that she sees a table in front of her, for example. To be personally justified, all competitors must be beaten or neutralized. Now, and this is the crucial point, the isolation objection is a competitor. Consider the following justification game:

Claimant: I see a table in front of me.
Skeptic: You are isolated from the external world.
Claimant: It is more reasonable for me to accept that I see a table in front of me than that I am isolated from the external world. (I am visually connected with the external world and not isolated from it.)

The acceptance system of the claimant enables her to beat the skeptical objection because she accepts that she is appropriately connected with the external world and not isolated from it. If, finally, she is correct in accepting this, then her victory in this round of the justification game will be sustained in other rounds and transformed into a victory in the ultra justification game as well. Her justification will go undefeated.

If, on the other hand, she really is isolated from the external world and not visually connected as she accepts, perhaps because she is deceived by the Cartesian demon, then she will lose the following ultra justification game:

Claimant: I see a table in front of me.
Skeptic: Replace 'I am visually connected with external world' with 'I am not visually connected with the external world'. You are isolated from the external world.

The claimant loses the round because after the replacement the competitor cited by the skeptic cannot be beaten or neutralized. The justification is defeated.

Thus, the reply to isolation objection is a dilemma. The claimant must accept that she is visually connected with external reality to win the justification game yielding personal justification. Either she is correct in accepting this, and she is so connected, or she is incorrect, and she is not connected. Suppose that she is connected with the external world as she accepts. In that case, she will be victorious in the ultra justification game, her justification will be undefeated, and she will turn out to have knowledge on our account. That is the appropriate result in such a case. Suppose, on the contrary, that she is not connected with the external world though she accepts that she is. Then she loses in the ultra justification game, and she will not turn out to have knowledge on our account. That is the proper result in such an instance since she is truly ignorant. Whether she is isolated or not, our coherence theory of justification yields the appropriate result concerning whether she knows.

The conclusion is that victory in the ultra justification game insures the appropriate truth connection between internal coherence and external reality. Such victory insures this result because the objection that the connection is lacking is a skeptical objection. The objection must be met in terms of what one accepts for one to be personally justified. So what one accepts must imply that one is appropriately connected. For personal justification to remain undefeated, it must be true that one is connected in the way one accepts that one is. The truth connection transforms personal justification into knowledge.

Perception, Memory, and Introspection

The isolation objection is related to another kind of objection to the coherence theory of justification and knowledge. The objection is based on alleged sources of knowledge.[10] Perception, memory, and introspection are, it is alleged, sources of knowledge. It appears that we know that beliefs arising from these sources are justified because they originate in this way, because they are the products or outputs of our faculties, rather than because they cohere with some acceptance system or correction thereof. If I see something, or remember something, or introspect something, I appear to acquire a justified belief simply because it arises from sight, memory or introspection regardless of what else I might happen to accept. Thus, the objection runs, we may have justified beliefs because they arise from some source or faculty of the mind independently of what else we accept and, therefore, coherence is inessential to the justified beliefs and knowledge emanating from them.

The sort of positive theory that generates an objection of this kind will be critically discussed in detail in the next chapter. It is, however, worthwhile indicating how the objection can be answered in terms of the justification game and the ultra justification game that we have developed. Any claim that we see, remember, or introspect that something is the case immediately confronts the skeptical objection that the belief does not emanate from a trustworthy source but arises in some un-trustworthy manner. To be personally justified in accepting that one sees, remembers, or introspects something, one must, therefore, accept that these are trustworthy sources of information or the skeptic will win the justification game.

Consider the following justification game concerning memory as an illustration:

Claimant: I remember drinking coffee for breakfast.
Skeptic: Your memory is untrustworthy in the matter.
Claimant: It is more reasonable for me to accept that I remember drinking coffee for breakfast than that my memory is untrust-worthy in the matter. (My memory is clear and distinct, and memory of this sort is trustworthy.)

The last sort of reply is required for the justification of the memory belief and depends on accepting that memory is trustworthy. It is not sufficient for knowledge that a belief arise from a trustworthy source when one has no idea that this is so. The justification of the belief depends on acceptance of the unstated assumption that the source of the belief is trustworthy and not deceptive. Victory in the justification game depends on our accepting that perception, memory, and introspection are trustworthy sources of information in general and in our special circumstances. Victory in the ultra justification game depends in turn on our being correct in accepting these assumptions.

Personal justification of what we accept from perception, memory, and introspection results from our accepting that these sources are trustworthy, and personal justification is transformed into undefeated justification and knowledge only when we are correct in accepting that these sources are trustworthy. The transformation argument meets the objection appealing to the sources of knowledge in the same way that it meets the isolation objection. Both objections give rise to a skeptical competitor that must be met in order for a person to be personally justified. One competitor is that one is isolated from the external world, and the other is that one's belief did not arise from a trustworthy source. What one accepts to meet such objections in order to obtain personal justification must turn out to be correct to yield undefeated justification. The correctness of what we accept about the sources and origins of the beliefs of perception, memory, and introspection transform such beliefs into knowledge. Coherence transforms sources of information into fountains of knowledge.

A Definition of Undefeated Justification

Consider any system, M, resulting from making one or more of the changes in a claimant's acceptance system which a skeptic may require in the ultra justification game. Suppose I am personally justified in accepting that p. If the skeptic can require me to form a system M with the result that I am not justified in accepting p on the basis of M, then the skeptic wins the game, and my justification is defeated. If, on the other hand, my acceptance is such that no such system M has the result that I am not justified in accepting p on the basis of M, then I win, and my justification is undefeated.

There is obviously a set of systems, M, resulting from different changes the skeptic might require. Let us call the set of such systems the ultrasystem of S at t. We may then define undefeated justification as follows:

(*ivd*) S is justified in accepting that p in a way that is undefeated if and only if S is justified in accepting p on the basis of every system that is a member of the ultrasystem of S.

Similarly, we may define what it means to say that a system M defeats a personal justification of S for accepting that p as follows:

> M defeats the personal justification of S for accepting p if and only if S is personally justified in accepting p, but S is not justified in accepting p on system M where M is a member of the ultrasystem of S.[11]

It should be noted that it is not necessary for a person to know what the members of her ultrasystem are in order to know that she has undefeated justification for accepting something and, therefore, to know that she knows. A person lifting her hand before her eyes accepts that she has a hand, and she also knows that her acceptance of this does not depend on any error of hers. She might not know what the members of her ultrasystem are, but she does know that whatever they are they will leave her justified in accepting that she has a hand. So, she may know and know that she knows. As a close analogy, a person may know that a set of theorems validly deduced from axioms contains no errors, even though she does not know exactly which theorems have been deduced, just because she knows the axioms are true and the person who deduced the theorems would not make any errors. A person can know that no correction of errors in her acceptance system will yield a system to defeat her justification for a specific claim because she knows that her justification for that claim is based on truths. It is not hard to know that you know when your evidence is good enough.

Knowledge Reduced to Undefeated Justification

The foregoing complicated set of definitions permits us to reduce knowledge to a simple formula. Knowledge is undefeated justified acceptance. The reduction is easily effected. We began in the first chapter with the following definition of knowledge:

> DK. S knows that p if and only if (i) S accepts that p, (ii) it is true that p, (iii) S is completely justified in accepting that p, and (iv) S is completely justified in accepting that p in a way that is not defeated by any false statement.

We then undertook to analyze conditions (iii) and (iv) by means of a complicated set of definitions. The first definition specifies the system, the acceptance system, with which something must cohere to yield justification.

D1. A system X is an acceptance system of S if and only if X contains just statements of the form, S accepts that p, attributing to S just those things that S accepts with the objective of accepting that p if and only if p.

The second definition expresses the idea that justification is coherence with a system.

D2. S is justified in accepting p at t on the basis of system X of S at t if and only if p coheres with X of S at t.

The next definitions articulate the idea that coherence with a system means that all skeptical objections, competitors, can be met because they are either beaten or neutralized on the basis of the system.

D3. S is justified in accepting p at t on the basis of system X of S at t if and only if all competitors of p are beaten or neutralized for S on X at t.

D4. c competes with p for S on X at t if and only if it is more reasonable for S to accept that p on the assumption that c is false than on the assumption that c is true, on the basis of X at t.

D5. p beats c for S on X at t if and only if c competes with p for S on X at t, and it is more reasonable for S to accept p than to accept c on X at t.
D6. n neutralizes c as a competitor of p for S on X at t if and only if c competes with p for S on X at t, the conjunction of c and n does not compete with p for S on X at t, and it is as reasonable for S to accept the conjunction of c and n as to accept c alone on X at t.

We thus arrive at a definition of personal justification.

D7. S is personally justified in accepting that p at t if and only if S is justified in accepting that p on the basis of the acceptance system of S at t.

To proceed beyond personal justification to complete justification, we require a notion of justification based on that part of the acceptance system that remains when all errors have been eliminated, the verific system. This kind of justification is called verific justification. The next three definitions accomplish this and result in a definition of complete justification as the combination of personal and verific justification.

D8. A system *V* is a verific system of *S* at *t* if and only if *V* is a subsystem of the acceptance system of *S* at *t* resulting from eliminating all statements of the form, *S* accepts that *p*, when *p* is false. (*V* is a member of the ultrasystem of *S*.)

D9. *S* is verifically justified in accepting that *p* at *t* if and only if *S* is justified in accepting that *p* on the basis of the verific system of *S* at *t*.

D10. *S* is completely justified in accepting that *p* at *t* if and only if *S* is personally justified in accepting *p* at *t* and *S* is verifically justified in accepting *p* at *t*.

Finally, we require a definition of undefeated justification which amounts to justification on the basis of those systems resulting from the corrections of errors in the acceptance system by either elimination of the acceptance of the error or replacement by the acceptance of denial of the error.

D11. *S* is justified in accepting that *p* at *t* in a way that is undefeated if and only if *S* is justified in accepting *p* at *t* on the basis of every system that is a member of the ultrasystem of *S* at *t*.

D12. A system *M* is a member of the ultrasystem of *S* at *t* if and only if either *M* is the acceptance system of *S* at *t* or results from eliminating one or more statements of the form, '*S* accepts that *q*,' when *q* is false, replacing one or more statements of the form, '*S* accepts that *q*,' with a statement of the form, '*S* accepts that not *q*' when *q* is false, or any combination of such eliminations and replacements in the acceptance system of *S* at *t* with the constraint that if *q* logically entails *r* which is false and also accepted, then '*S* accepts that *r*' must also be eliminated or replaced just as '*S* accepts that *q*' was.

Needless to say, the attempt to analyze justification and undefeated justification in terms of acceptance, reasonableness, and truth has yielded a complicated analysis. As is often the case, however, thorough analysis enables us to find the underlying simplicity. We are now in a position to provide an elegant reduction of the original analysis of knowledge (DK). Knowledge reduces to undefeated justification, a just reward for our arduous analytical efforts.

The reduction of knowledge to undefeated justified acceptance is a consequence of our explication of condition (iv). This condition implies the other three. It is easiest to see that undefeated justification implies complete justification. The verific system is one of the members of the ultrasystem and, therefore, if a person is justified in accepting that p on the basis of every member of the ultrasystem as our definition of undefeated justification requires, the person is justified in accepting that p on the basis of the verific system. Thus, if a person's justification for accepting that p is undefeated, then the person is verifically and completely justified in accepting that p. Undefeated justified acceptance obviously implies acceptance, and the implication of the truth condition is trivial. If a person accepts that p and it is false that p, then any justification the person has for accepting p will be defeated. The reason for this is that if it is false that p, then the skeptic in the ultra justification game may require the claimant to replace acceptance of p with acceptance of the denial of p and the claimant will lose the game starting with the claim that p. This is equivalent to saying that if a person accepts that p when p is false, then some member of the ultrasystem containing acceptance of the denial of p will defeat the person's justification for accepting p. Hence, condition (iv), the defeasibility condition of (DK), our original definition of knowledge, logically implies the other three conditions, and knowledge is reduced to undefeated justification.

The reduction is a formal feature of the theory. The substance of it is the coherence theory of justification in which personal justification results from coherence with an acceptance system, just as other necessary kinds of justification, verific, complete, and undefeated, result from modifications of the acceptance system. The soul of the theory is personal acceptance. This is entirely an internal matter. One is personally justified in accepting something because what one accepts informs one that such acceptance is a trustworthy guide to truth. Even the conclusions that one accepts from perception and inference must cohere with one's background information articulated in an acceptance system to insure that they are trustworthy. Without such insurance, one may possess information but lack knowledge, for, the trustworthiness of perception and inference is not a necessary *a priori* truth. When they prove trustworthy, this is the result of the nature of our faculties, the circumstances we find ourselves in and, most importantly, our background information about the circumstances in which our faculties are worthy of our trust. The soul of personal justification requires a body of truth to provide knowledge, however. A truth connection between an acceptance system and worldly fact is essential. There must be a match between what one accepts as a trustworthy guide to truth and what really is a trustworthy guide to truth. The match must be close enough to sustain justification when error is eliminated or replaced with truth.

Given the importance of the trustworthiness of acceptance in yielding undefeated justification and knowledge, the theory might be regarded as a form of *reliabilism*, but, given that the acceptance of our trustworthiness yields, in the normal case, justification of its own acceptance, the theory might as well be called foundational coherentism. To obtain knowledge we need the right mix of internal and external factors. Our theory may appear dialectically promiscuous, but fidelity to a single approach is epistemic puritanism. The simple theory, though ever seductive, is usually the mistress of error. The queen of truth is a more complicated woman but of better philosophical parts.

Determining Justification

How can a person ascertain that she is completely justified in accepting that p or that her justification is undefeated except by checking to determine whether she is personally justified in accepting that p? At a given point in time, a person can only evaluate such a claim in terms of her acceptance system at that time. Her acceptance system summarizes her information; it is her repository of information about the world and it alone is the basis for evaluation. That is the fundamental truth in the subjective approach. The acceptance system is the first and last court of appeal of an individual at any specific point in time. It is the only epistemic court for synchronic adjudication, judgment at a time.

We are, however, diachronic creatures spanning time and considering our cognitive accomplishments through time. As a result, an individual remembers that, however many successes he has had, he also has had his failures. In the past, some of the things that he accepted were false, and, therefore, at those times there was a distinction between his acceptance system and his verific system. He may take what steps he can to make the two coincide as closely as possible in the future, of course, but when the time for evaluation of various claims to truth arrives, the basis for evaluation must be the system he has then. When I consider whether I am completely justified in accepting something now, I can only determine whether I am personally justified and, if I am, conclude that I am completely justified. Others with the information about where I have erred may disagree, and I may come to agree with them at some later date when further information has won my acceptance.

We have thus arrived at a coherence theory of justification. Coherence with an acceptance system yields personal justification, and the addition of coherence with a verific system yields complete justification. Coherence with members of the ultrasystem keeps the justification undefeated. Knowledge, or undefeated justification, results from the right combination of coherence, acceptance, and truth. We may put the matter this way: We accept what we do with the objective of reaching truth and avoiding error. What we are personally justified in accepting depends on what we accept with these objectives. Whether our justification is complete and undefeated depends on whether we succeed in our attempt. If we win the original justification game without depending on error, our justification is complete and undefeated and we gain knowledge. If our victory rests on error, we have won a game of justification but lost the prize of knowledge.

Introduction to the Literature

The original very readable brief article that spawned a vast literature is Edmund Gettier's "Is Justified True Belief Knowledge?" in which Gettier argued for the negative. There are many important articles written to deal with the problem that Gettier raised. One excellent collection is *Knowing: Essays in the Analysis of Knowledge*, edited by Michael Roth and Leon Galis. Another important collection is by George S. Pappas and Marshall Swain, *Essays on Knowledge and Justification*. For those who become fascinated with the problem, the literature is summarized critically in *The Analysis of Knowing* by Robert K. Shope.

8

Externalism and
Epistemology Naturalized

OUR ANALYSIS of complete and undefeated justification in terms of coherence and truth within an acceptance system brings us into conflict with an important competing theory of knowledge called *externalism*. The fundamental doctrine of externalism is that what must be added to true belief to obtain knowledge is the appropriate connection between belief and truth. An earlier account presented by Goldman affirmed that the appropriate connection is causal.[1] This is a very plausible sort of account of perceptual knowledge. The fact that I see something, the hand I hold before me, for example, causes me to believe that I see a hand. The fact that my seeing a hand causes me to believe I see a hand results, it is claimed, in my knowing that I see a hand. According to such an analysis, it is the history of my belief, a matter of external causation, rather than coherence with some internal system, that yields knowledge. The central tenet of externalism is that some relationship to the external world accounting for the truth of our belief suffices to convert true belief to knowledge without our having any idea of that relationship. It is not our conception of how we are related to a fact that yields knowledge but simply our being so related to it.

The early analysis, though providing a plausible account of perceptual knowledge, was a less plausible account of our knowledge of generalities, that men do not become pregnant, for example, or that neutrinos have a zero rest mass, or that there is no largest prime number. For here the nature of the required causal relationship between what is believed and the belief of it evades explication. That objection is, however, one of detail. Later analyses of others, and of Goldman himself, aim at preserving the thesis of externalism that some relationship of the belief to what makes it true yields knowledge, whether we have any idea of that relationship or not.[2] Armstrong and Dretske have argued that the relationship should be construed as nomological, one resulting from some law of nature connecting the belief with what makes it true.[3] This account is closely connected with the proposal of Nozick that belief track truth in a sense explicated, in part, by the counterfactual claim that the person would not have believed what she did if it were not for the truth of the belief.[4] Goldman now claims that justified belief must be the result of a belief-forming process that reliably yields truth.[5] Beliefs resulting from such a process are justified, he contends, while other externalists deny that justification is necessary for knowledge. They all agree, however, that a belief resulting from a certain kind of process or relationship connecting belief with truth can yield knowledge without the sustenance or support of any other beliefs or system of beliefs.

Naturalism

Assuming that the required relationship is something like causation, externalist theories are *naturalistic*. What is a naturalistic theory? It is one in which all the terms used in the analysis are ones that describe phenomena of nature, such as causation, for example, or that can be reduced to such terms. Hume's theory of belief was naturalistic in this sense. He restricted his account of human knowledge to relations of causation, contiguity, and resemblance.[6] It was, however, Quine who introduced the term *epistemology naturalized* and suggested that inquiry into the nature of human knowledge be restricted to accounts of how belief arises and is altered.[7] Other philosophers have adopted the term to refer simply to all those accounts of knowledge couched in naturalistic vocabulary or reducible to such a vocabulary. The early account of Goldman considered above according to which S knows that p if and only if S's believing that p is caused in the appropriate way by the fact that p is, in this extended sense, an example of epistemology naturalized. Other early naturalistic accounts offered by Armstrong and Dretske rested on the assumption that the conversion relation was based on nomological rather than causal relations, that is, relations articulated in laws of nature.[8] Dretske's basic idea was that the reasons we have for believing what we do should be nomologically connected with the truth of what is believed, that is, that it should be a law of nature that a person having such reasons for believing what she does will have a true belief. Assuming a naturalistic account of having a reason which Dretske supplies, such an account is also naturalistic.

One interesting aspect of some externalistic theories which naturalize epistemology is the way in which they attempt to avoid the problems of foundationalism. According to Dretske or Nozick, for example, there is no need either to justify beliefs or posit self-justified beliefs blindly because, contrary to the traditional analysis, the justification of beliefs is not required to convert true beliefs into knowledge. Beliefs or true beliefs having the appropriate sort of naturalistic external relationships to the facts are, as a result of such relationship, converted into knowledge without being justified. It is the way true beliefs are connected to the world that makes them knowledge rather than the way in which we might attempt to justify them. Notice how plausible this seems for perceptual beliefs. It is the way my belief that I see a bird is related to the facts, for example, when my seeing a bird causes the belief that I do, which accounts for my knowing that I see a bird, rather than some justification I have for that belief. What matters for knowledge is how the belief arises, not how I might reason on behalf of it. The traditional analysis says that knowledge is true belief coupled with the right sort of justification. One sort of externalist analysis says that knowledge is true belief coupled with the right sort of naturalistic relation. It is plausible to assume that the naturalistic relationship will be one concerning how the belief arises, in short, the natural history of the belief. Looked at in this way, the justification requirement can be eliminated altogether in favor of the right sort of historical account.

The Advantages of Externalism

Before turning to details and objections, it is useful to notice the advantages of externalism. First of all, according to some externalists, the need for justification and a theory of justification is eliminated as a component of an analysis of knowledge. On such an account, it is admitted that inference may play some role in the natural history of a true belief, but it is also possible to hold that some beliefs are non-inferential. They are beliefs arising from experience without the intervention of inference. This may be offered as an account of what the foundationalist was searching for, but in the wrong place. True beliefs that arise in the appropriate way from experience are knowledge because of the way they arise. There is no need to affirm that such beliefs are self-justified to maintain that they convert to knowledge. We might think of such beliefs as naturalized basic beliefs. Such basic beliefs might, of course, serve as the premises for inferring other beliefs and such inference might convert those beliefs to knowledge as well. It is the history of the belief rather than some sort of justification of the belief that converts it to knowledge.

A Reply to Skepticism

It is helpful, as well, to notice how neatly this sort of theory deals with traditional and modern forms of skepticism. The skeptic, confronted with a commonsense perceptual claim, that I see a tree, for example, has traditionally raised some skeptical doubt, the Cartesian one, for example, that we might be deceived by an evil demon who supplies us with deceptive sensations which lead us to believe we see external objects when we do not see them at all. Or consider the case of a small object, a 'braino', implanted in our brain which, when operated by a computer, provides us with sensory states which are all produced by the computer influencing the brain rather than by the external objects we believe to exist.[9] In neither case, affirms the skeptic, do I know I see a tree. The reply is simple. If my beliefs are, indeed, produced by the demon or by the braino, then they are false and I am ignorant. On the other hand, if the beliefs are true and produced in the appropriate way, then I do know.

To this the skeptic is wont to reply that I only know that I see a tree if I know that it is not the demon or the braino that produces my belief and, furthermore, to insist that I do not know this. Why do I not know that there is no demon or braino? I do not know so because my experience would be exactly the same if there were; that is what the demon and braino do, produce exactly the same experiences as I would have if I were to see a tree. I have no evidence whatever against these skeptical hypotheses and, therefore, the skeptic concludes, I do not know them to be false. The reply of the externalist is simple. I do not need to *know* that the skeptical hypotheses are false to know that I see a tree, though, of course, the skeptical hypotheses must *be* false. Otherwise, my belief that I see a tree will be false. All that is necessary is that my belief be true and that it arise in the appropriate way, that it have a suitable history, for knowledge to arise. If my belief is true and has arisen in the appropriate way, then I know that I see a tree, even if I do not know that the conflicting skeptical hypotheses are false. I might never have considered such skeptical machinations. Confronted with them, I might be astounded by them and find them so bizarre as not to be worthy of consideration.

The skeptic might retort that I cannot so easily escape the clutches of skepticism. For example, she might suggest that when I claim to know that I am seeing a car, a Mazda RX7, for example, I must have the information required to tell a Mazda RX7 from cars of another sort, and lacking such information, I do not know that I see a Mazda RX7. Hence, I must know that the car is not a Toyota MR2 or a Porsche 944, which bear some resemblance to a Mazda RX7. Going on, the skeptic might argue that to know that I see a Mazda RX7, I must have the information required to tell seeing a Mazda RX7 from experiences of another sort, those supplied by the demon or braino, and lacking such information, I do not know that I am seeing a Mazda RX7, or even that I am seeing a car. So, the skeptic concludes, just as I must know that the car I am seeing is not of another manufacture, so I must know that my experiences are not of skeptical manufacture. That, she insists, is precisely what I do not know. Skepticism wins.

Relevant Alternatives: A Reply to the Skeptic

The reply of the externalist is a combination of counterassertion and explanation. The counterassertion is that my true belief that I see a tree arising in the way it does is knowledge, even if I do not know that it has arisen in that way rather than in the way the skeptic suggests. If the skeptical hypothesis is true and the belief has not arisen in the way I suppose, then I lack knowledge, but if it has arisen in the way I suppose, then I have knowledge, even if I do not know competing hypotheses about the origin of the belief to be false. It does not matter whether I know that the belief originated in the appropriate manner. All that matters is that it have originated in that way. Then I know. The explanation about the Mazda, for example, is that there will be some cases, but not all, in which some information excluding other alternatives, will be necessary for knowledge. The alternative that I am seeing a Porsche 944 and not a Mazda RX7 is a relevant alternative. The alternative that I am being deceived by an evil demon or a braino is not.[10] What is the difference? My information about what a Mazda RX7 looks like must be sufficient to enable me to distinguish it from other cars, and that information plays a role in the formation of my belief that I am seeing a Mazda RX7. In other cases, particularly those suggested by the skeptic in which there is no such distinguishing information, no such information enters into the appropriate origination of the belief. Where the distinguishing information is a necessary component in the suitable generation of the belief, the alternatives to be distinguished from the truth are relevant, but where it is not a necessary component, the alternatives are not relevant ones. To be sure, a skeptic might find the distinction between relevant and irrelevant alternatives capricious and question-begging as a counterargument. Nevertheless, the initial reply to the skeptic to the effect that true belief originating in the appropriate manner is knowledge, even if we do not know the skeptical hypotheses to be false, is a straightforward consequence of epistemology naturalized whether or not it satisfies the demands of the skeptic.

Knowing That One Knows:
Rejection of Deductive Closure

There remains, of course, the question whether I know that I know that I see a tree when I do not know that the skeptical hypotheses are false. If I know that I see a tree, then it follows that the skeptical hypotheses concerning the demon and braino are false. It follows, first of all, from the fact that if I know that I see a tree, then I do see a tree, and, therefore, my experiences are not a result of demonic be-witchment or computer wizardry. It follows, further, from my knowing that I see a tree that my belief originates in the appropriate natural way and not from the demon or braino. In short, it follows both from the fact known and from the knowing of the fact that the skeptical hypotheses are false.

Some naturalists in epistemology would deny that I know that the skeptical hypotheses are false or that I need to know this in order to know that I know that I see a tree. They do this by denying what they call a *deductive closure* condition, namely, the condition that if I know that p and that q is a logical consequence of knowing that p, then I, therefore, know that q. Thus, I might know that p, and know that q is a consequence of knowing that p, even though I do not know that q.[11]

The denial of closure is directly relevant to replying to the skeptic. I might know that I see a tree, know that the falsity of the demon hypothesis is a consequence of my seeing a tree, even though I do not know that the demon hypothesis is false. If, however, I might know that I see a tree without knowing that the demon hypothesis is false, then might I also know that I know that I see a tree without knowing that the demon hypothesis is false? On the naturalist account, it appears that we may answer in the affirmative. If I can know something without knowing what I know to be the consequences of it, then I can know that I know something without knowing what I know to be the consequences of my knowing it.

The falsity of the demon hypothesis is something I know to be a consequence of my knowing that I see a tree, but I may, nevertheless, know that I see a tree without knowing what I know to be a consequence of my knowing it, to wit, the falsity of the demonic hypothesis. Once we deny the closure condition, we may agree with the skeptic that the falsity of the skeptical hypotheses is a necessary condition of what we know, while cheerfully admitting that we do not know that the skeptical hypotheses are false. Such are the joys of naturalism and rejection of the closure condition. Given that the appropriate origination of a true belief converts it to knowledge, it becomes obvious that the closure condition must be rejected. My true belief that I see a tree may originate in the appropriate way without a belief in the logical consequences of that true belief originating in the appropriate way. Indeed, I might fail to believe in the truth of the logical consequences. It may strike one as odd that a person should know that she sees a tree, know that the falsity of the skeptical hypothesis is a consequence, and yet fail to know the skeptical hypothesis to be false. The oddity is in the eye of the epistemologist, however, for there is no logical contradiction in this position.

The Naturalistic Relation

The advantages of naturalism are robust, but the theory must be true, not merely advantageous, to solve the problems with which we began. To ascertain whether the theory is true, we must have some account of the naturalistic relationship that is supposed to convert true belief into knowledge. Before proceeding to consideration of such accounts, however, let us consider the rejection of the justification condition. At least one defender of epistemology naturalized, Goldman in his later work, is inclined to argue that the notion of justification is a naturalistic notion. One might be a naturalist about justification and maintain that justification is reducible to some naturalistic relationship. In fact, a philosopher eager to connect the naturalistic analysis with the traditional one might argue that a person has the requisite sort of justification for knowledge if and only if true belief arises in the appropriate naturalistic manner. This would provide us with a naturalistic reduction of justification. Thus, the externalist theory can be construed as a naturalistic account of justification or as a repudiation of a nonnaturalistic account of justification. As we shall see later, however, there are objections to externalist accounts of justification that might lead an externalist to prefer the repudiation strategy.

What exactly is the external relationship that converts true belief into knowledge? It is typical of epistemological theories to take some sort of example as a paradigm of knowledge, to fine-tool the theory to fit that sort of example and, at least at the outset, to ignore less felicitous examples whose subsequent consideration necessitates rather substantial modification of the theory. That is the history of externalism. The paradigm example is perception. In the case of perception, it is indeed very plausible to contend that what converts perceptual belief into knowledge is the way that the belief arises in perceptual experience. My belief that I see a tree is converted into knowledge by being caused by my actually seeing a tree. Another kind of example is communication. You tell me that Holly Smith is Department Head and that causes me to believe that Holly Smith is Department Head. Do I know that Holly Smith is

Department Head as a result of this causation? It might be contended, and has been, that if my informant knows that what he tells me is true, then I know because he knows and his communication caused me to believe this. Of course, his knowing remains to be explicated. The assumption is that there is a causal chain beginning with the fact that Holly Smith is Department Head and ending with my believing it which accounts for my knowing it.

Thus, following Goldman's early proposal, we might consider the following as characteristic of externalistic theories which eliminate the justification condition.

(CK) S knows that p if and only if S believes that p and this belief is caused in the appropriate way by the fact that p.[12]

This account leaves us with the need to explain the difference between being caused in an appropriate way and being caused in a way that is not appropriate. Typical cases of perception provide a model of the appropriate kind of causation.

Dretske has suggested that when x is something S perceives, then

(DK) S knows that x is F if and only if S's belief that x is F is caused or causally sustained by the information that x is F received from the source x by S.[13]

Dretske's analysis, though restricted to perceptual knowledge, highlights two needed qualifications recognized by other authors as well. The first is that the belief need not be caused but only causally sustained by the information that p. This is necessary because the originating causation of a belief might involve an error which is corrected by subsequent information one receives.

If I see two men in the distance, I might take the one on the left to be Buchanan and believe that I see Buchanan when, in fact, it is not Buchanan, as I note when I move closer, but Harnish instead. At the same time, I note that the other man, the one on the right, is Buchanan and that Buchanan and Harnish are dressed in such a way that each appears to be the other in preparation for Tolliver's halloween party. My belief that I see Buchanan was caused by my seeing Harnish dressed as Buchanan, and I continue to hold that belief subsequently when I receive the further information which corrects my mistake about the man on the right but sustains my belief that I see Buchanan and, indeed, that I saw him earlier, though I did not recognize him. Moreover, on this sort of account the appropriate kind of causal relation is explicated in terms of receiving information from a source.

The foregoing analyses are, however, too restricted in scope to provide us with a general analysis of knowledge. There is more to knowledge than perceptual knowledge, and not all knowledge that p can be supposed to be caused by the fact that p. The most obvious example is general knowledge, my knowledge that all human beings die, for example. That fact includes the fact of death of as yet unborn humans which cannot now cause me to believe that all humans die or causally sustain that belief. Our knowledge that all neutrinos have zero rest mass is yet more difficult to account for on such a model, since no one has ever perceived a neutrino at rest. Assuming there to be mathematical knowledge, for example, that integers are infinite, the causal theory seems inappropriate. The integers appear to lie outside the temporal order and to be incapable of causing anything.

Accounts of knowledge in terms of causation or the receipt of information fail to provide an account of our knowledge of general and theoretical truths. Moreover, it is easy to see that externalism in no way requires such a restrictive conception of the external relationship. Causal or information-receiving analyses of knowledge have the virtue of explicating knowledge in a way that explains the connection between truth and belief, between reality and thought, and provides an answer to skepticism. We may, however, maintain the connection between truth and belief without committing ourselves to a restrictive causal connection. Instead, we may require that the *history* of the belief connect the belief with truth.

There are two popular accounts of how the history of a belief might connect the belief with truth. The first and perhaps best known is the later account of Goldman according to which true belief is converted to knowledge *via* justification when the belief is the result of a reliable belief-forming process. Goldman's basic idea, which he has modified and refined, is as follows:

> If S's believing that p at t results from a reliable cognitive belief-forming process (or set of processes), then S's belief in p at t is justified.[14]

The refinements include an account of reliable rules, methods, and processes. The other account, offered by Nozick, requires that a belief must track truth in order to convert to knowledge in the sense that the person would believe that p if p were true and would not believe that p if p were not true.[15]

The two theories share some advantages. Both retain the reply to the skeptic considered above. They both accomplish this without assuming that we have any guarantee that our beliefs are true, moreover. That my belief is the outcome of a reliable belief-forming process does not presuppose that I have any guarantee of the truth of the belief. Similarly, I might believe that something is true when I would not have believed it, had it not been true even though I have no guarantee that this is so. Thus, given either account of knowledge, the skeptic may be answered while allowing, what seems obvious, that we are fallible in the way in which we form our beliefs, even those converting to knowledge. The result is a fallibilistic epistemology without the postulation of self-justified beliefs.

Objections to Externalism:
Information Without Knowledge

There is, however, a general objection to all externalist theories which is as simple to state as it is fundamental. It is that a person who has no idea that her beliefs are caused or causally sustained by a reliable belief-forming process might fail to know because of her ignorance of this. Alternatively, the person who has no idea that she would not have believed what she did had it not been true might fail to know because of her ignorance of that. Any purely externalist account faces the fundamental objection that a person totally ignorant of the external factors connecting her belief with truth, might be ignorant of the truth of her belief as a result. All externalist theories share a common defect, to wit, that they provide accounts of the possession of information rather than of the attainment of knowledge. The appeal of such theories is their naturalistic character. They assimilate knowledge to other natural causal relationships between objects. Our attainment of knowledge is just one natural relationship between facts among all the rest. It is a relationship of causality, or nomological correlation, or frequency correlation, or counterfactual dependence. But this very attractive feature of such theories is their downfall. The relationship in question may suffice for the recording of information, but if we are ignorant of the relationship, we lack knowledge. As in our refutation of foundationalism, what is missing from the accounts of externalists is the needed supplementation of background information. To convert the specified relationships into knowledge, we need the additional information of the existence of those relationships. Such additional information is, however, precisely the sort of information required for coherence and complete justification.

The general problem with externalism can be seen most graphically by considering the analogy proposed by Armstrong. He suggested that the right model of knowledge is a thermometer.[16] The relationship between the reading on a thermometer and the temperature of the object illustrates the theories mentioned above. Suppose that the thermometer is an accurate one and that it records a temperature of 104 degrees for some oil it is used to measure. We can say, with Armstrong, that there is a nomological connection between the temperature and the thermometer reading, with Dretske that the thermometer receives the information, with Nozick that the thermometer would not record a temperature of 104 degrees if it were not true that the oil was at 104 degrees, and with Goldman that the reading is the outcome of a reliable temperature-recording process. The problem with the analogy is that the thermometer is obviously ignorant of the temperature it records. The question is—why?

One might be inclined to suggest that the thermometer is ignorant of temperature only because it lacks the capacity of thought. If, contrary to fact, the thermometer could entertain the thought that the oil is 104 degrees, would that suffice? Would the thermometer know that the temperature is 104 degrees? What are we to say of this fanciful thought experiment? One might protest, of course, that it is too farfetched to turn the philosophical lathe. The thermometer does record information accurately, however, and, given the capacity for thought, it may be said that the thermometer not only contains the information but possesses that information as well. But our thoughtful thermometer does not *know* that the temperature of the oil is 104 degrees as a result of thinking that this is so. The reason is that it might have no idea that it is an accurate temperature-recording device. If it has no idea that this is so, then, even if it thinks the temperature of the oil is 104 degrees when it records that temperature, it has no idea that the recorded temperature is correct. To obtain the benefits of these reflections, however, it is necessary to move to the human case.

Suppose a person, whom we shall name Mr. Truetemp, undergoes brain surgery by an experimental surgeon who invents a small device which is both a very accurate thermometer and a computational device capable of generating thoughts. The device, call it a tempucomp, is implanted in Truetemp's head so that the very tip of the device, no larger than the head of pin, sits unnoticed on his scalp and acts as a sensor to transmit information about the temperature to the computational system in his brain. This device, in turn, sends a message to his brain causing him to think of the temperature recorded by the external sensor. Assume that the tempucomp is very reliable, and so his thoughts are correct temperature thoughts. All told, this is a reliable belief-forming process. Now imagine, finally, that he has no idea that the tempucomp has been inserted in his brain, is only slightly puzzled about why he thinks so obsessively about the temperature, but never checks a thermometer to determine whether these thoughts about the temperature are correct. He accepts them unreflectively, another effect of the tempucomp. Thus, he thinks and accepts that the temperature is 104 degrees. It is. Does he know that it is? Surely not. He has no idea whether he or his thoughts about the temperature are reliable. What he accepts, that the temperature is 104 degrees, is correct, but he does not know that his thought is correct. His thought that the temperature is 104 degrees is correct information, but he does not know this. Though he records the information because of the operations of the tempucomp, he is ignorant of the facts about the tempucomp and about his temperature telling reliability. Yet, the sort of causal, nomological, statistical, or counterfactual relationships required by externalism may all be present. Does he know that the temperature is 104 degrees when the thought occurs to him while strolling in Pima Canyon? He has no idea why the thought occurred to him or that such thoughts are almost always correct. He does not, consequently, know that the temperature is 104 degrees when that thought occurs to him.

The preceding example is not presented as a decisive objection against externalism and should not be taken as such. It is possible to place some constraint on relationships or processes converting belief to knowledge to exclude production by the tempucomp. The fundamental difficulty remains, however. It is that more than the possession of correct information is required for knowledge. One must have some way of knowing that the information is correct. Consider another example. Someone informs me that Professor Haller is in my office. Suppose I have no idea whether the person telling me this is trustworthy. Even if the information I receive is correct and I believe what I am told, I do not know that Haller is in my office, because I have no idea of whether the source of my information is trustworthy. The nomological, statistical, or counterfactual relationships or processes may be trustworthy, but I lack this information.

When we considered the distinction between belief and acceptance in the third chapter, we noted the argument to the effect that a person who receives the information that p and believes that p as a result may fail to know that p. The reason is that the person may not know that the information she thus receives and believes is correct information. If a person does not know that the information, that p, which she receives is correct information, then she does not know that p. All forms of externalism fail to deal with this problem adequately. To know that the information one possesses is correct, one requires background information about that information. One requires information about whether the received information is trustworthy or not, and lacking such information, one falls short of knowledge. This is a line of argumentation we have already encountered, in earlier chapters. A necessary condition of knowledge is coherence with background information, with an acceptance system, informing us of the trustworthiness of the information we possess.

Externalism and Justification

Some forms of externalism repudiate justification as a condition of knowledge, according to Nozick and Dretske, for example.[17] Such accounts may provide an interesting account of what it is like for belief to constitute correct information or to track truth, but they provide no account of knowledge. The reason is that no one knows that what she accepts is true when it would have been just as reasonable for her to have accepted the opposite on the basis of her information. A necessary normative condition of a person knowing that *p* is that it be more reasonable for her to accept that *p* than to accept the denial of *p* on the basis of her information. This condition implies the need for a justification condition of the sort we have proposed.

One may, as Goldman illustrates, combine externalism with the affirmation of a justification condition, but such an account, if it takes account of background information in an acceptable manner, will introduce a coherence factor. Goldman insists, for example, that a justified belief resulting from a reliable belief-forming process must not be undermined by other evidence the subject possesses.[18] The condition requiring that the belief not be undermined by other evidence is a kind of negative coherence condition to the effect that the belief not be incoherent with background information. Nevertheless, the source of justification on this account is the reliability of the belief-forming process, that is, the fact that the belief has the sort of history frequently producing true beliefs. As a result of providing a justification condition, a normative constraint is supplied.

The objection raised against externalism in general still applies to such a theory, however. A person totally ignorant of the reliability of the process producing his belief would not know that what he believes is true, even if he had no information that would undermine his belief. The example of Mr. Truetemp illustrates this perfectly. He has no evidence that his thoughts about the temperature are incorrect. Had he taken time to consider evidence, he would have discovered that his thoughts about the temperature are correct, but he did not consider any evidence concerning the matter, and that is why he does not know that his thoughts about the temperature are correct.

Take a more commonplace example. If I read a thermometer at the local gas station, and it says that the temperature is 104 degrees, I do not know simply from reading the thermometer that the temperature is 104 degrees. I may not have any evidence that it is untrustworthy, but the competitor to the effect that gas station thermometers are often inaccurate is not one I can beat or neutralize, at least not without inquiring about the thermometer. Whether or not the belief-forming process is reliable, which perhaps it is, I do not know whether the information about the temperature is trustworthy or not. Indeed, I may have no view on the matter. I may believe what I see out of habit, but this is not knowledge. This is a central problem for externalism, to wit, that ignorance of our reliability or of other external relationships leaves us ignorant of whether our information is trustworthy. Trust sharpens the epistemic blade.

The Invincibility Objection

There is another objection to historical reliabilism that leads to an important lesson. The objection raised by Cohen is that if we are deceived in such a way that we are invincibly ignorant of the deception, we are justified in what we believe, nonetheless.[19] Cohen's example was the Cartesian demon who deceives us in all our perceptual beliefs. The details of the deception may vary, but let us suppose that the demon clouds our senses and supplies us with deceptive sensory data leading us to believe that we perceive the world though we actually perceive nothing at all. Since our perceptual beliefs are virtually all erroneous, the process that produces them is not reliable. Yet, Cohen suggests, we are certainly justified in our beliefs. We may have done the best we could to ensure that we were not deceived, attended to what we observe with the greatest circumspection, and noticed no error. Having done the best we could, indeed, the best anyone could do, we are certainly justified in believing what we do.

The intuition is reinforced by noting the difference between two people, one who examines his sensory data with the sort of care that would keep him virtually free from error in normal circumstances, and one who forms perceptual beliefs so casually that he would frequently err under the best of circumstances. The former puts together all his information and concludes that he is seeing the path of an alpha particle in a cloud chamber. The other believes this because some person, whom he knows to be scientifically ignorant, has told him that this is what he is seeing. We would wish to say that the former but not the latter was justified in believing that he sees the path of an alpha particle in a cloud chamber, even though both beliefs are produced by processes that are unreliable, given the interventions of the demon.

Externalism might be modified to meet the objection, and Goldman has suggested more than one way.[20] The example shows that it is internal factors, not external ones, that make us justified and explain the difference between the circumspect and casual observers above. The sort of justification appealed to in the example is personal justification as explicated in the last chapter. The circumspect observer wins the justification round arising when the skeptic claims that casual observations are often in error by replying that his observation is circumspect and not casual. The casual observer loses that round to the skeptic.

The Absentminded Demon

There is, however, an important lesson to be learned from reliabilism. It is that the sort of justification required for knowledge is not entirely an internal matter, either. On the contrary, the needed form of justification depends on the appropriate match between what one accepts about how one is related to the world and what is actually the case. To see this, consider a minor amendment in the preceding example in which the demon, in a moment of cosmic absentmindedness, forgets for a moment to cloud our senses with the result that we really perceive what we think we do. If this moment is one that occurs very briefly as we suddenly awake and is immediately followed by further slumber to conceal the demonic error, we might believe we perceive what, in this instance, we actually do perceive. I might perceive my hand for the first time and believe I see a hand, only to lose consciousness after this formidable event. Do I know that I see a hand in that brief moment? I believe I do, but, since such beliefs are almost all false, I am almost totally untrustworthy in such matters as is everybody else, though accepting myself to be worthy of trust.

I am as much deceived about my trustworthiness in this case as I would be when confronted with a convincing liar who tells me almost all falsehoods about some party he attended except for one fact which, in a moment of absentmindedness, he accurately conveyed, namely, that he arrived before the host. If I accept all that he tells me and also that he is a trustworthy source of information about the event, I may be personally justified in accepting all that he says, but I do not know that the one truth he has conveyed is a truth. I do not know that he arrived before the host. The reason is that my assumption that my informant is trustworthy is in error, even if he has told me the truth in this one instance, and this error is sufficient to deprive me of the sort of justification I require for knowledge. This is the truth about justification contained in reliabilism.

Complete Justification and Reliabilism

The account that we have offered of complete justification in the last chapter is sufficient to deal with the sort of problem we have just considered. To be personally justified in accepting what another says, one must accept that the person is trustworthy, for, otherwise, the skeptic can win the justification game by claiming that informants are sometimes untrustworthy, or more directly, that the informant from whom I received the information is an untrustworthy informant. Thus, to be personally justified, I must accept that the informant is trustworthy. Since that is false, however, I will not be justified in accepting that my informant arrived before the host on the basis of my verific system, what is left of my acceptance system when all errors are deleted. I will not be verifically justified, and so I will not be completely justified either. Hence, the account offered above incorporates the reliabilist insight and explains how we fail to obtain knowledge when the source of information is unreliable.

The appeal of reliabilism and the other forms of externalism may, moreover, be easily understood in terms of the coherence theory and the account of complete justification contained therein. To oversimplify a bit, personal justification depends on our background information about the relationship of acceptance to the truth of what is accepted, about nomological or statistical correlations, about counterfactual dependence, or about reliable processes. This information is contained in my acceptance system. I know that I see my cat sitting on papers on the desk. I accept that I would not believe that I see a cat if it were not true that I see him. I accept that my believing I see a cat is correlated with my seeing a cat, though I would not put it that way. I accept that always, or almost always, I see a cat when I think I see one because my accepting that I see a cat results from a reliable process. It is my acceptance of these things that converts merely accepting that I see a cat into personal justification, into victory in the justification game. For that victory to be converted into complete justification, however, what I accept about these things must also be true. The conversion of mere acceptance into personal justification depends on my accepting the things about myself whose bare existence the externalist mistakenly assumes to be sufficient to convert true belief into knowledge. The conversion also depends, as the externalist says it does, on these things I accept about myself being true. The error of externalism is to fail to notice that the subject of knowledge must accept that the externalist conditions hold true. The insight of externalism is the claim that the conditions must, indeed, hold true.

Causation and Justification: The Basing Relation

The truth contained in reliabilism is, however, concealed by an error. What a person originally believes as a result of prejudice may later be accepted on the basis of scientific evidence. Therefore, the reliabilist must be in error when he claims that it is what originates a belief that converts it into a justified belief and knowledge. This is, in effect, to confuse the *reason* a person has for believing something with the *cause* of his believing it. The confusion is such a common one that we might name it the *causal fallacy*.

It is easy to see how the fallacy arises. When a person's justification for her belief is based on evidence, then she believes what she does *because* of the evidence. This suggests a causal account of what is involved when the justification of a belief is based on evidence. It suggests that the notion of a justification being based on evidence should be explicated in causal terms. Following this proposal, a person's justification for her belief is based on certain evidence if and only if her belief is causally related in some specified way to the evidence. How to specify the exact way in which the belief must be causally related to the evidence would remain a problem on this approach, but it would be a problem of detail rather than of principle. All such theories must be rejected, however.

Often the evidence on which a justification is based does causally explain the existence of the belief, and it may even be admitted that sometimes the belief is justified because of the way in which it is causally explained by the evidence. Nevertheless, it is also possible for a justified belief to be causally independent of the evidence that justifies it. Indeed, it may well be that the evidence in no way explains why the person holds the belief, even though her justification for the belief is based on the evidence. The evidence that justifies a person's belief may be evidence she acquired because she already held the belief, rather than the other way round. This is to be expected, since it is commonsense to distinguish between the reasons that justify a belief and the causes that produce it. The causes of belief are various, and, though the reasons we have for a belief sometimes cause the belief to arise, the belief may also arise from some other cause than having the reasons that justify it. Having the reasons we do may justify the belief, however, even though they have no causal influence upon the belief at all.

An example will illustrate. It is easy to imagine the case of someone who comes to believe something for the wrong reason and, consequently, cannot be said to be justified in his belief, but who, as a result of his belief, uncovers some evidence which completely justifies his belief. Suppose that a man, Mr. Raco, is racially prejudiced and, as a result, believes that the members of some race are susceptible to some disease to which members of his race are not susceptible. This belief, we may imagine, is an unshakable conviction. It is so strong a conviction that no evidence to the contrary would weaken his prejudiced conviction, and no evidence in favor would strengthen it. Now imagine that Mr. Raco becomes a doctor and begins to study the disease in question. Imagine that he reads all that is known about the disease and discovers that the evidence, which is quite conclusive, confirms his conviction. The scientific evidence shows that only members of the race in question are susceptible to the disease. We may imagine as well that Mr. Raco has become a medical expert perfectly capable of understanding the canons of scientific evidence, though, unfortunately, he becomes no less prejudiced as a result of this. Nevertheless, he understands and appreciates the evidence as well as any medical expert and, as a result, has reason for his belief that justifies it. He has discovered that his conviction is confirmed by the scientific evidence. He knows that only members of the other race are susceptible to the disease in question. Yet, the reasons that justify him in this belief do not causally explain the belief. The belief is the result of prejudice, not reason, but it is confirmed by reason which provides the justification for the belief. Prejudice gives Mr. Raco conviction, but reason gives him justification.

Harman and others, most notably Marshall Swain and Alvin Goldman, have suggested that a belief is based on evidence only if the evidence conditionally or partially explains the belief.[21] The idea is that, even if the belief is not originated by the evidence on which it is based, it must be causally sustained by the evidence. Again, in the typical case, this will be true. Usually, the reasons a person has for a belief can be expected to have some causal influence on the belief, even if they do not originate that belief. It is, unfortunately, difficult to evaluate the claim that the reasons that justify a belief must always partially explain or causally sustain the belief because a sufficiently precise account of partial explanation and causal sustenance is lacking. There appears to be no better reason for supposing that the evidence that justifies a belief must partially explain or causally sustain the belief than for supposing that it must originate it. The explanation for this is that we may suppose that the evidence justifying Mr. Raco's beliefs does not in any way explain or causally sustain his belief. What explains and sustains his belief is his prejudice. His belief is neither strengthened nor explained by his discovering the evidence for it. His prejudice gives him the strongest level of conviction, and the evidence adds nothing to the strength of it.

One might, however, suggest that his conviction is conditionally or counterfactually explained or sustained by the evidence, nonetheless. It might be proposed that if Mr. Raco were not to believe what he does out of prejudice, he would believe it as a result of the evidence. This is again likely, but it need not be so. Imagine that Mr. Raco is so dependent on his prejudice that if he were to cease to believe what he does out of prejudice, he would become quite mad and become uninfluenced by reason. To avoid such an objection one might propose, as Swain did, that to say the belief is sustained by the evidence is only to say that if Mr. Raco were not to believe what he does out of prejudice but were to continue to believe it nonetheless, then he would believe it as a result of the evidence. Perhaps this is to be expected, but must it be so? Again suppose that were Mr. Raco to cease to believe what he does out of prejudice, he would become quite mad and uninfluenced by reason; then were he to believe the same thing though not out of prejudice, he would believe it as a result of madness.

The point is the one with which we began. Though evidence ordinarily has some influence over belief or would have if other factors were to lose their influence, this is really incidental to justification. The analogy between justification and validity explains why. If a person validly deduces a conclusion from something he knows, this may cause him to believe the conclusion or influence his belief in the conclusion. But the validity of the inference does not depend on this causal influence. If valid deduction had no influence whatever on whether a person believed the conclusion, that would not undermine the validity of the inference. Similarly, if someone justifies some conclusion on the basis of something he knows, this may cause him to believe the conclusion or influence his belief in the conclusion. The justification of his conclusion, however, does not depend on the causal influence. Thus, a person may justify a second belief in terms of a first belief and the justification of the second belief may be based on the first without the second belief being causally influenced thereby.

The preceding discussion rests on a distinction between explaining why a person believes something, on the one hand, and explaining how he knows it, on the other. When a person knows that his belief is true, the explanation of why he believes what he does may have something to do with his having the evidence he does, but it need not. The explanation may rest on political, erotic, or other extraneous influences, but the explanation of how a person knows that his belief is true, when the justification of the belief is based on evidence, must be in terms of the evidence. It is how a person knows that is explained by evidence. Why he believes what he does may be explained by anything whatever. Therefore, a justification of a belief that is known to be true is based on certain evidence if and only if his having that evidence explains how he knows that the belief is true. The evidence explains how the person knows, moreover, if and only if the evidence justifies the person's belief. The manner in which evidence justifies a belief is explained in the account of complete justification in the last chapter. Evidence that justifies a belief consists of that part of the acceptance system of a person which yields complete justification.

The idea of evidence explaining how a person knows may be further clarified by recalling once again that our primary concern is to provide a theory to explain how people know that the information that they possess is correct. If the evidence that a person has justifies her belief that p, then the evidence explains how she knows that the information that p is correct. She knows this from the evidence. Similarly, if a person is asked how she knows that p, her reply will be to justify the claim that p in terms of her evidence. It is appeal to her evidence that shows that she knows and how she knows. Thus, a justification based on evidence explains how a person knows that p if that justification would be a correct answer to the question 'How do you know that p?'

Reliability and the Justification Game

The example of Mr. Raco, a person originally believing out of racial prejudice that the members of some race suffer a disease which members of other races do not suffer and later accepting this on the basis of scientific evidence, shows that a belief need not be produced or, as the example further indicated, even sustained by the evidence that justifies accepting it. Reliability enters into justification not by originating belief but by backing acceptance in the justification game. Consider the justification game played by the prejudiced man before obtaining the scientific information.

> *Claimant:* The members of that race suffer a disease to which members of other races are not susceptible.
> *Skeptic:* You believe what you do as the result of prejudice.
> *Claimant:* It is more reasonable for me to accept that I do not believe what I do as a result of prejudice than to accept that I believe what I do as a result of prejudice. (I am quite unprejudiced concerning members of the race in question, it is just that they are inferior.)

This personal justification would fail to convert into verific and complete justification. The claimant's error concerning his prejudice would disqualify this move in the verific justification game.

After acquiring the scientific information, the claimant is in a position to neutralize the claim of the skeptic in the justification game by making the following reply to the claim of the skeptic above:

> *Claimant:* It is as reasonable for me to accept that I believe what I do out of prejudice and that the best scientific evidence shows that what I thus believe is, in fact, true than to accept merely that I believe what I do out of prejudice. (In the standard medical reference work concerning this disease, it is stated that only

> members of the race in question are susceptible to the disease.
> This has been confirmed by recent studies cited in . . .)

This move succeeds in the verific justification game. The claimant wins the round, and his move cannot be disqualified. Whatever his moral failings, as a result of obtaining scientific understanding, he is victorious in the justification game. He is, therefore, personally and verifically justified in accepting what he does.

The preceding reflections illustrate the point that the evidence which justifies a person in accepting something must explain how the person knows that *p* rather than why he believes it. The scientific evidence explains how the person knows by explaining how he is victorious in the justification game. Usually, what makes a person victorious in the justification game is closely connected to what makes him believe what he does. But the connection is not essential to justification. As a result, the reliability essential to justification is not the reliability of the process which produces or causally sustains belief. What is essential is the reliability or trustworthiness of the evidence for what we accept to guide us to acceptance of what is true rather than false. The trustworthiness of the evidence makes us trustworthy in the matter, whatever our general defects. In epistemology as in life generally, you do not have to be perfect in order to be justified.

Externalism, Foundationalism, and Coherence: An Ecumenical Reconsideration

The foregoing articulation of the coherence theory of justification suggests that there is some merit in the foundation theory and in externalism which we have preserved in our theory. It is, therefore, time to turn from criticism to ecumenicalism. The foundation theory held some introspective, perceptual, and memory beliefs to be self-justified. We argued that the justification of all such beliefs depends on background information concerning our trustworthiness in such matters. Thus, it is coherence with such information in our acceptance system that produces the justification. Nevertheless, we concede that some beliefs are justified without inference because we accept ourselves to be trustworthy in such matters, and that a principle of our trustworthiness is needed to convert mere acceptance into justified acceptance.

Moreover, though the principle of our trustworthiness must cohere with what we accept about our successes and failures in past epistemic employments, the principle of our own trustworthiness provides its own personal justification. We are, at least in part, personally justified in accepting that we are trustworthy precisely because we accept that we are. If we did not accept that we were trustworthy, there would be an unbeatable skeptical challenge to any claim we made in the justification game, to wit, that we are untrustworthy in what we accept. To beat that move, we must accept that we are trustworthy. So, there appears to be at least one thing that we accept, one important and fundamental thing, that is self-justified as the foundationalist contended, even if it is not those introspective, perceptual, and memory beliefs that he most favors. To be personally justified one must accept some principle of trustworthiness which is, in part, self-justified.

To be verifically and completely justified as well, some principle of trustworthiness we accept must be true. Otherwise, the skeptical challenge that we are not trustworthy in what we accept would not be beaten in the verific justification game. The insight of externalism is the contention that there must be some truth connection between our accepting something and the truth of what we accept. It is our acceptance of our trustworthiness and the correctness of what we thus accept that yields the truth connection.

Externalism is motivated by the doubt about whether what we accept can supply the truth connection. The reason for the doubt is the assumption that it is psychologically unrealistic to suppose that beliefs about our beliefs are necessary for knowledge. Such higher order beliefs about beliefs are not, of course, necessary for receiving and relaying information. Even a thermometer is capable of that. Such beliefs are, however, necessary for knowledge. Is it unrealistic to suppose that people believe themselves to be trustworthy? Some unrealistic theory of belief may yield that consequence, but our theory of acceptance avoids it. The mental state of acceptance is a functional state, one that plays a role in thought, inference, and action. We think, infer, and act in a way manifesting our trust in what we accept.

Thus, it is appropriate and not at all unrealistic to suppose that, in addition to the other things we accept, we accept our own trustworthiness as well. We have supplied the truth that supplies the truth connection required by the externalist in the form of a self-justified principle of our own trustworthiness. We cannot be accused of chauvinism in claiming that complete justification is the result of coherence with an acceptance system incorporating the principle. Unless we are trustworthy in what we accept, neither we nor our adversaries can be justified in what we accept and we must all concede the day to the skeptic. If we are trustworthy, as we accept ourselves to be, what we accept will cohere with our acceptance system and our verific system to yield complete justification. The attainment of knowledge, like so many other benefits in life, rests on self-trust.

Introduction to the Literature

The most important defenders of externalism and reliabilism are Alvin Goldman, *Epistemology and Cognition*, D. M. Armstrong, *Belief, Truth and Knowledge*, Fred Dretske, *Knowledge and the Flow of Information*, and Robert Nozick, *Philosophical Explanations*, Chapter 3. A refined attempt to combine reliabilism with a theory of justification is in *Reasons and Knowledge* by Marshall Swain. For an important critical account of reliabilism, see Stewart Cohen's "Justification and Truth," as well as Richard Feldman's "Reliability and Justification." The original and classic article on naturalized epistemology is W.V.O. Quine's "Epistemology Naturalized," in his *Ontological Relativity and Other Essays*.

9

Skepticism

WE SAY WE KNOW, but do we? Skeptics have denied it and they have had an influential history. We shall, in the light of our epistemology, assess the genuine merits of skepticism. We have used the skeptic as a heuristic opponent in the justification game, but now we must turn to the philosophical skeptic who really genuinely challenges our claim to knowledge.

Skepticism and Agnoiology

Skepticism comes in different depths. Shallow forms deny that we know the few things we claim to, and the deepest form denies that we know anything at all.[1] Deeper forms of skepticism are based on the ubiquitous chance for error. Plain people, who comfort themselves in the snug foothills of accepted opinion, overlook the possibilities for error residing in our most familiar beliefs. In the minds of the dogmatic, what is familiar comes, through long acquaintance, to appear completely dependable and wins unquestioning confidence. The philosophical skeptic, inclined to question when others are drawn to dogmatic tranquillity, discovers the risk of error in our most trusted convictions. On this discovery, she constructs an *agnoiology*, a theory of ignorance.

Of course, skeptics who have denied that we know what we say we do have frequently been moved by more than a passion for the study of agnoiology. Often, they espouse some theory that conflicts with common opinion. Skepticism is defended to win consideration for their own theories. In reply, commonsense philosophers, like Reid and Moore, have rejected such speculative theories on the sole grounds that they conflict with common sense.[2] The beliefs of commonsense are innocent, they say, until proven guilty and constitute knowledge unless they are shown not to. Skeptics have been accused of semantic deviation, logical absurdity, and triviality. In an earlier chapter, we argued that what the skeptic says is semantically acceptable, logically consistent, and highly contentious. Rather than attempting to dismiss her abruptly by some superficial artifice, let us consider what sustains her argument.

There are a number of classical skeptical arguments appealing to dreams and hallucinations purporting to show that, whatever we take to be true, there remains some chance of error.[3] However, skeptical argumentation does not depend on these appeals. They are simply familiar ways of explaining how people err. It matters little what the source of error may be. What is critical is most simple. People often accept what is false, and, when what they accept happens to be true, there was some chance that they might have erred. This is the fundamental skeptical premise.

Conception and the Chance of Error

There are a variety of ways in which a skeptic may press this premise. Such arguments have the merit of calling our attention to some possibility of error we overlook. For example, a skeptic may base his argument on the nature of human conception. Experience by itself, as we have noted, tells us nothing. Knowledge requires the application of concepts and background information to experience. The best entrenched concept remains constantly subject to total rejection. In the pursuit of truth, we may discard any concept as lacking a denotation. Any concept may be thrown onto the junk-heap of repudiated concepts along with demons, entelechies, and the like. Moreover, any discarded concept can be refurbished. Because the concepts we reject may be better than the ones that supplant them, we may have to recycle what we discard. No concept or belief is sacrosanct in the quest for truth, and there is always some chance that any one may be cast off as misleading and erroneous.

The foregoing remarks describe more than a mere logical possibility. It is not only logically possible that any belief is in error, there is some genuine chance that it is so. The beliefs that have been most cherished and in which people have placed their greatest confidence, for example, the belief in witches, have been demoted from literal truths to figures of speech. Strictly speaking, there is no such thing. The concept of a witch, aside from use as a figure of speech, is a relic of religious conceptualization which is no longer tenable in an impartial and disinterested search for truth. This merely illustrates how, in the flux of conceptual change and innovation, any concept may be rejected for the sake of conceptual improvement and increased veracity.

We must note in passing that the concept of belief, indeed, even the concept of a concept, is no more secure than any other. Some materialists have said that belief is mental, and, consequently, that there is no such thing as belief. We cannot consider such materialism and the implications of it for our theory of knowledge here. Such materialism would require that, if we have referred to anything real in the world when speaking incorrectly of belief, what is real may be correctly described within a materialistic vocabulary.

The skeptic is correct, we concede, in affirming that the chance of error is always genuine. We grant the skeptical premise that if S accepts that p, then there is some chance that S is incorrect.

A Refutation of Skepticism: Fallibility, Not Ignorance

To sustain skepticism, a skeptic must go on to argue that if there is some chance that S is incorrect in accepting that p, then S does not know that p. On the analysis of knowledge that we have articulated, this premise is unavailable. It does not follow from the premise that there is some chance that S is incorrect in accepting that p, that p is not true, or that S does not accept that p, or that S is not completely justified in accepting that p, or that S's justification is defeated. Even if S accepts that there is some chance that he is incorrect in accepting that p, it may, nevertheless, be just as reasonable for him to accept that p in addition.

In the interests of obtaining truth, it may be as reasonable to accept something one does while also accepting one's fallibility, that is, accepting that there is some chance that one might be in error. The skeptic in the justification game may always cite the chance of error as a competitor in the justification game, but the player can also neutralize it. Our fallibility is an insufficient basis for skeptical victory. We may accept the premise of the skeptic concerning conceptual change and the universal chance of error implicit therein without accepting the deep skeptical conclusion of universal ignorance.

With this reply to skepticism set forth, we hasten to note that in some ways our position is very close to that of the skeptic, for very often when people claim to know something, they claim to know for certain. If they do know for certain, then there must be no chance that they are in error. Hence, in agreeing that there is always some chance of error, we are agreeing with the skeptic that nobody ever knows for certain that anything is true. Joining hands with the skeptic in this way will win us little applause from those dogmatists who never doubt that people know for certain many of the things they claim to know.

Thus, our theory of knowledge is a theory of knowledge without certainty. We agree with the skeptic that if a person claims to know for certain, he does not know whereof he speaks. However, when we claim to know, we make no claim to certainty. We conjecture that to speak in this way is a departure from the most customary use of the word 'know'. Commonly, when people say that they know, they mean they know for certain and they assume that there is no chance of being in error. This assumption enables them to lay aside theoretical doubts and to pretend they proceed on certain grounds. Such a pretense offers comfort and security in practical affairs and often in scientific investigation, as well. Nonetheless, it is a pretense exposed by the skeptic and repudiated by those who seek the truth. We, like the skeptic, deny that our beliefs have any guarantee of truth. We, like the skeptic, admit there to be a genuine chance that any of our beliefs may be false. We, like the skeptic, acknowledge that there is some chance, however small and remote, that the hypotheses are true which skeptics have conceived to call our dogmatic assumptions into doubt, and these cannot be ruled out by semantic shenanigans or appeal to the fiat of commonsense.

Our only reply to the skeptic is that, even if there is some chance that any of our beliefs may be in error and, even if, therefore, we do not know for certain that any of them are true, still some of the things we accept are things we are justified in accepting because all competitors are beaten or neutralized on the basis of our acceptance system. Of course, what we accept may be wrong—we are fallible—but if enough of what we accept is correct, then our justification will be undefeated and we will have knowledge. If we are sufficiently correct in what we accept so that we can distinguish between when our acceptance of something is trustworthy and when it is not, then we may know what we think we do despite the risk of error that we confront. If we were massively mistaken, as we would be if the Cartesian demon were loose in the land, then we would lack knowledge. A merely conceivable demon cannot reduce us to ignorance, however.

The Merits of Skepticism

Before celebrating victory over the skeptic, however, it should be carefully noted that the agnoiology of some skeptics is closer to the truth than the epistemology of many dogmatists. We offer no proof that the skeptic is wrong. A skeptic, reflecting on the harrowing vicissitudes of human conception, may come to accept that we are not trustworthy in what we accept and that it is as reasonable to accept one thing as another, or, put more moderately, that everything we accept has at least one competitor that can be neither beaten nor neutralized, namely, its denial. Such a skeptic will not be completely justified in anything she accepts, and therefore on our theory will not know that any statement is true. Even if she is incorrect in denying that we have knowledge, she will be correct in denying that she does. She will know as little as she says she does. If she is correct in what she accepts, and we are in error, however, the beliefs in our acceptance systems which personally justify us in accepting what we do may be erroneous. Consequently, we would not be completely justified in accepting what we do. The skeptic would enjoy victory.

Thus, on our theory of knowledge, whether we win or the skeptic wins the day depends on whether what we accept is correct, and especially on what we accept about when we are trustworthy and when we are not. We cannot refute the skeptic by appeal to demonstration. We argue against her from our acceptance system which is precisely what she calls into question. We may, nonetheless, know that she is wrong. Assuming that our complete justification for some of the things we accept is sustained within the members of our ultrasystem, we know those things to be true, and, indeed, we know that we know. If we do know that we know, then, of course, we know that the skeptic is mistaken in denying we know.

We avoid skepticism by constructing a theory of justification without a guarantee of truth. On our theory, if people know anything at all, it is because of the correctness of what they accept in their quest for truth. It is what they accept that makes them personally justified in their acceptance and, if enough of what they accept is true, their justification will be undefeated and become knowledge. The mere possibility or risk of error is not sufficient to sustain the skeptic. She must deny what we accept, especially what we accept about our own trustworthiness, and she must be correct and we in error to render her victorious. So, whether we know or not depends on whether what we accept about ourselves and our trustworthiness is correct. Surely, that is exactly what we should expect.

To put the matter more precisely, consider principle T, to wit, that I am a trustworthy guide to truth. If T is true, the justification a person has for accepting T based on accepting T would, in normal circumstance, be undefeated. One would expect all competitors of T to be beaten or neutralized on the basis of the verific system and the ultrasystem of S and, therefore, would expect the following principles to be true:

If S accepts that T and T is true, then S is completely justified in accepting that T

and

> If S accepts that T and T is true, then S is justified in accepting that T in a way that is undefeated.

Thus, the acceptance of T, if T is true, may be expected to yield knowledge of the truth of T. We may not be able to refute the skeptic who denies the truth of T or who advances some skeptical hypotheses implying the falsity of T. If, however, we are correct in thinking the skeptic is in error and, in accepting the truth of T, then, skeptical machinations notwithstanding, we know that T is true and know many other things as a result of this knowledge. We may not have the satisfaction of demonstrating that the skeptic is in error, for the attempt to do so would beg the question. We may, nevertheless, know that the skeptical hypotheses are false.

Skepticism and Closure: An Externalist Caveat

Some externalists have dealt with the skeptic in a way that resembles the preceding argument but is, nevertheless, distinct from it. They have rejected a closure principle affirming that if a person knows that p and that if p, then q, all at once, so to speak, then the person knows that q. The closure principle might be formulated with greater precision, of course, but this rough formulation suffices to understand how rejecting such a principle may be useful against a skeptic. The skeptic advances a skeptical hypothesis, the hypothesis that we are now asleep and dreaming rather than perceiving the external world as we suppose. She goes on to argue that we have no way of knowing that this skeptical hypothesis is false and concludes, therefore, that we do not know that we perceive the things we perceive. The externalist who rejects the closure principle concedes to the skeptic that we do not know her hypothesis is false but denies her inference. He says that we do know that we are perceiving external objects, a piece of paper before us, for example, even though we do not know that we are not now asleep and dreaming. True, he admits, if we are now asleep and dreaming, then we are not now perceiving the piece of paper, but we know that the latter is true even though we do not know that the former is false. Epistemic closure fails, he concludes, and with it all skeptical hypotheses.

The preceding line of thought is typical of externalists, though not advocated by all, because a belief resulting from a reliable process or a belief that tracks truth may have a consequence that does not result from a reliable process or track truth. I may have no way of telling whether I am asleep and dreaming or not, and hence the belief that I am not may not be the output of a reliable process nor track truth. I cannot, on this account, claim that I would not now believe that I am now awake and not asleep and dreaming if it were not true. The reason for this is that if I were asleep and dreaming it were true, I would believe just what I do. Dretske has suggested that, though one must be able to exclude relevant alternatives to what one believes in order to have knowledge, the skeptical alternatives fall short of relevance.[4]

The foregoing approach has some appeal. Since we do not think of skeptical hypotheses concerning dreams, hallucinations, Cartesian demons, or brains in vats as we go about our daily rounds, it is natural to suppose that we do not need to know anything about such matters in order to know the many things we suppose we do, for example, that we perceive external objects. If we know we perceive those things and do not know that the skeptical hypotheses are false, then the reason for denying epistemic closure is clear. Still, is the externalist correct in supposing we do not know the skeptical hypotheses to be false? The contrary is the case. I know that I am not now dreaming. I know that I am not now hallucinating. I know that no Cartesian demon deceives me and that no powerful scientist has my brain in a vat in his laboratory. I may find it hard to explain just how I know these things. I am, however, personally justified in accepting that the skeptical hypotheses are false because my acceptance of their falsity is trustworthy. If, moreover, this personal justification is undefeated and my acceptance trustworthy as I suppose, then I know that these skeptical hypotheses are all false. The skeptical hypotheses are relevant, are genuine competitors, but they are beaten by my acceptance system, and their defeat is sustained in my ultrasystem yielding knowledge. This knowledge does not result from the irrelevance of the skeptical alternatives but from our being personally justified in accepting that we are not dreaming, hallucinating, deceived by an evil demon, brains in vats, and, assuming that we are right in this, from our justification being complete and undefeated.

The skeptic provides a competitor to our various claims to knowledge, to the claims of perception, memory, and introspection. She shows that it is possible that we are in error, and she is right in this. We may go further and admit not only the metaphysical possibility that we may err but also that we are genuinely fallible in what we accept. We make genuine errors of perception, memory, and introspection. Consequently, there is always some chance of error in what we accept, however small and not worth worrying about in our daily transactions. While we applaud the skeptic for reminding us that a sound epistemology must acknowledge that we sometimes err and are ever fallible in our judgment, we may at the same time neutralize her objection.

We acknowledge that we are fallible in perception, memory, and introspection, but when we accept that the chances of error are negligible, we also accept that we are trustworthy in such cases. It is then as reasonable for us to add that we are trustworthy and accept both the possibility of error and our trustworthiness to avoid it as to accept the skeptical worry alone. It is, therefore, our trustworthiness that neutralizes the skeptical worries. In those instances in which we are trustworthy as we accept, we have undefeated justification and knowledge. In those instances in which false pride leads us to accept that we are trustworthy when we are not, the neutralization fails and our justification is defeated. The possibility or even some small risk of error does not bring the skeptic victory, however. The possibility and risk of error may be worthwhile in the quest for truth. A simple moral suffices to answer the skeptic: One can be both fallible and trustworthy.

Why not, however, reject the closure principle and refute the skeptic twice over? Her ability to survive criticism has given her greater longevity than Methuselah, after all, and a double refutation seems appropriate. The problem is that rejection of the closure principle yields problematic results concerning other matters. Of course, as Harman has noted, the mere deduction of some result from what one knows does not ensure that one will know the thing deduced.[5] What one knows at one time, one may fail to know at a later time because of what transpires in the interval, and the deduction of a consequence may have that result. The closure principle is intended to concern what one knows at a single time, however, and then it seems correct. The principle says that if one knows that p and that if p then q all at once, then one knows that q as well.

The problem that arises from denying this principle is illustrated by an example from Kripke based on an earlier example from Goldman.[6] It would seem that if I know that I see a blue barn, then I know that I see a barn. How could I know the former and not the latter? If we deny the epistemic closure principle, then I might. Moreover, if externalist theories were correct, it also might be the case that I might. We may illustrate the connection by supposing that I am in a part of the country where a clever stage builder put up barn facades here and there, which, to the unsuspecting, look exactly like barns. Suppose, however, that no such facades are blue, and that I, innocent of the industry of facade builders, see a blue barn. Imagine, moreover, that there are no other real barns in the area, only red barn facades, and that I would not be able to tell the difference between such facades and a barn.

Do I know that I see a blue barn? It would seem that I do not, since I cannot here tell a barn from a barn facade in my present circumstances. Notice, however, that I would not believe that I see a blue barn if I did not see a blue barn, for there are no blue barn facades. My belief tracks truth, as Nozick requires. Were tracking truth sufficient for knowledge, I would know that I see a blue barn. Notice, however, that if I also believe I see a barn, this belief would not track truth. Since there are many barn facades, it would be incorrect to say that I would not believe that I see a barn if I did not see a barn. I might believe I see a barn because I see a barn facade. Thus, if tracking truth were sufficient for knowledge, I would know that I see a blue barn but not know that I see a barn. Closure would fail.

The foregoing problem might, perhaps, be avoided by some modification of externalism, but it is naturally avoided by the account we have offered. Suppose that I see a blue barn, ignorant of the existence of barn facades, as in the example. Then I will accept that I can tell a barn where I am when I see one. This is false, however. When replaced in a member of my ultrasystem by the acceptance of its denial, that is, by acceptance of the claim that I cannot tell a barn where I am when I see one, any justification I have for accepting that I see a blue barn, as well as for accepting simply that I see a barn, will be defeated. The result on our theory is that I do not know that I see a blue barn anymore than I know that I see a barn in a barn facade-infested environment. The moral is that if we try to escape from skepticism by rejecting the closure principle, we shall find ourselves committed to saying that we know that we see a blue barn when we do not know that we see a barn. For this reason, when the externalist replies to the skeptic that we know that we see a barn when we do not know that we are awake and not asleep and dreaming we see a barn, he can hardly expect any more tolerant response from her than a smile of unknowing contempt.

In summary, we may in our quest for truth become confident of some modest success and communicate our confidence to others by affirming that we know. We may then proceed to justify that claim to other inquirers. We thus elicit their rejoinders and sometimes change what we accept as a result. By so doing, we hope to correct what we accept and come to know our world. It is the purpose of our theory of knowledge and justification to explicate the product of this uncertain epistemic adventure. One necessary step in this explication has been to repudiate the dogmatic prejudice that we often proceed without any chance of error. Our epistemology closely approaches the agnoiology of skepticism. We affirm that there is no security against failure or guarantee of success in our search for truth. The nobility of our objective must suffice to sustain our quest. If we are, nevertheless, correct in enough of what we accept about ourselves, the external world, and our trustworthiness, we may, contrary to the skeptic, know what we think we do, including the falsity of her ingenious hypotheses. We should, however, have the modesty to concede that we do not know for certain that we are right nor can we demonstrate that she is in error. She is the touchstone of sound epistemology and merits our conscientious regard.

Introduction to the Literature

There are many important works on skepticism. The most influential traditional work was probably *Meditations* by René Descartes, and the most important traditional defense of common sense against skepticism was *Essays on the Intellectual Powers of Man* by Thomas Reid. The most important twentieth century article on skepticism is G. E. Moore's "A Defense of Common Sense." Four important recent works are *The Significance of Philosophical Scepticism* by Barry Stroud, *Ignorance: A Case for Scepticism* by Peter Unger, *Skepticism* by Nicholas Rescher, and *Certainty: A Refutation of Scepticism* by Peter Klein. There are important articles on skepticism in the volume *Essays on Knowledge and Justification* edited by George S. Pappas and Marshall Swain and in a forthcoming volume, *Doubt*, edited by Michael Roth and Glenn Ross.

Notes

Chapter 1

1. Plato, *Symposium, Phaedo.*
2. Aristotle, *Metaphysics,* Z.
3. Descartes, *Meditations,* II.
4. For an account of knowledge intended to unify these conceptions, see Colin McGinn, "The Concept of Knowledge," *Midwest Studies in Philosophy* 9 (1984): 529–54.
5. See John Hartland-Swann, *An Analysis of Knowing* (London: Allen & Unwin, 1958), Chapter 4; Gilbert Ryle, "Knowing How and Knowing That," *Proceedings of the Aristotelian Society* 46 (1945–46): 1–16.
6. Bertrand Russell uses the expression "knowledge by acquaintance" but in a somewhat more technical sense. See his "Knowledge by Acquaintance and Knowledge by Description," *Proc. of Aris. Soc.* 11 (1910–11): 108–28, and reprinted with some alterations as Chapter 5 in *The Problems of Philosophy* (London: Oxford University Press, 1959): 46–59.
7. Fred Dretske, *Knowledge and the Flow of Information* (Cambridge: MIT Press, 1981).
8. For example, see A. J. Ayer's *The Foundations of Empirical Knowledge* (New York: St. Martin's Press, 1955), and *The Problem of Knowledge* (Harmondsworth, Middlesex: Penguin, 1957).
9. Rudolf Carnap, "Introduction," *The Logical Foundations of Probability* (Chicago: University of Chicago Press, 1962); W.V.O. Quine, "Two Dogmas of Empiricism," in *From a Logical Point of View* (Cambridge: Harvard University Press, 1953): 20–46.
10. The attack on this distinction is due, most recently and impressively, to Quine's discussion in "Two Dogmas of Empiricism." The theme is developed further in his later works, e.g., "Epistemology Naturalized," in *Ontological Relativity and Other Essays* (New York: Columbia University Press, 1969).
11. Colin Radford, "Knowledge—By Examples," *Analysis* 27 (1966): 1–11.
12. See G. E. Moore's "Certainty," in *Philosophical Papers* (London: Allen & Unwin, 1959): 226–51; and A. J. Ayer's *The Problem of Knowledge,* Chapter 1, section 3, 14–26.

13. Ayer, *The Problem of Knowledge*, 31–35, formulates the condition as the right to be sure. Chisholm formulates it as having adequate evidence in *Perceiving: A Philosophical Study* (Ithaca: Cornell University Press, 1957): 5 and 17 and as something being evident for a man in *Theory of Knowledge* (Englewood Cliffs, NJ: Prentice-Hall, 1966), 1st ed., 18–23. (Chisholm made changes in the second and third editions of this book, the most substantive being in the third. The third edition appeared just as this book was sent off for copy-editing, thus, it was impossible to discuss Chisholm's most recent ideas.)

14. Foundation theories are defended in J. L. Pollock, *Contemporary Theories of Knowledge* (Totowa, NJ: Rowman and Littlefield, 1986), Chapter 5, part 7; R. M. Chisholm, *The Foundations of Knowing* (Minneapolis: University of Minnesota Press, 1982); and Paul Moser, *Empirical Justification* (Dordrecht and Boston: Reidel, 1985). Pollock's theory is unusual in that the foundational states are not beliefs; he calls his theory a "non-doxastic" version of "direct realism." Some might not call such a theory a foundation theory at all, but it is more closely allied with a foundation theory than with any other type of epistemological theory.

15. Coherence theories are defended in Keith Lehrer, *Knowledge* (Oxford: Clarendon Press, 1974), and Laurence BonJour, *The Structure of Empirical Knowledge* (Cambridge: Harvard University Press, 1985).

16. Representative externalist theories can be found in Robert Nozick, *Philosophical Explanations* (Cambridge: Harvard University Press, 1981); Fred Dretske, *Knowledge and the Flow of Information;* and Alvin Goldman, *Epistemology and Cognition* (Cambridge: Harvard University Press, 1986).

17. Ayer and Chisholm defend similar analyses. See Ayer, *The Problem of Knowledge* and *The Foundations of Empirical Knowledge;* Chisholm, *Perceiving.*

18. See Edmund Gettier, Jr., "Is Justified True Belief Knowledge?" *Analysis* 23 (1963): 121–23. Russell made a similar observation in *The Problems of Philosophy:* 132.

19. These examples and related ones are taken from Keith Lehrer, "Knowledge, Truth, and Evidence," *Analysis* 25 (1965): 168–75. This article and others on the same topic are included in Michael Roth and Leon Galis, eds., *Knowing: Essays in the Theory of Knowledge* (New York: Random House, 1970).

20. Gettier, "Is Justified True Belief Knowledge?"

21. The sheep example comes from R. M. Chisholm, *Theory of Knowledge,* 23, fn. 22.

22. This proposal is similar to one made in the article by Lehrer cited above, and by others as well, in the series of articles elicited by the Gettier example.

Chapter 2

1. Alfred Tarski, "The Semantic Conception of Truth," in L. Linsky, ed., *Semantics and the Philosophy of Language* (Urbana: University of Illinois Press, 1952); "The Concept of Truth in Formalized Languages," in *Logic, Semantics, and Metamathematics* (Oxford: Clarendon Press, 1969).

2. Tarski, "The Semantic Conception of Truth."

3. *Ibid.*

4. George Berkeley, *A Treatise Concerning the Principles of Human Knowledge,* Colin M. Turbayne, ed., sections 23 and 24 (Indianapolis: Bobbs-Merrill, 1957).

5. This kind of argument is more popular with philosophers than the literature of the field reveals, and it would be hard to say who first formulated it. The late Austin Duncan-Jones remarked, "Yet obviously, if 'I think *p*' is used in the colloquial way, as equivalent to, 'I am inclined to think *p*', it doesn't follow from 'I think *p*' at all but is consistent with it." In a footnote on the same page he remarks in support that we say, 'I don't think, I know'. These remarks appear in "Further Questions About 'Know' and 'Think'," Margaret Macdonald, ed., *Philosophy and Analysis* (Oxford: Blackwell, 1966): 97.

6. J. L. Austin, "Other Minds," in A.G.N. Flew, ed., *Logic and Language.* Second Series (Oxford: Blackwell, 1959): 123–58.

7. *Ibid.:* 144.

8. *Ibid.*

9. *Ibid.:* 146–47.

10. Colin Radford, "Knowledge—By Examples," *Analysis* 27 (1966): 1–11. Much of Radford's attack in this article is directed against the thesis that a person knows that *p* only if he is sure or feels sure that *p*.

11. Radford, "Analyzing 'Knows That'," *Philosophical Quarterly* 20 (1970): 228–29.

12. E. J. Lemmon, "If I Know, Do I Know That I Know?" in A. Stroll, ed., *Epistemology: New Essays in the Theory of Knowledge* (New York: Harper and Row, 1967): 54–83, particularly 63.

13. Radford, "Knowledge—By Examples," 4, fn. 1.

14. Stephan Kröner, *Experience and Theory* (London: Routledge and Kegan Paul, 1966): 19–47.

15. Fred Dretske, *Knowledge and the Flow of Information* (Cambridge: MIT Press, 1981).

16. David Armstrong, "Does Knowledge Entail Belief?" *Proceedings of the Aristotelian Society* 70 (1969–70): 21–36.

Chapter 3

1. Fallible foundations are defended in J. L. Pollock, *Contemporary Theories of Knowledge* (Totowa, NJ: Rowman and Littlefield, 1986), Chapter 5, part 7, and in R. M. Chisholm, *The Foundations of Knowing* (Minneapolis: University of Minnesota Press, 1982). See discussion in Chapter 1, fn. 13.

2. Descartes is often claimed to be such a rationalist. Historically, this position is probably mistaken. In a late section of the *Discourse on Method,* Descartes mentions how he had recourse to experiment to decide between competing hypotheses. See *Discourse on Method,* part 6. Thus, it is doubtful that Descartes was a strict rationalist. He seems to have agreed that at least on some occasions justification is derived from sense experience.

3. Panayot Butchvarov in *The Concept of Knowledge* (Evanston, IL: Northwestern University Press, 1970), and Arthur C. Danto in *Analytical Philosophy of Knowledge* (Cambridge: Cambridge University Press, 1968) have expounded this view. See

Butchvarov's discussion of the notion of sufficient evidence on pp. 49–50, and Danto's discussions of both direct knowledge and adequate evidence on pp. 26–49 and 147, and 122, resp. A. J. Ayer in *Foundations of Empirical Knowledge* (New York: St. Martin's Press, 1955): 74–84, proceeds with the same assumptions and attempts to found justification on incorrigible statements.

4. J. L. Pollock, *Knowledge and Justification* (Princeton: Princeton. University Press, 1974) and *Contemporary Theories of Knowledge;* Mark Pastin, "Modest Foundationalism and Self-Warrant," in *American Philosophical Quarterly,* monograph series 9 (1975); Ernest Sosa, "Epistemic Presupposition," in G. S. Pappas, ed., *Justification and Knowledge* (Dordrecht: Reidel, 1979): 79–92; Richard Foley, *A Theory of Epistemic Rationality* (Cambridge: Harvard University Press, 1987); and William Alston, "Two Types of Foundationalism," *Journal of Philosophy* 73 (1976): 165–85.

5. For example, see R. M. Chisholm, *Theory of Knowledge* (Englewood Cliffs, NJ: Prentice-Hall, 1966), 1st ed., Chapter 2, "The Directly Evident," and *Perceiving: A Philosophical Study* (Ithaca: Cornell University Press, 1957), particularly Chapter 5, "Justification and Perception."

6. Pollock has suggested this; see *Contemporary Theories of Knowledge,* Chapter 2. See also Jonathan Kvanvig, "How to be a Reliabilist," *Amer. Phil. Q.* 23 (1986).

7. See Laurence BonJour, *The Structure of Empirical Knowledge* (Cambridge: Harvard University Press, 1985), particularly Chapters 1, 2, and 4.

8. Another method for dealing with these problems is presented by George Nakhnikian in "Incorrigibility," *Philosophical Quarterly* 28 (1968): 207–15, but Nakhnikian defines incorrigibility in terms of knowledge, and this would be unacceptable in the present context.

9. Katherine Pyne Parsons in, "Mistaking Sensations," *Philosophical Review* 79 (1970): 201–13, raises some similar objections to the doctrine that statements about mental states are incorrigible.

10. David Armstrong, "Is Introspective Knowledge Incorrigible?" *Phil. Rev.* 72 (1963): 424.

11. *Ibid.*

12. George Berkeley, *A Treatise Concerning the Principles of Human Knowledge,* Colin M. Turbayne, ed. (Indianapolis: Bobbs-Merrill, 1957), part 1.

13. *Ibid.*

14. Ayer, *Foundations,* 74–84.

15. See Ayer's defense of this thesis in *Foundations,* 74–84, and in "Basic Propositions," in *Philosophical Essays* (New York: St. Martin's Press, 1954): 105–24, particularly 113ff.

16. See Chisholm, *Perceiving,* appendix, 190–93.

Chapter 4

1. Thomas Reid, *Essays on the Active Powers of Man* from *The Works of Thomas Reid, D.D.,* Sir William Hamilton, ed. (Edinburgh: James Thin, 1895): 617.

2. This argument is derived from Chisholm in *Perceiving: A Philosophical Study* (Ithaca: Cornell University Press, 1957), Chapter 5, "Justification and Perception": 54–66.

3. Thomas Reid, *Essays on the Active Powers of Man.*

4. See, for example, Alvin Goldman, "What Is Justified Belief?" in G. S. Pappas, ed., *Justification and Knowledge* (Dordrecht: Reidel, 1979), and *Epistemology and Cognition* (Cambridge: Harvard University Press, 1986), Chapter 5.

5. Gilbert Harman, "How Belief Is Based on Inference," *Journal of Philosophy* 61 (1964): 353–59.

6. R. M. Chisholm develops his doctrine concerning the noncomparative use of words in *Perceiving*, Chapter 4, and discusses it again in *Theory of Knowledge* (Englewood Cliffs, NJ: Prentice-Hall, 1966), 1st ed., Chapter 2.

7. Chisholm offers such an argument in *Theory of Knowledge*, Chapter 2, p. 36, fn. 20.

8. This argument has been influenced by a similar argument in W. F. Sellars, "Empiricism and the Philosophy of the Mind," in his book *Science, Perception, and Reality* (London: Routledge and Kegan Paul, 1963), section 18, 146–47.

9. See J. L. Pollock, *Knowledge and Justification* (Princeton: Princeton University Press, 1974).

10. See John Lyons, *Structural Semantics* (Oxford: Blackwell, 1963), Chapter 4; Adrienne Lehrer, "Semantic Cuisine," *Journal of Linguistics* 5 (1969): 39–55.

11. James Van Cleve, "Foundationalism, Epistemic Principles, and the Cartesian Circle," *Philosophical Review* 88 (1979): 55–91; William Alston, "Two Types of Foundationalism," *Journal of Philosophy* 73 (1976): 165–85.

12. This thesis may be questioned by those who defend a nonprobabilistic account of inductive support, for example, L. Jonathan Cohen in *The Implications of Induction* (London: Methuen, 1970); *The Probable and the Provable* (Oxford: Clarendon Press, 1977).

13. The frequency concept is articulated by Hans Reichenbach in *The Theory of Probability* (Berkeley: University of California Press, 1949), the logical concept is developed by Rudolf Carnap in *The Logical Foundations of Probability* (Chicago: University of Chicago Press, 1972), and the subjective concept is argued by Richard Jeffrey in *The Logic of Decision* (New York: McGraw-Hill, 1965).

14. See Jaakko Hintikka, "A Two-Dimensional Continuum of Inductive Methods," in J. Hintikka and P. Suppes, eds., *Aspects of Inductive Logic* (Amsterdam: North Holland, 1966): 113–32; Rudolf Carnap, *The Continuum of Inductive Methods* (Chicago: University of Chicago Press, 1952).

Chapter 5

1. See Robert Fogelin, *Evidence and Meaning* (New York: Humanities Press, 1967): 94–98.

2. They also conceive of coherence as truth. See Brand Blanshard's *The Nature of Thought* (London: Allen and Unwin, 1939), particularly Vol. 2, Chapters 26 and 27, 250–331.

3. See Wilfrid Sellars, "Some Reflections on Language Games," in *Science Perception, and Reality* (London: Routledge and Kegan Paul, 1963): 321–58; and Gilbert Harman's article, "Induction," in Marshall Swain, ed., *Induction, Acceptance, and Rational Belief* (Dordrecht: Reidel, 1970): 3–99, as well as his book, *Thought* (Princeton: Princeton University Press, 1973). The author defended a similar view in "Justification, Explanation, and Induction" in Swain, 100–33.

4. Bertrand Russell, *The Problems of Philosophy* (London: Holt, 1912): 22–26.

5. See Paul Ziff, "The Simplicity of Other Minds," in H. Feigl, W. F. Sellars, and K. Lehrer, eds., *New Readings in Philosophical Analysis* (New York: Appleton-Century-Crofts, 1972): 418–23.

6. Carl G. Hempel, "Studies in the Logic of Explanation," in *Aspects of Scientific Explanation* (New York: Free Press, 1965): 245–90.

7. See R. Eberle, D. Kaplan, and R. Montague, "Hempel and Oppenheim on Explanation," in *Philosophy of Science* 28 (1961): 418–28.

8. Sylvain Bromberger, "Why-Questions," in Robert Colodny, ed., *Mind and Cosmos* (Pittsburgh: University of Pittsburgh Press, 1966): 105.

9. Bromberger, "An Approach to Explanation," in Ronald Butler, ed., *Studies in Analytical Philosophy*, 2nd series (Oxford: Blackwell, 1965): 72–105.

10. Hempel, *Aspects of Scientific Explanation*, 425–28.

11. See Sellars' remarks on language entry transitions in "Some Reflections on Language Games," 321–58. It should be noted that Sellars explicitly denies that such conditioned responses are sufficient for establishing the meaning or justification of observation statements. Nevertheless, they do play a role in such justification. See Quine's remarks on stimulus meaning in *Word and Object* (Cambridge: MIT Press, 1960), Chapters 1 and 2.

12. Laurence BonJour, *The Structure of Empirical Knowledge* (Cambridge: Harvard University Press, 1985): 141–46. A detailed statement and defense of coherentism regarding empirical knowledge is found in Chapters 1, 4, 6, 7, and 9.

13. See the introduction to C. I. Lewis' *Mind and the World Order* (New York: Dover, 1929), and R. M. Chisholm, *Perceiving: A Philosophical Study* (Ithaca: Cornell University Press, 1957), Chapter 3, "The Problem of 'the Criterion'," 30–39.

14. See Alan Goldman, *Empirical Knowledge* (Berkeley: University of California, 1988).

15. Bromberger, "Why-Questions," 96–102.

16. This example was provided by Frederick Schick.

17. In articles and books cited above.

18. Sellars, "Some Reflections on Language Games," section 85, p. 356.

19. Quine in *Word and Object*, Chapter 1, pp. 20–21; and Harman in *Thought*, 159.

20. The importance of the objective of truth-seeking in a coherence theory has been systematically emphasized by BonJour in *Structure*, while the opposite view that explanation suffices is defended by William Lycan, *Judgement and Justification* (New York: Cambridge University Press, 1988).

Chapter 6

1. Descartes, *Meditations*, II; Hilary Putnam in *Reason, Truth and History*, Chapter 1, "Brains in a Vat" (Cambridge: Cambridge University Press, 1984).

2. Thomas Reid, *Essays on the Active Powers of Man*, from *The Works of Thomas Reid, D.D.*, Sir William Hamilton, ed. (Edinburgh: James Thin, 1895): 617.

3. See W.V.O. Quine, *Word and Object* (Cambridge: MIT Press, 1960); Wilfrid Sellars, "Some Reflections on Language Games," in *Science, Perception, and Reality* (London: Routledge and Kegan Paul, 1963): 321–58; Gilbert Harman, *Thought* (Princeton: Princeton University Press, 1973); Bruce Aune, *Knowledge, Mind, and Nature* (New York: Random House, 1967); Jay Rosenberg, *One World and Our Knowledge of It* (Dordrecht: Reidel, 1980); Laurence Bonjour, *The Structure of Empirical Knowledge* (Cambridge: Harvard University Press, 1985).

4. Decision theory is applied to epistemic issues by Carl G. Hempel in his article, "Deductive-Nomological vs. Statistical Explanation," in Herbert Feigl and Grover Maxwell, eds., *Minnesota Studies in the Philosophy of Science*, Vol. 3 (Minneapolis: University of Minnesota Press, 1962): 98–169; by J. Hintikka and J. Pietarinen in "Semantic Information and Inductive Logic," in *Aspects of Inductive Logic* (Amsterdam: North-Holland Publishing Co., 1966); and by Issac Levi in *Gambling With Truth: An Essay on Induction and the Aims of Science* (New York: Knopf, 1967).

5. See Henry Kyburg, *Probability and the Logic of Rational Belief* (Middletown, CT: Wesleyan University Press, 1961): 167.

Chapter 7

1. See Donald Davidson, "Truth and Meaning" and "Radical Interpretation," in his *Inquiries Into Truth and Interpretation* (Oxford: Clarendon Press, 1984), especially 27 and 136–37. See also Davidson's "A Coherence Theory of Truth and Knowledge" in Ernest LePore, ed., *Truth and Interpretation: Perspectives on the Philosophy of Donald Davidson* (Oxford: Blackwell, 1986): 307–19. Davidson's claims have been cogently criticized by Peter Klein, "Radical Interpretation and Global Skepticism," *Truth and Interpretation*, 369–86; and Ernest Sosa, "'Circular' Coherence and 'Absurd' Foundations," in *Truth and Interpretation*, 387–97.

2. Edmund Gettier, Jr., "Is Justified True Belief Knowledge?" *Analysis* 23 (1963): 121–23. The example in the text is taken from Keith Lehrer, "Knowledge, Truth and Evidence," *Analysis* 25 (1965): 168–75.

3. Gettier made an observation to this effect in a symposium of the Eastern Division meetings of the American Philosophical Association, December 1970, in reply to Gilbert Harman's "Knowledge, Reasons and Causes," *Journal of Philosophy* 67 (1970): 841–55.

4. See Irving Thalberg, "In Defense of Justified True Belief," *Journal of Philosophy* 66 (1969): 794–803; Joseph Margolis, "The Problem of Justified Belief," *Philosophical Studies* 23 (1972): 405–09.

5. R. M. Chisholm, *Theory of Knowledge* (Englewood Cliffs, NJ: Prentice-Hall, 1966), 1st ed., 23, fn. 22.

6. This argument appeared originally in the author's "Knowledge, Truth, and Evidence," *Analysis* 25 (1965): 168–75, and was reprinted in Michael Roth and Leon Galis, eds., *Knowing: Essays in the Theory of Knowledge* (New York: Random House, 1970): 55–66.

7. Peter Klein, "A Proposed Definition of Propositional Knowledge," *Journal of Philosophy* 67 (1971): 471–82; and Risto Hilpinen, "Knowledge and Justification," *Ajatus* 33 (1971): 7–39.

8. Keith Lehrer and Thomas Paxson, Jr., "Knowledge: Undefeated Justified True Belief," *Journal of Philosophy* 66 (1966): 225–37.

9. Gilbert Harman, *Thought* (Princeton: Princeton University Press, 1973).

10. Robert Audi, *Belief, Justification, and Knowledge* (Belmont, CA: Wadsworth, 1988).

11. The notion of something being a member of an ultrasystem explained above may be defined as follows: (M) A system M is a member of the ultrasystem of S at t if and only if either M is the acceptance system of S at t or results from eliminating one or more statements of the form 'S accepts that q' when q is false, replacing one or more statements of the form 'S accepts that q' with a statement of the form 'S accepts that not-q' when q is false, or any combination of such eliminations and replacements in the acceptance system of S at t with the constraint that if q logically entails r, which is false and also accepted, then 'S accepts that r' must also be eliminated or replaced in the same way as 'S accepts that q' was.

Chapter 8

1. Alvin Goldman, "A Causal Theory of Knowing," *Journal of Philosophy* 64 (1987): 357–72.

2. Alvin Goldman, *Epistemology and Cognition* (Cambridge: Harvard University Press, 1986).

3. D. M. Armstrong, *Belief, Truth, and Knowledge* (Cambridge: Cambridge University Press, 1973); Fred Dretske, *Knowledge and the Flow of Information* (Cambridge: MIT Press, 1981).

4. Robert Nozick, *Philosophical Explanations* (Cambridge: Harvard University Press, 1981), Chapter 3.

5. Alvin Goldman, "What Is Justified Belief?" in G. S. Pappas, ed., *Justification and Knowledge* (Dordrecht: Reidel, 1979); see also his *Epistemology and Cognition*.

6. David Hume, *A Treatise of Human Nature* (Indianapolis: Bobbs-Merrill, 1977).

7. W.V.O. Quine, "Epistemology Naturalized," *Ontological Relativity and Other Essays* (New York: Columbia University Press, 1969).

8. Armstrong, *Belief, Truth, and Knowledge*; Fred Dretske, *Seeing and Knowing* (London: Routledge and Kegan Paul, 1969).

9. The 'braino' example comes from James M. Cornman, Keith Lehrer, and G. S. Pappas, eds., *Philosophical Problems and Arguments: An Introduction* (New York: Hackett, 1987), 3rd ed., 54–55.

10. Dretske and Goldman have both discussed replies to skepticism that distinguish relevant from irrelevant alternatives. See Goldman, "Discrimination and Perceptual Knowledge," *Journal of Philosophy* 73 (1976): 771–91, and Dretske, "Conclusive Reasons," *Australasian Journal of Philosophy* 49 (1971): 1–22. See also Dretske, *Knowledge and the Flow of Information*.

11. See Nozick, *Philosophical Explanations*, Chapter 3, and Dretske, *Knowledge and the Flow of Information*.

12. Goldman, "A Causal Theory of Knowing."

13. Dretske, *Knowledge and the Flow of Information*.

14. Goldman, "What Is Justified Belief?"

15. Nozick, *Philosophical Explanations*.

16. Armstrong, *Belief, Truth, and Knowledge*.

17. Nozick, *Philosophical Explanations*; Dretske, *Knowledge and the Flow of Information*.

18. Goldman, *Epistemology and Cognition*: 62–63, 111–12.

19. Stewart Cohen, "Justification and Truth," *Philosophical Studies* 46 (1984): 279–96; see also Keith Lehrer and Stewart Cohen, "Justification, Truth, and Coherence," *Synthese* 55 (1983): 191–207.

20. Goldman, *Epistemology and Cognition*, 107–09, and "Strong and Weak Justification," in J. Tomberlin, ed., *Philosophical Perspectives*, Vol. 2 (Atascadero, CA: Ridgeview, 1988): 51–70.

21. See Gilbert Harman, "Knowledge, Reasons, and Causes," *Journal of Philosophy* 67 (1970): 844–55; also his *Change in View* (Cambridge: MIT Press, 1986) and *Thought* (Princeton: Princeton University Press, 1973); and Marshall Swain, *Reason and Knowledge* (Ithaca: Cornell University Press, 1981). For an argument that no revision of Swain's account can succeed, see Jonathan Kvanvig, "Swain on the Basing Relation," *Analysis* 45 (1985): 153–58.

Chapter 9

1. The author defended the deepest skepticism in "Why Not Scepticism?" in *Philosophical Forum* 2 (1971): 283–98, and Peter Unger defended a very deep, if not the deepest, form in "A Defense of Skepticism," *Philosophical Review* 80 (1971): 198–219. See also Unger, *Ignorance: A Case for Skepticism* (Oxford: Clarendon Press, 1975); Barry Stroud, *The Significance of Philosophical Scepticism* (Minneapolis: University of Minnesota Press, 1981); Nicholas Rescher, *Skepticism: A Critical Reappraisal* (Tototwa: Rowman and Littlefield, 1980), and Peter Klein, *Certainty: A Refutation of Scepticism* (Oxford: Clarendon Press, 1984).

2. Thomas Reid, *The Philosophical Works of Thomas Reid*, Sir William Hamilton, ed., 234, and G. E. Moore in "A Defense of Common Sense" in *Contemporary British Philosophy*, J. H. Muirhead, ed., 2nd series (London: Macmillan, 1925): 193–223.

3. The most famous, of course, is René Descartes in *Meditations* I.

4. See Fred Dretske, *Knowledge and the Flow of Information* (Cambridge: MIT Press, 1981): 123–24.

5. Gilbert Harman, "Induction," in "Induction, Acceptance, and Rational Belief," *Rational Belief,* Marshall Swain, ed. (Dordrecht: Reidel, 1970): 91.

6. Saul Kripke, unpublished review of Robert Nozick, *Philosophical Explanations,* Chapter 3 (Cambridge: Harvard University Press, 1981).

Bibliography

THIS LIST is not a complete bibliography of the subject. It contains all of the books mentioned in the Introduction to the Literature sections that follow each chapter as well as other references that may be useful to students.

Ackermann, Robert. *Belief and Knowledge*. Garden City, NY: Anchor Books, 1972.

Adler, Jonathan E. "Knowing, Betting and Cohering." *Philosophical Topics* 14 (1986).

Alston, William. "Varieties of Privileged Access." *American Philosophical Quarterly* 8 (1971).

——— . "Two Types of Foundationalism." *Journal of Philosophy* 73 (1976).

——— . "Self-Warrant: A Neglected Form of Privileged Access." *American Philosophical Quarterly* 13 (1976).

——— . "Level-Confusions in Epistemology." In *Midwest Studies in Philosophy*, Vol. 5: *Studies in Epistemology*, edited by P. A. French, T. E. Uehling, and H. K. Wettstein. Minneapolis: University of Minnesota Press, 1980.

——— . "What's Wrong with Immediate Knowledge?" *Synthese* 55 (1983).

——— . "Concepts of Epistemic Justification." *The Monist* 68 (1985). Reprinted in *Empirical Knowledge: Readings in Contemporary Epistemology*, edited by Paul K. Moser. Totowa, NJ: Rowman and Littlefield, 1986.

——— . "Internalism and Externalism in Epistemology." *Philosophical Topics* 14 (1986).

——— . "The Deontological Conception of Epistemic Justification." In *Philosophical Perspectives*, Vol. 2: *Epistemology*, edited by J. Tomberlin. Atascadero, CA: Ridgeview, 1988.

Annis, David B. "A Contextualist Theory of Epistemic Justification." *American Philosophical Quarterly* 15 (1978).

Aristotle. *Metaphysics*, Z.

Armstrong, D. M. "Is Introspective Knowledge Incorrigible?" *Philosophical Review* 72 (1963).

——— . *A Materialistic Theory of the Mind*. London: Routledge and Kegan Paul, 1968.

——— . "Does Knowledge Entail Belief?" *Proceedings of the Aristotelian Society* 70 (1969–70).

————. *Belief, Truth and Knowledge.* Cambridge: Cambridge University Press, 1973.

Audi, Robert. "Believing and Affirming." *Mind* 92 (1982).

————. "Belief, Reason, and Inference." *Philosophical Topics* 14 (1986).

————. *Belief, Justification, and Knowledge.* Belmont, CA: Wadsworth, 1988.

Aune, Bruce. *Knowledge, Mind, and Nature.* New York: Random House, 1967.

Austin, J. L. "Other Minds." In *Logic and Language,* Second Series, edited by A.G.N. Flew. Oxford: Blackwell, 1959.

Ayer, A. J. *Philosophical Essays.* New York: St. Martin's Press, 1954.

————. *The Foundations of Empirical Knowledge.* New York: St. Martin's Press, 1955.

————. *The Problem of Knowledge.* Harmondsworth, Middlesex: Penguin, 1957.

————. "Verification and Experience" (1936). In *Logical Positivism,* edited by A. J. Ayer. New York: Free Press, 1959.

Bender, John W. "The Ins and Outs of 'Metaknowledge'." *Analysis* 48 (1988).

————. "Knowledge, Justification, and Lehrer's Theory of Coherence." *Philosophical Studies* 54 (1988): 355–81.

Bender, John W., ed. *The Current State of the Coherence Theory.* Boston: Kluwer, 1989.

Berkeley, George. *A Treatise Concerning the Principles of Human Knowledge,* edited by Colin M. Turbayne. Indianapolis: Bobbs-Merrill, 1957.

Blanshard, Brand. *The Nature of Thought.* London: Allen and Unwin, 1939.

BonJour, Laurence. "Can Empirical Knowledge Have a Foundation?" *American Philosophical Quarterly* 15 (1978).

————. "Externalist Theories of Empirical Knowledge." In *Midwest Studies in Philosophy,* Vol. 5: *Studies in Epistemology,* edited by P. A. French, T. E. Uehling, and W. K. Wettstein. Minneapolis: University of Minnesota Press, 1980.

————. *The Structure of Empirical Knowledge.* Cambridge: Harvard University Press, 1985.

————. "A Reconsideration of the Problem of Induction." *Philosophical Topics* 14 (1986).

————. "The Coherence Theory of Empirical Knowledge." In *Empirical Knowledge: Readings in Contemporary Epistemology,* edited by Paul K. Moser. Totowa, NJ: Rowman and Littlefield, 1986.

Brandt, R. B., and Ernest Nagel, eds. *Meaning and Knowledge.* New York: Harcourt, Brace and World, 1965.

Bromberger, Sylvain. "An Approach to Explanation." In *Studies in Analytical Philosophy,* edited by Ronald Butler. 2nd series. Oxford: Blackwell, 1965.

————. "Why-Questions." In *Mind and Cosmos,* edited by Robert Colodny. Pittsburgh: University of Pittsburgh Press, 1966.

Butchvarov, Panayot. *The Concept of Knowledge.* Evanston, IL: Northwestern University Press, 1970.

Carnap, Rudolf. *The Continuum of Inductive Methods.* Chicago: University of Chicago Press, 1952.

————. *The Logical Foundations of Probability.* 2nd ed. Chicago: University of Chicago Press, 1962.

Castañeda, Hector-Neri. "Knowledge and Epistemic Obligation." In *Philosophical Perspectives*, Vol. 2: *Epistemology*, edited by S. Tomberlin. Atascadero, CA: Ridgeview, 1988.

Chisholm, R. M. *Perceiving: A Philosophical Study*. Ithaca, NY: Cornell University Press, 1957.

_____ . *Theory of Knowledge*. 1st ed. Englewood Cliffs, NJ: Prentice-Hall, 1966.

_____ . *Theory of Knowledge*. 2nd ed. Englewood Cliffs, NJ: Prentice-Hall, 1977.

_____ . *Theory of Knowledge*. 3rd ed. Englewood Cliffs, NJ: Prentice-Hall, 1989.

_____ . "On the Nature of Empirical Evidence." In *Essays on Knowledge and Justification*, edited by G. S. Pappas and Marshall Swain. Ithaca, NY: Cornell University Press, 1978.

_____ . *The Foundations of Knowing*. Minneapolis: University of Minnesota Press, 1982.

_____ . "The Place of Epistemic Justification." *Philosophical Topics* 14 (1986).

_____ . "The Evidence of the Senses." In *Philosophical Perspectives*, Vol. 2: *Epistemology*, edited by J. Tomberlin. Atascadero, CA: Ridgeview, 1988.

Chisholm, R. M., and Robert Swartz, eds. *Empirical Knowledge*. Englewood Cliffs, NJ: Prentice-Hall, 1973.

Chomsky, Noam. *Language and Mind*. New York: Harcourt, Brace & World, 1968.

_____ . *Reflections on Language*. New York: Pantheon, 1975.

_____ . *Rules and Representations*. New York: Columbia University Press, 1980.

Clay, Marjorie, and Keith Lehrer, eds. *Knowledge and Skepticism*. Boulder, CO: Westview Press, 1989.

Cohen, L. Jonathan. *The Implications of Induction*. London: Methuen, 1970.

_____ . *The Probable and the Provable*. Oxford: Clarendon Press, 1977.

Cohen, Stewart. "Justification and Truth." *Philosophical Studies* 46 (1984).

_____ . "How to be a Fallibilist." In *Philosophical Perspectives*, Vol. 2: *Epistemology*. Atascadero, CA: Ridgeview, 1988.

Cornman, James W. *Materialism and Sensations*. New Haven: Yale University Press, 1971.

_____ . "Foundational versus Nonfoundational Theories of Empirical Justification." *American Philosophical Quarterly* 14 (1977). Reprinted in *Essays on Knowledge and Justification*, edited by G. S. Pappas and Marshall Swain. Ithaca, NY: Cornell University Press, 1978.

_____ . "On Justifying Non-Basic Statements by Basic-Reports." In *Justification and Knowledge*, edited by G. S. Pappas. Dordrecht: Reidel, 1979.

_____ . *Skepticism, Justification and Explanation*. Dordrecht: Reidel, 1980.

Cornman, James W., Keith Lehrer, and George S. Pappas. *Philosophical Problems and Arguments: An Introduction*. 3rd ed. New York: Hackett, 1987.

Dancy, Jonathan. *An Introduction to Contemporary Epistemology*. Oxford: Blackwell, 1985.

Danto, Arthur C. *Analytical Philosophy of Knowledge*. Cambridge: Cambridge University Press, 1968.

Davidson, Donald. "The Individuation of Events." In *Essays in Honor of Carl G. Hempel*, edited by Nicholas Rescher. Dordrecht: Reidel, 1969.

_____ . *Essays on Actions and Events*. Oxford: Clarendon Press, 1980.

––––––. *Inquiries into Truth and Interpretation*. Oxford: Clarendon Press, 1984.

––––––. "A Coherence Theory of Truth and Knowledge." In *Truth and Interpretation: Perspectives on the Philosophy of Donald Davidson*, edited by Ernest LePore. Oxford: Blackwell, 1986.

Davis, Wayne, and John W. Bender. "Technical Flaws in the Coherence Theory." *Synthese*, forthcoming.

Descartes, René. *Meditations*.

––––––. *Discourse on Method*.

Dicker, Georges. *Perceptual Knowledge*. Dordrecht: Reidel, 1980.

Dretske, Fred I. *Seeing and Knowing*. London: Routledge and Kegan Paul, 1969.

––––––. "Conclusive Reasons." *Australasian Journal of Philosophy* 49 (1971).

––––––. *Knowledge and the Flow of Information*. Cambridge: MIT Press, 1981.

Duncan-Jones, Austin. "Further Questions About 'Know' and 'Think'." In *Philosophy and Analysis*, edited by Margaret Macdonald. Oxford: Blackwell, 1966.

Eberle, R., D. Kaplan, and R. Montague. "Hempel and Oppenheim on Explanation." *Philosophy of Science* 28 (1961).

Feldman, Richard. "Reliability and Justification." *The Monist* 68 (1985).

––––––. "Epistemic Obligations." In *Philosophical Perspectives*, Vol. 2: *Epistemology*, edited by J. Tomberlin. Atascadero, CA: Ridgeview, 1988.

Fogelin, Robert. *Evidence and Meaning*. New York: Humanities Press, 1967.

Foley, Richard. *A Theory of Epistemic Rationality*. Cambridge: Harvard University Press, 1987.

Fumerton, Richard A. *Metaphysical and Epistemological Problems of Perception*. Lincoln: University of Nebraska Press, 1985.

Gettier, Edmund, Jr. "Is Justified True Belief Knowledge?" *Analysis* 23 (1963).

Ginet, Carl. *Knowledge, Perception and Memory*. Dordrecht and Boston: Reidel, 1975.

Goldman, Alan. *Empirical Knowledge*. Berkeley: University of California Press, 1988.

Goldman, Alvin I. "Discrimination and Perceptual Knowledge." *Journal of Philosophy* 73 (1976).

––––––. "A Causal Theory of Knowing." *Journal of Philosophy* 64 (1967). Reprinted in *Essays on Knowledge and Justification*, edited by G. S. Pappas and Marshall Swain. Ithaca, NY: Cornell University Press, 1978.

––––––. "What is Justified Belief?" In *Justification and Knowledge*, edited by G. S. Pappas. Dordrecht: Reidel, 1979.

––––––. *Epistemology and Cognition*. Cambridge: Harvard University Press, 1986.

––––––. "Strong and Weak Justification." In *Philosophical Perspectives*, Vol. 2: *Epistemology*, edited by J. Tomberlin. Atascadero, CA: Ridgeview, 1988.

Hamlyn, D. W. *The Theory of Knowledge*. London: Macmillan, 1971.

Harman, Gilbert. "How Belief Is Based on Inference." *Journal of Philosophy* 61 (1964).

––––––. "The Inference to the Best Explanation." *Philosophy Review* 74 (1965).

––––––. "Knowledge, Reasons, and Causes." *Journal of Philosophy* 67 (1970).

––––––. "Induction." In *Induction, Acceptance, and Rational Belief*, edited by Marshall Swain. Dordrecht: Reidel, 1970.

————. *Thought*. Princeton: Princeton University Press, 1973.

————. *Change in View*. Cambridge: MIT Press, 1986.

Hartland-Swann, John. *An Analysis of Knowing*. London: Allen and Unwin, 1958.

Heil, John. *Perception and Cognition*. Berkeley and Los Angeles: University of California Press, 1983.

Hempel, Carl G. "Deductive-Nomological vs. Statistical Explanation." In *Minnesota Studies in the Philosophy of Science*, Vol. 3, edited by Herbert Feigl and Grover Maxwell. Minneapolis: University of Minnesota Press, 1962.

————. *Aspects of Scientific Explanation*. New York: Free Press, 1965.

Hill, Thomas. *Contemporary Theories of Knowledge*. New York: Macmillan, 1961.

Hilpinen, Risto. "Knowledge and Justification." *Ajatus* 33 (1971).

————. "Knowledge and Conditionals." In *Philosophical Perspectives*, Vol. 2: *Epistemology*, edited by J. Tomberlin. Atascadero, CA: Ridgeview, 1988.

Hintikka, Jaako. *Knowledge and Belief*. Ithaca, NY: Cornell University Press, 1962.

————. "A Two-Dimensional Continuum of Inductive Methods." In *Aspects of Inductive Logic*, edited by J. Hintikka and P. Suppes. Amsterdam: North-Holland, 1966.

Hintikka, Jaako, and J. Pietarinen. "Semantic Information and Inductive Logic." In *Aspects of Inductive Logic*, edited by J. Hintikka and P. Suppes. Amsterdam: North-Holland, 1966.

Honderich, Ted. *A Theory of Determinism*. Oxford: Clarendon Press, 1988.

Hume, David. *An Inquiry Concerning Human Understanding*. Indianapolis: Bobbs-Merrill, 1977.

————. *A Treatise of Human Nature*. Oxford: Clarendon Press, 1888. (Originally published in 1739)

James, William. "The Will to Believe." In *The Writings of William James: A Comprehensive Edition*, edited by John J. McDermott. Chicago: University of Chicago Press, 1977.

Jeffrey, Richard. *The Logic of Decision*. New York: McGraw-Hill, 1965.

Kant, Immanuel. *Prolegomena to Any Future Metaphysics*. Translated by Lewis White Beck (based on the Mahaffy-Carus trans.). New York: Liberal Arts Press, 1950.

Klein, Peter. "A Proposed Definition of Propositional Knowledge." *Journal of Philosophy* 68 (1971).

————. "Knowledge, Causality and Defeasibility." *Journal of Philosophy* 73 (1976).

————. *Certainty: A Refutation of Scepticism*. Oxford: Clarendon Press, 1984.

————. "Real Knowledge." *Synthese* 55 (1983).

————. "Radical Interpretation and Global Skepticism." In *Truth and Interpretation: Perspectives on the Philosophy of Donald Davidson*, edited by Ernest LePore. Oxford: Blackwell, 1986.

————. "Immune Belief Systems." *Philosophical Topics* 14 (1986).

Körner, Stephan. *Experience and Theory*. London: Routledge and Kegan Paul, 1966.

Kvanvig, Jonathan. "Swain on the Basing Relation." *Analysis* 45 (1985).

————. "How to be a Reliabilist." *American Philosophical Quarterly* 23 (1986).

Kyburg, Henry E., Jr. *Probability and the Logic of Rational Belief*. Middletown, CT: Wesleyan University Press, 1961.

_____ . *Epistemology and Inference*. Minneapolis: University of Minnesota Press, 1983.

Lehrer, Adrienne. "Semantic Cuisine." *Journal of Linguistics* 5 (1969).

Lehrer, Keith. "Knowledge, Truth, and Evidence." *Analysis* 25 (1965).

_____ . "Why Not Scepticism?" *Philosophical Forum* 2 (1971).

_____ . *Knowledge*. Oxford: Clarendon Press, 1974.

_____ . "The Knowledge Cycle." *Nous* 11 (1977).

_____ . "The Gettier Problem and the Analysis of Knowledge." In *Justification and Knowledge*, edited by G. S. Pappas. Dordrecht: Reidel, 1979.

_____ . "Self-Profile." In *Keith Lehrer*, edited by R. J. Bogdan. Dordrecht: Reidel, 1981.

_____ . "Knowledge, Truth, and Ontology." In *Language and Ontology: Proceedings of the Sixth International Wittgenstein Symposium*, edited by Werner Leinfellner. Vienna: Holder-Pichler-Tempsky, 1982.

_____ . "Belief, Acceptance, and Cognition." In *On Believing*, edited by Herman Parret. Berlin: Walter de Gruyter, 1983.

_____ . "The Coherence Theory of Knowledge." *Philosophical Topics* 14 (1986).

_____ . "Metamind: Belief, Consciousness, and Intentionality." In *Belief: Form, Content, and Function*, edited by R. J. Bogdan. Oxford: Clarendon Press, 1986.

_____ . "Personal and Social Knowledge." *Synthese* 73 (1987).

_____ . "Metaknowledge: Undefeated Justification." *Synthese* 74 (1988).

_____ . "Coherence, Justification, and Chisholm." In *Philosophical Perspectives*, Vol. 2: *Epistemology*, edited by J. Tomberlin. Atascadero, CA: Ridgeview, 1988.

Lehrer, Keith, and Thomas Paxson, Jr. "Knowledge: Undefeated Justified True Belief." *Journal of Philosophy* 66 (1969).

Lehrer, Keith, and Stewart Cohen. "Justification, Truth, and Coherence." *Synthese* 55 (1983).

Lehrer, Keith, and Carl Wagner. *Rational Consensus in Science and Society*. Dordrecht: Reidel, 1981.

Lemmon, E. J. "If I Know, Do I Know That I Know?" In *Epistemology: New Essays in the Theory of Knowledge*, edited by A. Stroll. New York: Harper and Row, 1967.

Levi, Issac. *Gambling with Truth: An Essay on Induction and the Aims of Science*. New York: Knopf, 1967.

Lewis, C. I. *An Analysis of Knowledge and Valuation*. Paul Carus Lectures. 7th series. LaSalle, IL: Open Court, 1946.

_____ . *Mind and the World Order*. New York: Dover, 1929.

Locke, Don. *Memory*. New York: Anchor Books, 1971.

Locke, John. *An Essay Concerning Human Understanding*. New York: Dutton, 1928. (Originally published in 1689)

Lycan, William. *Judgement and Justification*. New York: Cambridge University Press, 1988.

Lyons, John. *Structural Semantics*. Oxford: Blackwell, 1963.

Malcolm, Norman. "Knowledge and Belief." In *Knowledge and Belief*, edited by A. P. Griffiths. Oxford: Blackwell, 1967.

_____ . *Knowledge and Certainty*. Ithaca, NY: Cornell University Press, 1975.

Margolis, Joseph. "The Problem of Justified Belief." *Philosophical Studies* 23 (1972).

Martin, Robert, ed. *Recent Essays on Truth and the Liar Paradox.* Oxford: Clarendon Press, 1984.

McGee, Vann. *Truth, Vagueness and Paradox: An Essay on the Logic of Truth.* New York: Hackett, forthcoming.

McGinn, Colin. "The Concept of Knowledge." In *Midwest Studies in Philosophy,* Vol. 9: *Causation and Causal Theories,* edited by P. A. French, T. E. Uehling, and H. K. Wettstein. Minneapolis: University of Minnesota Press, 1984.

Mill, John Stuart. *A System of Logic.* London: Longmans, 1843.

Moore, G. E. "A Defense of Common Sense." In *Contemporary British Philosophy,* edited by J. H. Muirhead. 2nd series. London: Allen and Unwin, 1925.

———. *Philosophical Papers.* London: Allen and Unwin, 1959.

Morton, Adam. *A Guide Through the Theory of Knowledge.* Encino, CA: Dickenson, 1977.

Moser, Paul K. *Empirical Justification.* Dordrecht and Boston: Reidel, 1985.

———. "Critical Notice of *The Structure of Empirical Knowledge,* by L. Bonjour." *Philosophy and Phenomenological Research* 47 (1987).

———. "Propositional Knowledge." *Philosophical Studies* 52 (1987).

———. "Internalism and Coherentism: A Dilemma." *Analysis* 48 (1988).

———. *Knowledge and Evidence.* New York and Cambridge: Cambridge University Press, 1989.

———, ed. *Empirical Knowledge: Readings in Contemporary Epistemology.* Totowa, NJ: Rowman and Littlefield, 1986.

———, ed. *A Priori Knowledge.* Oxford: Oxford University Press, 1987.

Moser, Paul K., and Arnold Vander Nat, eds. *Human Knowledge: Classical and Contemporary Approaches.* New York and Oxford: Oxford University Press, 1987.

Nagel, Thomas. "Linguistics and Epistemology." *Philosophical Studies* 32 (1977).

Nakhnikian, George. "Incorrigibility." *Philosophical Quarterly* 18 (1968).

Nozick, Robert. *Philosophical Explanations.* Cambridge: Harvard University Press, 1981.

———. "Positive Epistemic Status and Proper Function." *Philosophical Perspectives,* Vol. 2: *Epistemology.* Atascadero, CA: Ridgeview, 1988.

Pappas, George S., and Marshall Swain, eds. *Essays on Knowledge and Justification.* Ithaca, NY: Cornell University Press, 1978.

Parsons, Katherine Pyne. "Mistaking Sensations." *Philosophical Review* 79 (1970).

Pastin, Mark. "Modest Foundationalism and Self-Warrant." *American Philosophy Quarterly* 9 (1975).

Plato. *Theaetetus, Symposium,* and *Phaedo.*

Pollock, John L. *Knowledge and Justification.* Princeton: Princeton University Press, 1974.

———. "A Plethora of Epistemological Theories." In *Justification and Knowledge,* edited by G. S. Pappas. Dordrecht: Reidel, 1979.

———. "Reliability and Justified Belief." *Canadian Journal of Philosophy* 14 (1984).

———. *Contemporary Theories of Knowledge.* Totowa, NJ: Rowman and Littlefield, 1986.

Posner, Michael. *Cognition: An Introduction.* Glenview, IL: Scott, Foresman, 1973.

Price, H. H. *Perception.* London: Methuen & Co., 1932.

_____ . *Truth and Corrigibility.* Oxford: Clarendon Press, 1936.

Prichard, H. "Knowing and Believing." In *Knowledge and Belief,* edited by A. P. Griffiths. Oxford: Blackwell, 1967.

Putnam, Hilary. *Reason, Truth, and History.* Cambridge: Cambridge University Press, 1984.

Quine, W.V.O. *From a Logical Point of View.* Cambridge: Harvard University Press, 1953.

_____ . *Word and Object.* Cambridge: MIT Press, 1960.

_____ . *Ontological Relativity and Other Essays.* New York: Columbia University Press, 1969.

Quine, W.V.O., and Joseph Ullian. *The Web of Belief.* 2nd ed. New York: Random House, 1978.

Quinton, Anthony. *The Nature of Things.* London: Routledge and Kegan Paul, 1973.

Radford, Colin. "Knowledge—By Examples." *Analysis* 27 (1966).

_____ . "Analyzing 'Knows That'." *Philosophical Quarterly* 20 (1970).

Reichenbach, Hans. *The Theory of Probability.* Berkeley: University of California Press, 1949.

Reid, Thomas. *The Works of Thomas Reid, D.D.,* edited by Sir William Hamilton. Eighth edition. Edinburgh: James Thin, 1895.

Rescher, Nicholas. *The Coherence Theory of Truth.* Oxford: Oxford University Press, 1973.

_____ . "Foundationalism, Coherentism, and the Idea of Cognitive Systematization." *Journal of Philosophy* 71 (1974).

_____ . *Cognitive Systematization.* Totowa, NJ: Rowman and Littlefield, 1979.

_____ . *Skepticism: A Critical Reappraisal.* Totowa, NJ: Rowman and Littlefield, 1980.

Rosenberg, Jay. *One World and Our Knowledge of It.* Dordrecht: Reidel, 1980.

Roth, Michael, and Leon Galis, eds. *Knowing: Essays in the Theory of Knowledge.* New York: Random House, 1970.

Roth, Michael, and Glenn Ross. *Doubt.* Boston: Kluwer, forthcoming.

Russell, Bertrand. "Knowledge by Acquaintance and Knowledge by Description." *Proceedings of the Aristotelian Society* 11 (1910–11).

_____ . *An Inquiry into Meaning and Truth.* London: Oxford University Press, 1940.

_____ . *The Problems of Philosophy.* London: Oxford University Press, 1959.

Ryle, Gilbert. "Knowing How and Knowing That." *Proceedings of the Aristotelian Society* 46 (1945–46).

Savage, C. W., ed. *Perception and Cognition: Issues in the Foundations of Psychology.* Minneapolis: University of Minnesota Press, 1978.

Schlick, Moritz. "The Foundation of Knowledge" (1934). In *Logical Positivism,* edited by A. J. Ayer. New York: Free Press, 1957.

Sellars, W. F. *Science, Perception, and Reality.* London: Routledge and Kegan Paul, 1963.

Shoemaker, Sydney. "On Knowing One's Own Mind." In *Philosophical Perspectives,* Vol. 2: *Epistemology,* edited by J. Tomberlin. Atascadero, CA: Ridgeway, 1988.

Shope, Robert. *The Analysis of Knowing.* Princeton: Princeton University Press, 1983.

Siegel, Harvey. "Justification, Discovery and the Naturalizing of Epistemology." *Philosophy of Science* 47 (1980).

Slaght, Ralph. "Is Justified True Belief Knowledge? A Selected Critical Survey of Recent Work." *Philosophy Research Archives* 3 (1977).

Sosa, Ernest. "Epistemic Presupposition." In *Justification and Knowledge,* edited by G. S. Pappas. Dordrecht: Reidel, 1979.

———. "The Raft and the Pyramid: Coherence versus Foundations in the Theory of Knowledge." In *Midwest Studies in Philosophy,* Vol. 5: *Studies in Epistemology,* edited by P. A. French, T. E. Uehling, and H. K. Wettstein. Minneapolis: University of Minnesota Press, 1980.

———. "Nature Unmirrored, Epistemology Naturalized." *Synthese* 55 (1983).

———. "Experience and Intentionality." *Philosophical Topics* 14 (1986).

———. "'Circular' Coherence and 'Absurd' Foundations" In *Truth and Interpretation: Perspectives on the Philosophy of Donald Davidson.* Oxford: Blackwell, 1986.

———. "Knowledge in Context, Skepticism in Doubt." In *Philosophical Perspectives,* Vol. 2: *Epistemology,* edited by J. Tomberlin. Atascadero, CA: Ridgeview, 1988.

Stroud, Barry. *The Significance of Philosophical Scepticism.* Oxford: Clarendon Press, 1984.

Swain, Marshall. *Reasons and Knowledge.* Ithaca, NY: Cornell University Press, 1981.

Tarski, Alfred. "The Semantic Conception of Truth." In *Semantics and the Philosophy of Language,* edited by L. Linsky. Urbana: University of Illinois Press, 1952.

———. "The Concept of Truth in Formalized Languages." *Logic, Semantics, and Metamathematics.* Oxford: Clarendon Press, 1969.

Thalberg, Irving. "In Defense of Justified True Belief." *Journal of Philosophy* 66 (1969).

Unger, Peter. "A Defense of Skepticism." *Philosophical Review* 80 (1971).

———. *Ignorance: A Case for Scepticism.* Oxford: Clarendon Press, 1975.

———. "The Cone Model of Knowledge." *Philosophical Topics* 14 (1986).

Van Cleve, James. "Foundationalism, Epistemic Principles, and the Cartesian Circle." *Philosophical Review* 88 (1979).

———. "Epistemic Supervenience and the Circle of Belief." *The Monist* 68 (1985).

Will, Frederick L. *Induction and Justification.* Ithaca, NY: Cornell University Press, 1974.

Williams, Michael. "Inference, Justification, and the Analysis of Knowledge." *Journal of Philosophy* 75 (1978).

———. "Do We (Epistemologists) Need a Theory of Truth?" *Philosophical Topics* 14 (1986).

Wittgenstein, Ludwig. *On Certainty.* Translated by Dennis Paul and G.E.M. Anscombe. Oxford: Blackwell, 1969.

Ziff, Paul. "The Simplicity of Other Minds." In *New Readings in Philosophical Analysis*, edited by H. Feigl, W. F. Sellars, and K. Lehrer. New York: Appleton-Century-Crofts, 1972.

Index

b denotes entry in Bibliography.

Acceptance, 10–11, 20–21, 113–114
  and belief, 26–27, 113–114
  as a condition of knowledge, 10–11
  and correspondence, 26
  functional role of, 35–36
  and information, 33–35
  and memory, 37–38
  and paradox, 24
  trustworthiness. *See* Principle of
    trustworthiness
  and truth. *See* Principle of
    trustworthiness
  See also Acceptance system; Belief
Acceptance system, 112, 114–115
  defined, 117, 148
  and the Principle of trustworthiness,
    122–124
  See also Reasonableness; Ultrasystem;
    Verific system
Ackerman, Robert, 197*b*
Adler, Jonathan E., 197*b*
Agnoiology, 176. *See also* Skepticism
Alston, William P., 74, 85, 190(n4),
  191(n11), 197*b*
Analysis, philosophical, 5–9
  as meaning analysis, 5
  and science, 7
  as specification of necessary and
    sufficient conditions, 5–6
  See also Explication
Annis, David B., 197*b*
Aristotle, 1, 187(n2), 197*b*
Armstrong, D. M. 38, 51, 154, 162–163,
  175, 189(n16), 190(nn 10, 11), 194(nn
  3, 8, 16), 197*b*, 198*b*

Audi, Robert, 19, 194(n10), 198*b*
Aune, Bruce, 111, 127, 193(n3), 198*b*
Austin, J. L., 27–28, 38, 189(nn 6, 9),
  198*b*
Ayer, A. J., 19, 59, 62, 187(nn 8, 12),
  188(nn 13, 17), 189(n3), 190(nn 14,
  15), 198*b*

Basic belief, 13, 41–42
  and contingent self-justification, 73–75
  fallible, 63–86
  as a guarantee of truth, 42–43
  and incorrigibility. *See* Incorrigibility
  and independent information, 73–75, 83
  infallible. *See* Infallible belief
  and necessary truth, 70–73
  and prima facie justification, 43
  and probability, 75–84
  and reliability, 66–67
  and semantic information, 68–70
  See also Foundationalism; Perceptual belief
Basing relation, 168–172
Belief, 10–11
  and acceptance, 26–27
  basic. *See* Basic belief
  and causation. *See* Basing relation
  fallible. *See* Basic belief, fallible
  and independent information, 64–68,
    73–75. *See also* Basic belief
  infallible. *See* Infallible belief
  innocent, 65–66. *See also* Basic belief
  perceptual. *See* Perceptual belief
  and probability, 75–84
  and reliability, 66–67
  self-justified. *See* Self-justification

See also Acceptance; Observation
  statement
Bender, John W., 131, 198*b*, 200*b*
Berkeley, George (bishop), 58, 189(n4),
  190(nn 12, 13), 198*b*
Blanshard, Brand, 191(n2), 198*b*
BonJour, Laurence, 101, 127, 131,
  188(n15), 190(n7), 192(nn 12, 20),
  193(n3), 198*b*
Brand, R. B., 198*b*
Bromberger, Sylvain, 96–98, 103, 192(nn
  8, 9, 15), 192(n15), 198*b*
Butchvarov, Panayot, 62, 189(n3), 198*b*

Carnap, Rudolf, 6, 187(n9), 191(n13), 198*b*
Castañeda, Hector-Neri, 199*b*
Chisholm, R. M., 17, 19, 60, 62, 67–68,
  86, 102, 137, 188(nn 13, 14, 17, 21),
  189(n1), 190(nn 5, 16), 191(nn 2, 6,
  7), 192(n13), 193(n5), 199*b*
Chomsky, Noam, 199*b*
Clay, Marjorie, 199*b*
Cohen, Jonathan L., 191(n12), 199*b*
Cohen, Steward, 166, 175, 194(n19), 199*b*,
  202*b*
Coherence
  and acceptance system, 115, 117
  as explanation, 91–96
  as implication, 90
  See also Reasonableness
Coherentism, 13–14, 87–152, 173–174
  and the circularity objection, 87–89
  explanatory. *See* Explanatory
    coherentism
  and the isolation objection. *See* Isolation
    objection
  and the regress objection, 87–89
  and self-justified beliefs, 89
  and the sources of knowledge, 145–146
  See also Coherence; Principle of
    trustworthiness
Competition, 117–118
Complete justification, 135, 149. *See also*
  Personal justification
Conditions of knowledge
  an acceptance condition, 10–11
  a fourth condition, 17. *See also* Gettier,
    Edmund
  a justification condition, 12–13
  a truth condition, 9–10
Cornman, James W., 199*b*

Dancy, Jonathan, 199*b*
Danto, Arthur, 62, 189(n3), 199*b*
Davidson, Donald, 132–133, 193(n1),
  199*b*, 200*b*
Davis, Wayne, 200*b*
Descartes, René, 2, 185, 187(n3), 189(n2),
  193(n1), 194(n3), 200*b*
Dicker, Georges, 200*b*
Dretske, Fred, 33, 38, 154–155, 163, 165,
  175, 182, 187(n7), 188(n16), 189(n15),
  194(nn 3, 8, 10, 11, 13, 17), 196(n4),
  200*b*
Duncan-Jones, Austin, 189(n5), 200*b*

Eberle, Rolf, 192(n7), 200*b*
Epistemic conservatism, 109–110
Epistemology
  critical, 2
  metaphysical, 1
  skeptical, 2
Explanation, 96–98
  deductive model of, 96–97
  epistemic analysis of, 97–98
  as a primitive, 98
  and self-explanation, 103–104
Explanatory coherentism, 91–111
  and conditioned response, 99–101
  defined, 95
  and inconsistent beliefs, 107–108
  and justification without explanation,
    105–106
  the maximization of coherence and the
    size of the explanation basis, 98–102
  and natural selection, 101–102
  and observation statements, 99–105
  and spontaneity, 101
  and weak explanations, 106–107
  See also Epistemic conservatism;
    Explanation; Observation statement;
    Simplicity
Explication, 6
Externalism, 14, 153–175
  and basic belief, 154–155
  and the basing relation, 168–172
  and deductive closure, 158, 181–185
  defined, 153
  and the invincibility objection, 166–167
  and justification, 155, 159, 165, 166
  and the possession of information vs.
    the attainment of knowledge, 162–166
  and probability, 77–79

and relevant alternatives, 157, 182
and skepticism, 156–159, 181–185
See also Naturalism

Fallible foundations, 40, 43–44, 63
compared with infallible foundations, 40
and contingent self-justification, 73–75
and *prima facie* justification, 72–73
and probability, 75–84
and truth, 84
See also Basic belief
Feldman, Richard, 175, 200*b*
Foegelin, Robert, 191(n1), 200*b*
Foley, Richard, 86, 190(n4), 200*b*
Foundationalism, 13, 39–86
fallible. *See* Fallible foundations
infallible. *See* Infallibe foundations
and nonbasic belief. *See* Phenomenalism
See also Basic belief
Fumerton, Richard A., 200*b*

Galis, Leon, 152, 188(n19), 204*b*
Gettier, Edmund, 16, 135–136, 152, 188(nn 18, 20), 193(nn 2, 3), 200*b*.
See also Gettier problem
Gettier problem, 16–17, 135–137, 141. *See also* Justification, and truth; Justification, undefeated
Ginet, Carl, 62, 200*b*
Goldman, Alan, 111, 192(n14), 194(n5), 200*b*
Goldman, Alvin, 153–154, 159, 161, 163, 165, 166, 170, 175, 188(n16), 191(n4), 194(nn 2, 3, 10, 12, 14, 18, 20), 200*b*

Hamlyn, D. W., 200*b*
Harman, Gilbert, 91, 108, 111, 127, 140, 170, 183, 191(n5), 192(nn 3, 19), 193(n3), 194(nn 9, 21), 196(n5), 200*b*, 201*b*
Hartland-Swann, John, 187(n5), 201*b*
Heil, John, 201*b*
Hempel, Carl G., 96, 98, 131, 192(nn 6, 10), 193(n4), 201*b*
Hill, Thomas, 201*b*
Hilpinen, Risto, 138, 194(n7), 201*b*
Hintikka, Jaakko, 191(n14), 193(n4), 201*b*
Hondrich, Ted, 201*b*
Hume, David, 154, 194(n6), 201*b*

Incorrigibility, 44–48
defined, 47
and logical necessity, 46
Infallible belief
and inference, 54
and meaning, 55–57. *See also* Principle of charity
and nomological necessity, 54–55
about sensation, 51–54
about thought, 48–51
Infallible foundations, 39–62
compared with fallible foundations, 40–41
and justification as guarantee of truth, 42–43
See also Basic belief; Incorrigibility; Infallible belief
Information, 4, 8, 33–35
correct, 8, 162–164
without knowledge, 162–166
and memory, 37–38
possession of, 4, 162–164
source of, 4
See also Knowledge
Isolation objection
ultra justification game and the, 143–144

James, William, 201*b*
Jeffrey, Richard, 86, 191(n13), 201*b*
Justification
and causation. *See* Basing relation
and coherence. *See* Coherentism
complete, 12–13, 16–17. *See* Basic belief
and conditioned response, 99–101
determination of, 151–152
and explanation. *See* Explanatory coherentism
and falsity, 135–143. *See also* Gettier problem; Justification game; Verific justification
and naturalism, 159
and natural selection, 101–102
and necessity, 71–73
and nonbasic belief. *See* Phenomenalism
personal. *See* Personal justification
and *prima facie* justification. *See* *Prima facie* justification
and probability, 75–84
and self-explanation, 102–105
and self-justification. *See* Self-justification

and semantics, 68–70
and spontaneity, 101
subjective. *See* Personal justification
theories of, 13–16
and trustworthiness. *See* Principle of
trustworthiness
and truth, 42–43, 84. *See also* Infallible
foundations
undefeated. *See* Undefeated justification
verific. *See* Verific justification
See also Acceptance system;
Coherentism; Externalism;
Foundationalism; Justification game;
Principle of trustworthiness
Justification game, 119–120
and personal justification, 126
and reliability, 172–173
and skepticism, 119–120
verific, 135–137
See also Ultra justification game

Kant, Immanuel, 201*b*
Kaplan, D., 192(n7), 200*b*
Klein, Peter, 138, 185, 193(n1), 194(nn 1,
7), 201*b*
Knowledge
and acceptance, 33–35, 36
acquaintance sense of, 3
analysis of, 9–18
and belief, 27–32
borderline cases of, 32–33, 35
characteristically human, 4, 36
competence sense of, 3
conditions of. *See* Conditions of
knowledge
defined, 18, 147
fallible, 178–179, 183. *See also*
Skepticism
information sense of, 4–5, 9
without justification. *See* Externalism
and memory, 31–32, 36–38
performative view of, 27–28
reduced to undefeated justification,
147–151
See also Acceptance; Coherentism;
Externalism; Foundationalism;
Information
Körner, Stephan, 32, 189(n14), 201*b*
Kripke, Saul, 183, 196(n6)
Kvanvig, Jonathan, 190(n6), 194(n21),
201*b*

Kyburg, Henry, Jr., 129, 193(n5), 201*b*,
202*b*

Lehrer, Adrienne, 70, 191(n10), 202*b*
Lehrer, Keith, 131, 188(nn 15, 19, 22),
192(n3), 193(n2), 194(nn 1, 6, 8, 19),
199*b*, 202*b*
Lemmon, E. J., 31, 189(n12), 202*b*
Levi, Isaac, 131, 193(n4), 202*b*
Lewis, C. I., 102, 192(n13), 202*b*
Locke, Don, 202*b*
Locke, John, 202*b*
Lottery paradox, 129–130
Lycan, William, 111, 192(n20), 202*b*
Lyons, John, 70, 191(n10), 202*b*

McGee, Van, 38, 203*b*
McGinn, Colin, 187(n4), 203*b*
Malcolm, Norman, 202*b*
Margolis, Joseph, 193(n4), 203*b*
Martin, Robert, 38, 203*b*
Meaning
and belief, 55–57
and skepticism, 69–70
Memory
and acceptance, 37–38
and information, 37–38
Mill, John Stuart, 203*b*
Montague, Richard, 192(n7), 200*b*
Moore, G. E., 176, 185, 187(n12), 194(n2),
203*b*
Morton, Adam, 203*b*
Moser, Paul K., 18, 62, 188(n14), 203*b*

Nagel, Ernest, 198*b*
Nagel, Thomas, 203*b*
Nakhnikian, George, 190(n8), 203*b*
Naturalism, 154–155
and causation, 159–161
and historical reliabilism, 161
and tracking, 161
See also Externalism
Neutralization, 124–126
Nozick, Robert, 154–155, 161, 163, 165,
175, 184, 188(n16), 194(nn 4, 11, 15,
17), 203*b*

Observation statement
and conditioned response, 99–101
and natural selection, 101–102
as self-explanatory, 102–105

and spontaneity, 101

Pappas, George S., 19, 152, 185, 199b,
203b
Parsons, Katherine Pyne, 190(n9), 203b
Pastin, Mark, 85, 190(n4), 203b
Paxson, Thomas, 194(n8), 202b
Perceptual belief, 64–68
and independent information, 64–68.
See also Basic belief
as innocent belief, 65–66
and the noncomparative use of words,
67–68
Personal justification, 112–126
as a basis of complete justification,
133–134
defeated, 147
defined, 126, 148
and reliability, 168, 172–173
and trustworthiness, 121–124
See also Acceptance system;
Competition; Neutralization
Phenomenalism, 58–62
Pietarinen, J., 193(n4), 201b
Plato, 1, 187(n1), 203b
Pollock, John L., 19, 62, 188(n14),
189(n1), 190(nn 4, 6), 191(n9), 203b
Posner, Michael, 204b
Price, H. H., 204b
Prichard, H., 204b
Prima facie justification, 72–73
and necessity, 72–73
See also Basic belief; Belief, innocent;
Perceptual belief
Principle of charity, 132–133
and belief ascription, 55–56
Principle of trustworthiness, 85, 121–122,
173–174, 180–181
and fallibility, 183
and truth, 121–122
Probability, 75–84
frequency concept of, 76–79
and independent information, 77, 82, 83
logical conception of, 79–80
subjective conception of, 80–81
and truth, 82–84
Putnam, Hilary, 193(n1), 204b

Quine, W.V.O., 6, 7, 99, 108, 127, 154,
175, 187(nn 9, 10), 192(nn 11, 19),
193(n3), 194(n7), 204b

Quinton, Anthony, 204b

Radford, Colin, 28–32, 33, 38, 187(n11),
189(nn 10, 11, 13), 204b
Reasonableness
and expected utility, 128–129
as a primitive, 127
and probability, 127–128
and skepticism, 116
and truth, 130–131
See also Acceptance system; Lottery
paradox
Reichenbach, Hans, 191(n13), 204b
Reid, Thomas, 63, 123, 176, 185, 190(nn
1, 3), 193(n2), 194(n2), 204b
Reliability
and belief, 66–67
and independent information, 66–67
Rescher, Nicholas, 131, 185, 194(n1), 204b
Rosenberg, Jay F., 111, 127, 193(n3), 204b
Ross, Glenn, 185, 204b
Roth, Michael, 152, 185, 188(n19), 204b
Russell, Bertrand, 19, 62, 91, 187(n6),
188(n18), 192(n4), 204b
Ryle, Gilbert, 187(n5), 204b

Savage, W. C., 204b
Schick, Frederick, 192(n16)
Schlick, Moritz, 204b
Self-justification, and necessary truth, 70–
73. *See also* Basic belief; Justification,
and semantics; Observation statement,
as self-explanatory
Sellars, Wilfrid, 91, 99, 108, 111, 127,
191(n8), 192(nn 3, 11, 18), 193(n3),
204b
Shoemaker, Sydney, 204b
Shope, Robert K., 152, 204b
Siegel, Harvey, 204b
Simplicity, 108–109
Skepticism, 15, 176–181
and conceptual change, 177
and deductive closure, 158, 181–185
and externalism, 156–159, 181–185
and fallible knowledge, 178–179
and ignorance. *See* Agnoiology
and meaning, 69–70
and the possibility of error, 176–177
and relevant alternatives, 157, 182
and trustworthiness, 179–180
See also Justification game

Slaght, Ralph, 204*b*
Sosa, Ernest, 85, 190(n4), 193(n1), 204*b*
Stroud, Barry, 185, 194(n1), 204*b*
Swain, Marshall, 19, 152, 170, 175, 185, 194(n21), 204*b*
Robert, 199*b*

Tarski, Alfred, 24, 38, 188(nn 1, 3), 204*b*
Thalberg, Irving, 193(n4), 204*b*
Truth, 21–26
  absolute theory of, 9, 25
  as a condition of knowledge, 9–10
  and correspondence, 25–26
  disquotational theory of. *See* Truth, minimal theory of
  minimal theory of, 23–24
  and paradox, 21–25
  See also Justification; Principle of trustworthiness

Ullian, Joseph, 204*b*

Ultra justification game
  and the isolation objection, 141–144
  and the truth connection, 141–144
Ultrasystem, defined, 149, 194(n11)
Undefeated justification, defined, 146, 149
Unger, Peter, 185, 194(n1), 204*b*

Van Cleve, James, 74, 85, 191(n11), 204*b*
Vander Nat, Arnold, 18, 203*b*
Verific justification, 134–135
  defined, 135, 149
  See also Justification game, verific; Verific system
Verific system, defined, 149. *See also* Verific justification

Wagner, Carl, 202*b*
Will, Frederick L., 204*b*
Williams, Michael, 204*b*
Wittgenstein, Ludwig, 204*b*

Ziff, Paul, 111, 192(n5), 204*b*